Three Weeks to
eBay
Profits

Library of Congress Cataloging-in-Publication Data

McGrath, Skip.
Three weeks to eBay profits : go from beginner to successful seller in less than a month /
Skip McGrath.
   p. cm.
Includes index.
ISBN-13: 978-1-4027-3281-2
ISBN-10: 1-4027-3281-3
1. eBay (Firm) 2. Internet auctions. 3. Consignment sales. I. Title.

HF5478.M3873 2006
658.8'7--dc22

2006008714

   4   6   8   10   9   7   5

Published by Sterling Publishing Co., Inc.
387 Park Avenue South, New York, NY 10016

Distributed in Canada by Sterling Publishing
C/o Canadian Manda Group, 165 Dufferin Street,
Toronto, Ontario, Canada M6K 3H6
Distributed in the United Kingdom by GMC Distribution Services,
Castle Place, 166 High Street, Lewes, East Sussex, England BN7 1XU
Distributed in Australia by Capricorn Link (Australia) Pty. Ltd.
P.O. Box 704, Windsor, NSW 2756, Australia

Sterling ISBN-13: 978-1-4027-3281-2
      ISBN-10: 1-4027-3281-3

For information about custom editions, special sales, premium and
corporate purchases, please contact Sterling Special Sales
Department at 800-805-5489 or specialsales@sterlingpub.com.

Three Weeks to
eBay
Profits

Go from Beginner
to Successful Seller
in Less than a Month

Skip McGrath

Sterling Publishing Co., Inc.
New York

This book is lovingly dedicated to my mom, June Springer. Mom never failed to encourage me in my endeavors, she taught me the value of hard work, and, at eighty-two, she herself still works every day. From a very young age, I learned from my mom to reach for my dreams—no matter how impossible they seemed—and that it was all right to be afraid of something as long as you didn't let your fear stop you from doing what you wanted to do or going where you wanted to go. She is gentle, sweet, and generous—sometimes to a fault—and none of my success in life would have been possible without her love and support. My gratitude to this extraordinary woman knows no bounds.

✦ CONTENTS ✦

WEEK
3

BUILDING AND GROWING YOUR BUSINESS 201

ACKNOWLEDGMENTS

When you pick up a book, you see the title and the author's name. However, unlike with a movie, where the credits roll across the screen at the end, you never get to see the names of all the people working behind the scenes to help bring that book to fruition. An author spends countless hours writing a book, but a lot of work by other people actually figures in the final product.

My editor, Meredith Peters Hale, got married in the middle of this project, and I had to get used to her new name. Meredith was enthusiastic about the book from day one, and worked tirelessly with me from the initial outline right up to the final edits. She contributed solid ideas and pointed out flaws in my organization, always keeping you, the reader, in mind. Editorial Assistant Lindsay Herman watched over both of us to make sure we didn't miss anything.

Copyeditor Diana Drew spent hours poring over every word of my prose—shortening run-on sentences; correcting grammar, spelling, and agreement problems; and coming up with simple ways to express complicated ideas. If you find this book easy to read, thank Diana.

Before a book is printed, much thought goes into the layout and design. The cover of *Three Weeks to eBay Profits* was designed by Kevin Baier. The interior was designed by Christine Heun and by Oxygen Design, and overseen by Sterling's art director Paula Schlosser. All details and issues, large and small, were overseen by the publisher, Michael Fragnito.

Lastly, I would like to thank my agent, Marilyn Allen. Marilyn understands what publishers are looking for and helps me channel my ideas into successful proposals and projects.

✦ INTRODUCTION ✦

Welcome to eBay, the world's greatest marketplace—electronic or otherwise. More than 80 million people in the United States alone have bought or sold items on eBay, and worldwide usage has surpassed 180 million in twenty-seven markets (according to eBay's own research). Over 1 million people list an item for sale on eBay every day; 600,000 of these are professional, full-time sellers.

In 2005, more than $40 billion worth of merchandise changed hands on eBay. In 2006, eBay estimates gross merchandise sales could top $48 billion. Yet eBay itself sells nothing but access to its platform. eBay does not sell one antique or collectible, one razor blade, even one digital camera—although 10,000-plus digital cameras are sold on eBay each month. It is you and I who do the selling. If every eBay seller were an employee of eBay, it would be the largest private employer in the world—larger than Wal-Mart and Lowe's combined.

When you launch an eBay business, you are opening a store in a city of 180 million people. Except you have no rent, no employees, no costly advertising, and very little overhead. What could be better?

I have been selling on eBay for over six years, and writing books and newsletters about selling on eBay for the past five. During that time, I have spoken to and answered e-mails from hundreds of my readers seeking advice. Although the questions always differ in their specifics, a basic theme recurs: "OK, I'm registered on eBay. What do I do next?" That question prompted me to write this book.

At first glance, selling an item on eBay looks simple. But once people become immersed in the process, they are confronted with dozens of choices and decisions related to auction titles, item descriptions, payment, shipping, image placement, eBay promotional options, and more. As they start to list their first two or three items for auction, new sellers begin to wonder if they can really build an eBay business—or is this whole thing just too complicated?

It *is* somewhat complicated—but not overly so. Almost anyone can master selling on eBay: You just need to take the time to understand the process and the unique nature of the eBay selling platform. Over 10 million people have sold items on eBay. With some guidance and perseverance, you, too, can join the ranks of those 600,000 full-time sellers.

What makes this book different from all the others that teach the ins and outs of selling on eBay? Most books on this subject tend to focus on mechanical aspects of the process, answering questions like the following: How do I upload photos? How do I get paid? How do I create a listing? Understanding how all these elements work is certainly important, and we do cover these points clearly. But rather than getting bogged down in details soon to become second nature, this book offers answers to one simple, yet all-encompassing, question: How do I make money on eBay?

Three Weeks to eBay Profits is designed to take you through the process, step by step in a logical manner, so you understand and master each step. Why three weeks? It won't take you three weeks to sell your first few items—you can do that within a few days of starting. But we are talking about achieving *success* on eBay—not just making a few quick sales.

Setting up and organizing your business, researching and finding the right products, and putting in place the automated systems and services to save you time will take the average person about three weeks. If you are not currently working and are doing this full time, you may actually master all these steps even sooner. On the other hand, if you have a full-time job and can only devote a few hours to your eBay business every evening, it may take you four or five weeks before everything is humming along and you are making money consistently week after week.

How you define success on eBay depends on your personal goals and how eBay fits into your life. If you are a single mom or a working person just looking to supplement your income, you might be looking to make an extra $100–$200 a week. However, if you are trying to replace your income from a job lost to downsizing, then your vision of success might be earning $500 or $1,000 a week—or more. Both scenarios are doable—it's just a matter of time, work, and learning the ropes.

If you enjoy selling on eBay, then this is the greatest gig in the world. Not only have I made a lot of money on eBay over the past six years, but I have had a fabulous time doing it. My wife, Karen, and I work together in the business and we still get as excited today watching the last few moments of an auction as we did when we entered an item in our very first auction more than six years ago. We now exhibit every year at eBay's annual convention, eBay Live (held every June in a different city), and there we get to meet thousands of fellow eBay professionals and enthusiasts.

If you are already registered and have sold things on eBay, you might be tempted to skip through the first few chapters. I suggest that, at the very least, you scan them for new information. I frequently see items being auctioned on eBay by veteran sellers who are still making rookie mistakes. Clearly, they didn't set up their business for success right from the start.

To get the most out of this book, take the time to set up and organize your business correctly (chapter 1) before you start launching your first auctions. Work through the first few chapters to do the research and select the products you will sell. This is one of the most important decisions you will make. Then set your goals and write your success plan (chapter 12). Benjamin Franklin once said, "An investment in knowledge pays the best interest." Make the investment now to maximize your interest and dividends later.

BIZ BUILDER

As you read this book, you will come across Web sites for various companies and products. To save you the trouble of typing each link into your browser, I have set up a special Web page just for the readers of this book at www.skipmcgrath.com/3_weeks.

Here's a quick outline of how this book is organized:

GETTING READY TO SELL

In the first week we concentrate on setting up your business correctly, learning the keys to operating on eBay, researching and settling on the products you will sell, and learning how and where to find sources for those products.

PUTTING YOUR AUCTIONS TO WORK

Almost anyone can use the eBay interface to launch an auction, but the devil is in the details. Learning how to make your auctions stand out from the millions of others, how to maximize your bids and final values, how to promote your auctions, and how to build a strong feedback profile are the keys to long-term success.

BUILDING AND GROWING YOUR BUSINESS

There's no great trick to selling on eBay, but only a professional can make money doing it week after week. In the third week, we show you how to control your costs, save time with automation, drive repeat business to your auctions, and open an eBay Store, as well as steps you can take to expand your business beyond eBay to the rest of the Web.

Here's to your success!

GETTING READY TO SELL

You are probably ready to jump right into selling on eBay, and I promise to get you there very soon. But, first, you need to take a few crucial steps to set up your business for the long term. If you have been buying on eBay or have sold a few items, you already may know some of this information or you may have performed some of the important tasks spelled out in the Week 1 chapters. Still, I would advise you to read through each chapter, looking for something you may have missed or for changes you may want to make to improve your current practices.

Strategies to help you conduct product research (chapter 4), select the right products (chapter 5), and figure out how to get products (chapter 6) are critical to your long-term success, and forgoing them makes most new eBay sellers wonder what is going wrong. Doing the research and going through the processes outlined here will help you avoid costly mistakes, and your first selling experience will be much more enjoyable—and profitable.

In Week 1, we will cover setting up and organizing your business, finding your way around eBay, and researching, choosing, and sourcing products to sell. In addition, we will explore the different types of auctions—and which may be right for your specific product—and then walk step-by-step through the process of launching your first auctions on eBay. Finally, we'll examine listing and pricing strategies, ways to quickly build positive feedback, and then to tie together everything you've learned into a targeted business plan that will ensure your success.

At the end of each chapter is a short checklist of actions for you to take. Some of these actions can be done within a few hours, while others might span a few days. You may opt to carry out each task right away, or you may want to keep reading and come back to certain ones later on. If you choose to return to some of them later on, make a list of the tasks you're setting aside, be sure to do each one at some point, and check it off as you complete it. Don't be intimidated if your list looks long. None of the tasks are that difficult or time-consuming—and many are actually fun. Just take them one at a time and you will see progress every day.

I also find it helpful to keep a three-ring binder near my computer so I can print out information as I come across it, punch three holes in the sheets, and file it for easy reference. You can organize the notebook into sections: one section for eBay information, and one for research and products. Once you begin launching auctions, you will want to add a section for storing printed-out copies of the results of your first few auctions. This way you can review and critique your auctions and make notes right on the auction copy. I started doing this five years ago and now have five very full binders next to my computer. I still refer to them to see which ideas worked and which did not.

CHAPTER 1

✦ SETTING UP AND ORGANIZING ✦ YOUR BUSINESS

To start selling on eBay, there's only one step that's absolutely required: registering an eBay selling account. However, following a number of other steps will make your path to success much smoother.

This chapter will walk you through how to register and set up your eBay and PayPal accounts, as well as how to create your About Me page, so that prospective bidders can learn about you and your business. Keep in mind that before learning how to sell on eBay, you need to understand the entire eBay process—both buying and selling. So we will first take a look at *buying* on eBay—how to gain experience, earn your first feedback ratings, and use your My eBay page to track your activity. Finally, we will address the issue of business licenses and explain how to get a state sales tax number, so you can buy inventory for resale from wholesalers and other distributors.

SETTING UP YOUR EBAY ACCOUNT

If you do not yet have an eBay account, the first thing you need to do is register as a buyer on eBay. You can do this by clicking on the link that says Register Now on the eBay homepage at www.eBay.com. eBay will ask for your name, address, telephone number, and e-mail address; then you will set up a username and password. Next, eBay will send you an e-mail with a link to click on and a confirmation code to enter. Once you do this, you are eligible to bid and buy on eBay. Note that when you create your eBay username, you cannot use any spaces. So, for example, *BidMoreOften* works, but *Bid More Often* will not be accepted. (However, you may use the underscore, as in *Bid_More_Often.*)

BIZ BUILDER

Give some thought to your username. Don't pick a name that will limit your business unless you will be concentrating on a specific niche. Something like *TheCameraDude* will work fine if all you plan to sell are cameras and photo equipment. A more generic name such as *HillsAndDales* or *SamsGreatStuff* will allow you to sell almost anything.

Next you need to register as a seller. Simply click on the *Sell* tab at the top of any eBay page (see Figure 1.1).

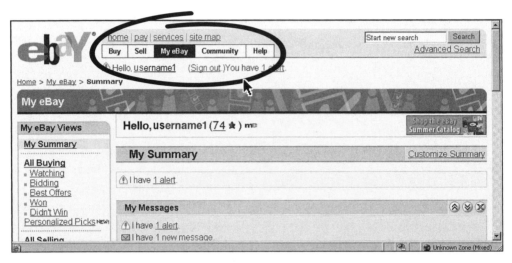

Figure 1.1 eBay Main Navigation Links

eBay will recognize that you are not yet registered to sell by the lack of a cookie in your computer and will direct you to register. To register as a seller, you have to provide a credit or debit card in the same name under which you registered and your checking account name and account number. Note that eBay will *not* charge your credit card or access your checking account unless you authorize them to charge your eBay selling fees. You also have the option of paying your eBay selling fees by check or PayPal. (We'll discuss eBay selling fees in chapter 21.)

Once you register as a seller, eBay will give you the option to verify your ID. You will see a link on your My eBay page that says *ID Verify* (see Figure 1.2). If you click on this link, eBay will ask you to enter your social security number. This prompts the software to pull an electronic credit report on you, and ask you two or three questions that only you could know the answer to, such as: What bank finances your auto loan? Or what is the amount of your monthly mortgage payment with such-and-such loan company? By answering these questions, you confirm that you really are Sally Jones from Moose Port, Michigan, and not Princess Motobuto from Nigeria or Sergei the Hacker from Russia.

This verification service costs $5, but is a very good investment. Once you are ID verified, eBay will place a little icon next to your name that tells everyone who bids on your auctions that you really are who you say you are. In addition to your feedback rating, credibility is very important to potential eBay bidders. If you are selling higher-priced items, many bidders will look for the *ID Verify* icon. Another advantage of becoming ID verified is that eBay will allow you to sell using the fixed-price *Buy It Now* feature we will discuss in chapter 8.

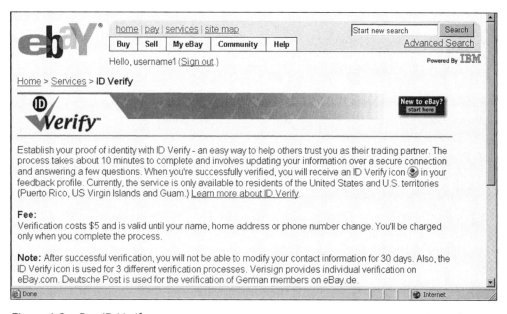

Figure 1.2 eBay ID Verify

OPENING YOUR PAYPAL ACCOUNT

The next step, if you haven't already done so, is to open a *PayPal* account. PayPal is the payment service owned by eBay. PayPal has a long record of reliability and service to eBay sellers. Over 75 percent of eBay users are registered with PayPal, and this is the only payment service that is integrated with the eBay checkout system—allowing you to automate the checkout process so you get paid quickly.

The basic PayPal account is free, but if you are going to receive funds on a regular basis, PayPal requires you to have a Business account. To register, simply go to www.paypal.com. To link your PayPal and eBay accounts, you will need to provide the same information you did when registering with eBay, as well as your eBay username.

Once you are registered and you sign into your account, you will notice a link on the upper left-hand corner of your account homepage that says: Verify Your Account.

When you click on this link, PayPal will ask you to enter your bank name, routing number, and account number. PayPal will then make two small deposits to your bank account—both in pennies—such as eight cents and seventeen cents. After that, PayPal will send you an e-mail instructing you to call your bank and determine the amount of the two deposits. You will then be given a link to click on where you enter the information. If the information you supplied was accurate, you will now be a PayPal Verified Account. This is very important because PayPal offers buyers up to $1,000.00 in fraud protection as long as they paid their money to a PayPal user who was verified.

When you buy something on eBay using your PayPal account, PayPal gives you several payment options. You can elect to use the credit or debit card you have on file, or you can write an e-check from your bank account. Of course, if you have cash in your PayPal account—which you will as soon as you become a seller and people start paying you—PayPal will first access the cash in your account whenever you authorize a payment. PayPal will *never* debit your credit card or your bank account without your authorization.

There is no fee to purchase using PayPal; however, there is a fee for sellers. Every time you receive a payment from PayPal, 2.9 percent of the selling price is deducted, plus $0.30 per transaction. This may sound like a lot, but it is actually cheaper than the rates and fees charged by merchant credit card companies like Visa and MasterCard. Depending on the bank where you open a merchant account, rates may vary from 2.5 percent to as high as 4 percent of the amount paid, plus transaction fees that can run as high as $0.40 per transaction. In addition to that, most merchant credit card companies have high setup fees and recurring monthly charges.

Not only is PayPal cheaper than merchant credit card companies, but it is the payment system eBay buyers prefer. Don't worry if one of your buyers doesn't have a PayPal account. You can still send him an electronic invoice via PayPal that allows him to enter his credit card information or send you an e-check online.

SETTING UP YOUR PREFERENCES

One of the most important benefits of using PayPal as your payment service is the automation eBay and PayPal offer to help you collect money quickly when an auction ends. Once you open your PayPal account, you have the option to set PayPal up as your preferred payment method and to insert the PayPal logo automatically into your auctions. Just click on the tab marked *Auction Tools* on your PayPal account page (see Figure 1.3). You should definitely do this because a lot of eBay buyers search for items with the term *PayPal* in their search. These buyers are looking for items that they can pay for by PayPal. So if you don't have the PayPal preference set for your auctions, your auction will not come up in this kind of search, even if what you're selling is exactly what the buyer is looking for.

Figure 1.3 The PayPal Auction Tools Tab

When you click on the Auction Tools tab, you will also see an option that says *End of Auction E-mail*. This allows you to have eBay send out a notice to the winning bidder of your auctions with a PayPal button embedded in the e-mail. All the winning bidder has to do is click on the button to pay you instantly via PayPal. You also have the opportunity to customize the e-mail by adding your own personal message.

GAINING EXPERIENCE

Now that you have a PayPal account, you are ready to buy and sell on eBay. Before you start selling on eBay, however, you should first bid on and win several auctions. *Don't skip this important step.* You can't really understand the selling process on eBay unless you become a buyer first. This way you learn how other sellers deal with winning bidders. For example:

✳ How do they communicate with you after the auction?

✳ How do they ask you for payment and what are their policies?

✳ How did they ship your goods, what did shipping cost, and how were the items packaged?

* Did the seller attempt an upsell—offering you a discount if you bought a greater quantity or a related product?

* How quickly did the seller post feedback for you, if at all?

* Just how smooth and comfortable was the process? Did you feel pleased with the transaction? If not, what could the seller have done better? If so, what aspect of the transaction really pleased you?

Bidding on items from several different sellers—and winning items from more than one seller—is a valuable part of your education as a seller. If you forgo this step, you will certainly make mistakes you could easily avoid. Hundreds of ordinary products are for sale on eBay, things that you use every day, such as shampoo, razor blades, diapers, and beauty products. Many of them are less expensive on eBay than at your local drugstore or supermarket, so bidding on them and buying them to gain experience in working through the process doesn't cost you much—and may even save you some money. The other advantage of buying on eBay is that you can start building your feedback rating, which we turn to next.

FEEDBACK

We will discuss feedback in detail in chapter 11, but we need to introduce the concept here because it is related to several of the initial steps you should take as a seller. When Pierre Omidyar started eBay in 1995, most observers thought it was an insane idea. *People are just not going to buy products over the Internet from strangers* was the recurring critique from the Silicon Valley know-it-alls. However, Pierre embedded in eBay two major concepts, which no one at the time understood: eBay would become a community of users and the community would become self-policing. Indeed, eBay became a community because of the intimacy and the direct contact the platform provided—and, yes, because the idea was just quirky enough to attract the same kind of people who were attracted to chat rooms and playing games online. Self-policing came about through the concept of *feedback*.

Here is how feedback works: Every time an auction ends, each party—both buyer and seller—is encouraged to post a short comment about the other party. Those comments become a *permanent* part of the buyer's and seller's reputations on eBay. If you open any eBay auction, you will see the username of the seller followed by a number in parentheses—for example, BidMoreOften (74). The number 74 represents the number of comments left by other eBay users about BidMoreOften. Before you bid on an item from a seller, you get to look at his feedback—what other actual customers have to say about their experience with that seller.

Figure 1.4 shows an example of feedback comments left for eBay user *BidMoreOften*.

Feedback Score:	74
Positive Feedback:	100%
Members who left a positive:	74
Members who left a negative:	0
All positive feedback received:	83

Learn about what these numbers mean.

Recent Ratings:		Past Month	Past 6 Months	Past 12 Months
⊕	positive	0	1	2
⊙	neutral	0	0	0
⊖	negative	0	0	0

Bid Retractions (Past 6 months): 0

Member since: May-09-00
Location: United States
* ID History
* Items for Sale
* Add to Favorite Sellers
* Learn more About Me

Contact Member

Feedback Received   From Buyers   From Sellers   Left for Others
83 feedback received by bidmoreoften (0 mutually withdrawn)   Page 1 of 4

Comment	From	Date / Time	Item #
⊕ Great communication. A pleasure to do business with.	Seller sellername1 (2808 ☆)	Apr-14-05 14:00	8179108315
⊕ Top Notch Transaction w/a Delightful eBayer! Thanks for making eBay great.	Seller sellername2 (991 ☆)	Sep-29-04 18:33	6924166926
⊕ very quick payment, enjoy the product! thanks!	Seller sellername3 (480 ☆)	Feb-22-04 12:11	3176419915
⊕ Lightning Fast Payment. Thank you for a smooth transaction. A++++	Seller sellername4 (4810 ★)	Feb-20-04 17:26	3552761450
⊕ Very prompt and courteous buyer, great to deal with, Thanks!	Seller sellername5 (6151 ☆)	Sep-28-03 09:10	2193086500
⊕ Excellent eBayer! Aces in my book! AAA+++	Seller sellername6 (94 ★)	Jul-30-03 18:58	2185019826
⊕ www.eFashionJewelry.com thanks you for a GREAT TRANSACTION!!!!	Seller sellername7 (10972 ☆)	May-22-03 06:15	2163084737

Done   Internet

Figure 1.4 Sample eBay Feedback Comments

Feedback is an enormously powerful tool and has now been copied in various formats by many other auction sites and Web shopping portals. Imagine if you walked into your local shopping mall and outside each store was a board where you could post comments about the quality of the products sold there and the customer service you received—and *the store was not allowed to remove those comments!* Don't you think the stores would work harder to provide good service? This is the power of feedback.

In addition to listing the comments from other eBay users, eBay also keeps track of how many comments are positive, neutral, or negative. Very few sellers have perfect feedback (100 percent positive), but over time eBay users have set the bar fairly high. A rating of less than 98 percent (two negatives out of one hundred transactions) is considered a yellow caution flag. Less than 95 or 96 percent, and you will find your bids dropping off substantially. So if you want to build a long-term business on eBay, protecting your feedback rating is critical to your success.

This brings us back to the importance of buying on eBay before you start selling. You also earn feedback comments when you buy; remember, both parties in a transaction get to leave feedback. When you start to sell on eBay, unless you have a feedback rating of at least ten to fifteen, it will be very hard to attract bids. Personally, I rarely buy from any seller with a rating lower than fifty, and at that low rating her feedback had better be 99 or 100 percent positive if she wants me to bid.

ABOUT ME PAGE

Whenever you open an auction on eBay, you will see the seller's username prominently displayed in the top section of the auction. If the seller has an About Me page, you will see a little icon after his name that says Me. If you click on this icon, it will take you to the seller's About Me page (see, for example, Figure 1.5). This is a page that eBay allows you to create to tell prospective bidders about you and your eBay business. There is no cost to set up your About Me page and it can help you to get more bids, especially when your are new and still have a low feedback score.

Figure 1.5 About Me Page

You can personalize the page any way you want. Some sellers use it to talk about themselves and where they live, often including photos. Others explain their policies and experience on eBay on their About Me page. Still others create an About Me page to help brand their business.

While eBay does not allow you to link to a Web site from your auction description, you *can* link to your personal or e-commerce Web site from your About Me page.

In chapter 25 we look more closely at ways to use your About Me page to drive additional revenue to your eBay business.

MY EBAY PAGE

Once you register, you will automatically be set up with a *My eBay* page. A link to your My eBay page appears at the top of every eBay page you access; it's located in the navigation links. When you click on this, you will be prompted to sign in with your User ID and password, because your My eBay page contains links to your account and personal information.

The My eBay page has four main sections: All Buying, All Selling, All Favorites, and My Account. Under All Selling, the first thing you see is a list of all the items you are selling, the current price and number of bids, whether or not your reserve has been met (if you have one), and the number of people who are watching your auction. If you click on the Sold link, you will see a list of the items you have sold and their status, as well as actions you can take just by clicking on the button next to each item. These actions include Send Invoice, Print Shipping Label, and Leave Feedback. Later, we address the issue of automation as it relates to selling on eBay. eBay sells a program called eBay Selling Manager, which, once it's integrated into your My eBay page, allows you to automate a lot of sales-related functions, such as sending out invoices and shipping notices, and posting feedback.

For the moment, just spend some time clicking on the various links on your My eBay page to become familiar with all the information that is available to you. Once you have some auctions launched and items sold, this page will become a useful tool for tracking your sold and unsold items, customer communications, payment and shipping status, and feedback.

Your My eBay Page also includes an important link to *My Messages*. Whenever eBay or a potential eBay bidder sends you an e-mail, you will receive the message in your personal eBay account, accessible via your My Messages page. If you ever question the authenticity of an eBay-related e-mail you receive in a personal e-mail account (such as Hotmail, Yahoo!, or Google), be sure to check your My Messages page to see if the message appears there. (See the box on page 24 for more about fraudulent e-mails.)

AVOIDING SPOOF E-MAILS

Be wary of spoof e-mails. These are messages that arrive in your e-mail inbox and *appear* to be from one of your bidders or buyers, often claiming that the buyer has not received an item he bought from you. The message will contain a link to sign into your eBay account. *Never click on one of these links in an e-mail.* The link is bogus: It will bring up a page that looks just like the eBay sign-in page—however, it is really a fraudulent Web site designed to capture your username and password. We delve into the topic of spoof e-mails and other types of fraud in chapter 20, but since you may receive one of these messages shortly after signing up with eBay, you need to be aware of this scam right off the bat as a lot of new eBay users fall for this.

If you receive an e-mail relating to an eBay auction or transaction purporting to be from eBay itself—or any message whose origin you are unsure of—just go to your My Messages page. If the message is authentic, it will also appear there. Remember: Neither eBay nor PayPal will ever send you an e-mail asking you to click on an embedded link to log into your account. Genuine e-mails from eBay and PayPal will instruct you to go to their respective homepages and log into your account.

BUSINESS LICENSES

If you are running your business out of your home, you will most likely *not* need to obtain a local business license from your town or county. Typically, local business licenses are for businesses that have customers visiting the business location. If, however, you open an office or rent space in a commercial location, you may need to get a local business license. This license is usually inexpensive—under $100 in most towns and cities. You can apply for it at the city clerk's office.

SALES TAX NUMBER

If you live in a state that charges sales tax, you need a *state sales tax number.* Other states that do not charge sales tax, such as Oregon and Idaho, typically issue a business-use tax number that serves the same purpose.

A sales tax number allows you to purchase merchandise for resale without paying sales tax to the vendor. Whenever you sell something in your state that is delivered to an address *in your state*, you must collect sales tax from the customer and remit the sales tax to your state's tax department. Most states require you to file and pay your sales taxes quarterly, although some states do it monthly, often depending on the volume of sales generated by your business.

You *do not* have to collect, or pay, sales tax on orders that you ship *out of state*. However, if you live in a state with a large population, such as New York, Illinois, or California, most likely you will sell a lot of items on eBay to buyers in your state.

You should always collect and pay this tax, because state tax authorities are aware that many Internet sellers are skirting this requirement, and they are cracking down. Sometimes a state compliance officer, masquerading as a legitimate eBay bidder, will purchase something low cost from you, or just send you an e-mail pretending to be a bidder, and ask if you charge sales tax. If you don't collect the tax, you will be subject to some serious fines. In some states, you're liable for criminal penalties as well.

BIZ BUILDER

Luckily, eBay makes it simple to collect sales taxes on in-state transactions. From the Sell Your Item page, you can enter the name of your state and the percentage of sales tax to collect. When an auction ends, if the buyer is located in your state, eBay automatically adds the sales tax to the final selling price and the shipping amount.

Most states require you to fill out a simple form once a quarter that lists all your taxable sales and mail it into the state with a check for the sales tax you collected. Later on, we'll look at a simple way to maintain these records and automate the process so it only takes a few minutes a week to keep track of sales tax collection and handle the payments.

Besides collecting and paying taxes, the other reason you need a state sales tax number is to purchase merchandise. Most legitimate wholesale companies simply will not sell to you unless you have a sales tax number.

It is very simple to get a sales tax number. In most states the fee is low, typically from $25 to $100, although some states require new businesses to put up a deposit as high as $500. This is usually returned after one year of paying your taxes on time.

To get the lowdown on state sales tax, visit the Web site for this book, www.skipmcgrath.com/3_weeks, and click on the navigation link *State Sales Tax*. This takes you to a page where you can link directly to the Web sites of the tax departments in all fifty states. There you can get all the information you need and download the required forms. In most cases you can apply for a number online.

COMMERCIAL CHECKING ACCOUNT

Since you are probably going to buy from wholesale companies, you will want to open a commercial checking account in the name of your business. Most legitimate wholesale companies and distributors prefer to deal with businesses, rather than individuals. They require you to have both a state sales tax number and a business checking account to do business with them. Later on, we give you tips on how to get into wholesale trade shows and merchandise marts, which also require this proof of business status. When you apply for a state sales tax number, you can register a business name at the same time. Simply take your certificate with the business name to your local bank and ask to open a commercial (or business) checking account. Most banks will do this for a minimum deposit of $100. At this time you should also apply for a credit or debit card for the account. You will be making wholesale purchases on the Web and paying online for different services, including your eBay fees. This way all your business expenses are handled through one account—and you will simplify both your record keeping and your taxes at the end of the year.

POWER MOVES

❏ Register your eBay account and sign up for a PayPal business account.

❏ If you haven't ever purchased anything on eBay, gain some experience by bidding on and winning a few items so your can learn about and get a good grasp of the process.

❏ As you are bidding and buying, be sure to look at each seller's feedback rating. When you win an auction, make sure the seller posts feedback for you. E-mail the seller a polite request if she forgets to do this.

❏ Set up your About Me page.

❏ Explore the resources on your My eBay Page.

❏ Apply for a sales tax number for your state.

❏ Open a commercial checking account and sign up for a business debit card.

CHAPTER 2

✦FINDING YOUR WAY AROUND EBAY✦

Besides the My eBay page and the About Me page, there are many more resource pages on eBay. As a seller you need to become familiar with pages that allow you to manage your items for sale, revise your auctions, end a listing early, and handle disputes from nonpaying bidders. You may not need to access these pages for your first few auctions, but if you do, it is imperative to know what actions eBay allows you to take and how to quickly find the tools you need.

SITE MAP

eBay's site map can be difficult to navigate, but it is still the best place to start investigating the tools available to you. Table 2.1 shows the most important links for sellers. As a seller, the middle column of the site map, Selling Activities (see Figure 2.1), contains several links you will be using often.

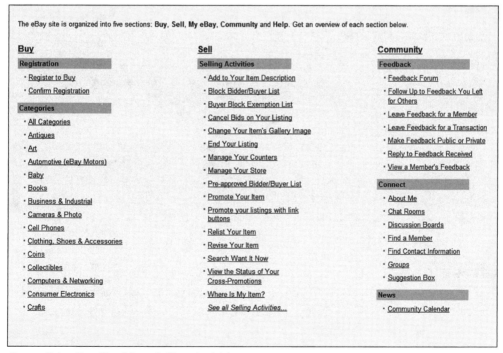

The eBay site is organized into five sections: **Buy, Sell, My eBay, Community** and **Help**. Get an overview of each section below.

Buy

Registration
- Register to Buy
- Confirm Registration

Categories
- All Categories
- Antiques
- Art
- Automotive (eBay Motors)
- Baby
- Books
- Business & Industrial
- Cameras & Photo
- Cell Phones
- Clothing, Shoes & Accessories
- Coins
- Collectibles
- Computers & Networking
- Consumer Electronics
- Crafts

Sell

Selling Activities
- Add to Your Item Description
- Block Bidder/Buyer List
- Buyer Block Exemption List
- Cancel Bids on Your Listing
- Change Your Item's Gallery Image
- End Your Listing
- Manage Your Counters
- Manage Your Store
- Pre-approved Bidder/Buyer List
- Promote Your Item
- Promote your listings with link buttons
- Relist Your Item
- Revise Your Item
- Search Want It Now
- View the Status of Your Cross-Promotions
- Where Is My Item?
- *See all Selling Activities...*

Community

Feedback
- Feedback Forum
- Follow Up to Feedback You Left for Others
- Leave Feedback for a Member
- Leave Feedback for a Transaction
- Make Feedback Public or Private
- Reply to Feedback Received
- View a Member's Feedback

Connect
- About Me
- Chat Rooms
- Discussion Boards
- Find a Member
- Find Contact Information
- Groups
- Suggestion Box

News
- Community Calendar

Figure 2.1 eBay Site Map: Selling Activities

Some of these links are quite valuable and you will refer to them often, so you will want to bookmark them (add them to your Favorites). To access the others, you can just refer to the site map when you need them.

Table 2.1: Useful eBay Links for Sellers

REVISE YOUR ITEM	Like all of us, you will occasionally make a mistake in one of your listings. This link allows you to fix any mistakes you made or add new information.
CANCEL BIDS ON YOUR ITEM	If you need to end an auction, you will first have to cancel any bids on your item. This is a page where you can do that.
END YOUR LISTING	You can end your listing at any time, but if there are bids, you must cancel them first (see above).
DISPUTE CONSOLE	This is where you can report buyers to eBay who have not paid for an item, or who failed to ship an item that you purchased. You can also link to the dispute console from your My eBay page.
BLOCK BIDDER/BUYER LIST	This is where you can block certain bidders from bidding on your auctions. If a bidder leaves me negative feedback, I always block him from bidding on my future auctions.
POWERSELLERS	Once you are a PowerSeller, bookmark this page because this is where you can access special tools for PowerSellers and communicate with PowerSeller support.

SELLER CENTRAL

Further down the middle column of the site map is a heading titled *Selling Resources.* Under this heading is a link to Seller Central. Seller Central contains many valuable resources for eBay sellers, including:

* **BEST PRACTICES:** These are listings of strategies and techniques developed by eBay PowerSellers to help you increase sales. I strongly recommend that you read them after you have read this book. Some of them might not make a lot of sense until you understand the context.

* **ADVANCED SELLING:** This section introduces you to some of eBay's advanced selling tools, such as eBay Keywords, the Trading Assistant program, and co-op advertising opportunities. Again, these are services best accessed after you have been selling for a while.

* **CATEGORY TIPS:** This is a very valuable section. The resources here include:

  > *Seller's Edge:* Strategies, features, and insights from the category managers and PowerSellers who specialize in the specific category.

  > *Seller Profiles:* An in-depth look at how successful sellers maximize their sales and profits on eBay.

  > *In Demand:* Lists of what's hot, with expert picks and top searches.

  > *Selling Guides/Zones:* Overview of the basics of selling in your category.

  > *Discussion Boards:* Your link to other sellers so you can share experiences and best practices.

  > *Contact Us:* A quick way to e-mail your eBay Category Management team.

* **WHAT'S HOT:** What's Hot is a PDF download that gives you a detailed report on the most searched-for terms during the previous month, plus the categories and products that are getting the most sales. This is a very valuable research tool.

* **NEWS & UPDATES:** Here's how you can keep up-to-date on all the changes going on with eBay—and there are a lot of them. If you are going to be a serious PowerSeller, you should get in the habit of checking the news and announcement boards daily. I like to do it first thing in the morning after I check my e-mails.

* **RESOURCES:** This is a great page to bookmark because it takes you to a site map of all the resources available to the seller, conveniently listed in one place. It is sort of a "sellers only" site map.

Further down the site map page is a series of links under the heading *My Account.* You do not have to bookmark these links because they are all easily accessible from your My eBay page.

THE EBAY TOOLBAR

The eBay toolbar (Figure 2.2) is a new feature released by eBay in late 2005. It is a toolbar you can download from eBay that installs automatically right below the URL window in your browser. At the moment it only works with Internet Explorer. eBay is supposedly working on versions for Mozilla Firefox and Mac Safari, but it is not known when they will become available.

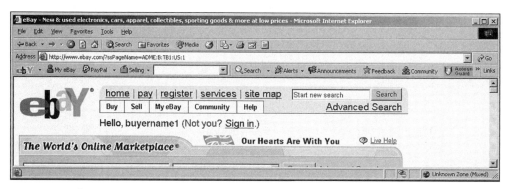

Figure 2.2 The eBay Toolbar

The eBay toolbar, which can be customized, contains a lot of useful features. There are instant links to the eBay homepage, My eBay, PayPal, new announcements, and the community message boards, as well as an alert feature that you can set to notify you of auctions ending soon.

EBAY COMMUNITY PAGE

eBay is a unique community. Its members have a long history (long, that is, in terms of the Internet Age) of helping each other out. You can connect to other members in several ways. On the eBay Community Page (see Figure 2.3) there are four Connect categories:

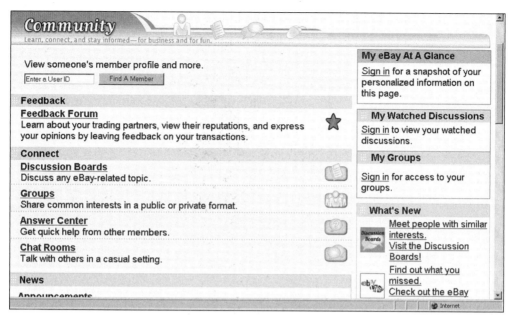

Figure 2.3 The eBay Community Page

✳ **DISCUSSION BOARDS:** Here you can post and reply to messages on thousands of topics. Special boards are geared to PowerSellers and trading assistants; other boards focus on subjects like PayPal and shipping and handling. Almost any eBay subject you can think of is covered here. And, if it's not, you can start a new board to discuss it.

✳ **GROUPS:** These are message boards arranged by category, so you can kibbitz with other collectors or sellers of merchandise in your category. Regional groups, by city and state, can be found here as well, so you can meet up online with folks in your local area.

✳ **ANSWER CENTER:** This is the place to ask any questions you may have, such as "How do I insert a photo into my auction?" or "How do I pack and ship a six-foot-long Didgeridoo?" Other sellers and eBay employees will answer almost any question you pose. You can identify employees by the color of their usernames—employee usernames are always pink. If you see someone refer to a "pink," she is talking about an eBay employee.

✳ **CHAT ROOMS:** eBay hosts over one hundred different chat rooms. Unlike the message boards, where it can take hours to get a reply to a post, the chat rooms are active 24/7. Once again, there are category-specific and feature-specific chat rooms.

POWER MOVES

❑ Familiarize yourself with the eBay site map, especially the links under *Selling Activities* and *Selling Resources.*

❑ Bookmark important pages in a special *eBay Pages* folder, so that you can readily access important tools without searching through the site map.

❑ Visit *Seller Central* and familiarize yourself with the resources and tools available to eBay sellers.

❑ Install the eBay toolbar on your desktop.

CHAPTER 3

✦WHAT SELLS ON EBAY?✦

With over 27,000 categories and subcategories, you can sell virtually anything on eBay. But choosing what to sell can often be overwhelming. You should first examine your own professional experience, hobbies, and interests. If you currently own a small retail store, gallery, or antiques shop, experiment to figure out which of your products will sell well on eBay.

If you want to start an eBay business from scratch, then you have to decide what business you are going to be in and what kind of products to sell. The biggest mistake new sellers make is jumping from product to product, trying to find the latest, hottest-selling gadget. If you are going to launch a sustainable business, you will have to specialize in something—preferably something where the competition is minimal.

In this chapter, we'll explore which products sell consistently well on eBay, and what categories might be right for you. We'll also focus on several product areas that are fairly easy for any eBay seller to enter. I am not suggesting that you choose one of these areas. Instead, I am trying to show you that there are plenty of categories where people can still make money, even with competition. Perhaps reading about some of the possibilities in this chapter will inspire some ideas of your own.

.... BEST PRACTICES ....

YOU CAN'T SELL *THAT* ON EBAY!

While you can sell anything from your kitchen sink to your pet rock collection on eBay, certain items are prohibited. Items you can't sell on eBay include human body parts; merchandise that has been recalled by the manufacturer; counterfeit brand-name goods, such as knock-off Rolex watches or Gucci handbags; any tobacco product; electronic surveillance equipment; animals and wildlife products; drugs and drug paraphernalia; firearms; bootleg recordings; and satellite or cable TV descramblers.

The complete list is quite long. In addition to prohibiting the sale of certain merchandise outright, eBay also places restrictions on other items, such as travel, real estate, paintball and Airsoft guns, and others. To find out more about prohibited and restricted items, click on the Help tab at the top of any eBay Page and type *prohibited items* into the search box.

CONSIDER YOUR INTERESTS

If you worked as an audiovisual technician, then you have the knowledge to sell AV equipment. Do you love cooking? Then get into cookware, restaurant equipment, or gourmet food items. Do you collect sports memorabilia? If so, start there. Perhaps you love to read and you always wanted to own a small bookstore, but you could never afford the overhead. On eBay, you can start with only a few dozen books and build your business from there. The same goes for art. You can buy art posters or prints wholesale just a few at a time. Thousands of art prints and posters sell every day on eBay.

If you are a computer or software whiz, look to the computer area for items to sell. Better still, write your own software or build a computer-related product or accessory and sell it on eBay.

Your business and product ideas are limited only by your imagination, *but make sure there is a market for the products and/or services you love and plan to sell.* (In the next chapter, we'll discuss researching a product to determine if there is a market for it on eBay, and what kind of prices you can realistically charge.)

Whatever you decide to sell, work to become an expert at it. Go to the library and read up on your products, talk to other merchants and collectors, research your competition, learn something about the history of your product, and study the manufacturers. Knowing your product category in depth will pay many dividends down the road.

If you don't believe in what you're selling, and you aren't willing to stand behind your product, your online business will most certainly fail. You should never sell a product you aren't enthusiastic about. If you wouldn't buy the product for yourself, or strongly recommend it to a friend or family member, then do not sell it to unwary consumers. (See chapter 11 on Feedback to understand how important this logic is.)

Certain items definitely outsell others. Information and software products are particularly hot sellers. Why? Because everyone buying on eBay already owns a computer. And using a computer means they need hardware and/or software. Therefore, almost anyone buying on eBay is a potential customer for computer hardware, software, or accessories.

Software is a huge seller on eBay. Here's why: If you wrote a highly specialized application, you would have a difficult time selling it to a software company. Such companies are not interested in a product unless it can generate millions of dollars in sales. But *you* could probably make a lot of money selling a few hundred or a few thousand copies on eBay and the other auction sites. Pokémon collecting software has become very popular (although there is so much of it around now that the price has fallen drastically). Or perhaps you have figured out a way to automate an eBay function. You can apply to work with the eBay Application Program Interface (API) and write (and sell) a software program for eBay users.

Computer games are also big with eBay buyers. Just make sure you are selling a popular game and not one that is considered passé. Yesterday's hot game that sold for $49.95 in the stores can be bought from the closeout dealers for $5.00 each. (You could still make this situation work, because there are people willing to buy old games for up to $15.00 each. Just don't expect to sell them for much more.)

A CPA with a large accounting firm here in Seattle collects sports memorabilia. He spent hundreds of hours scouring eBay for bargains. He realized right away that the market for common sports memorabilia was saturated and profit margins were too small for him to make much of a profit. So he decided to specialize in oddball and unusual items. He purchased a lot of five hundred unused tickets from the Ali-Fraser fight (the "Thrilla in Manila"), and began auctioning them off on eBay one ticket at a time. The last time I saw him, he was still selling them at up to $40 each. I believe he bought the whole lot for under $200.

My wife and I used to sell antiques. We worked through one of the largest antiques malls in upstate New York. The mall had a common Web site shared by all the vendors, and I ran auctions for the dealers. This gave us the image of being one large dealer with a high feedback rating. Whenever customers purchased from us, we would then introduce them to our Web site. Customers would link to our Web site over and over again because of the large variety of items available there.

At first I tried to use eBay to unload our slow-moving items. It didn't work! Slow-moving merchandise moves slowly for a reason; there isn't much interest in it on eBay, or in the store. After a few tries, I switched to selling our higher-quality, more expensive items. Our sales took off and we were getting bids 10–30 percent higher than we were selling the items for in the store.

Whatever your interest—clothing and fashion, sports, cars, cooking, high finance, antiques, art, books, collectibles—there are products you can sell on eBay and other auction sites. And, yes, eBay fortunes have been made on Furby toys, Pokémon cards, and Beanie Babies! Lately, anything related to Harry Potter, Sponge Bob, or Lord of the Rings will be a big seller. Next year it will be something else—guaranteed.

TARGET EBAY SELLERS

Another excellent sales strategy is to sell supplies to other eBay sellers. Bubble Pak envelopes, printer ink cartridges, and packing tape are big sellers on eBay. You can also sell supplies to collectors. Card collectors buy card holders and software to catalog their cards; doll collectors buy display cases; coin collectors buy coin holders; and so on. Look at a current fad and try to find some way to supply every collector with something he can use to give his collectibles extra value—instead of selling the collectible itself.

.... BEST PRACTICES ....

A WORD ABOUT CONSUMER ELECTRONICS

I always get e-mails from eBay sellers who want to sell the latest digital cameras, DVD players, plasma TVs, stereo equipment, and computers. Beware: *This is a very difficult business to enter.* First of all, the wholesale distributors for these products will not even talk to you unless you have a minimum $250,000 line of credit and can place orders of at least $50,000. I once spoke to Apple Computer's distributor about selling iPods online. The distributor's representatives were happy to sell the product to me at a wholesale cost of $122 for the $199 unit. However, I had to prove that I had a $200,000 line of credit and purchase one hundred units at a time.

If you have the kind of money it takes to place large wholesale orders and you want to find these goods, the best strategy is to contact the manufacturer of the product you wish to sell, and simply ask for the name and contact information of the company's wholesale distributor in your area. As long as you can meet the distributor's buying criteria, you can place an order.

USED GOODS

Hundreds of eBay sellers (many of them PowerSellers) sell used goods they pick up at flea markets, garage sales, and thrift shops. Almost any product you can think of has been sold used on eBay. Some of the best-selling products are children's clothing, women's plus-sized clothes, cowboy boots, ice skates, used athletic equipment, old cameras and any type of photo or darkroom equipment, old computers (that is, pre-1990), small appliances (such as Juiceman juicers, pasta machines, food processors, and mixers), and, of course, used watches and jewelry.

Used electronics, including vintage hi-fi equipment (pre-1980s), early computers, reel-to-reel tape decks, and 8-track players and cartridges, are excellent products—always in high demand on eBay. Because many eBay users consider themselves at the cutting edge of technology, used electronics often have a quaint appeal.

If you decide to sell used goods, you must first research what is selling. So before you buy that Juiceman at your local thrift store, check out the ones selling on eBay to make sure it's a desirable model and is going for a price that allows you to make a profit.

Only buy items that are in good-to-excellent condition. Don't attempt to sell anything defective or broken unless you are selling it for parts—and be sure to say this. If you sell anything used, it is critical that you completely and accurately describe its condition. In addition, you should take good photos and be sure to point out any defects. People will readily buy used goods with defects or blemishes as long as they understand the product's condition up front.

USED BOOKS

Used books are big sellers on eBay, and this is a very easy business to start. There are hundreds of eBay sellers making over $1,000 a week selling used books.

Unless you are an expert bookseller, forget about novels, literature, or rare expensive books. Any used bookstore owner will tell you that her daily bread and butter are nonfiction books on art, photography, crafts, cooking, history, sports, cars, trains, motorcycles, and music, as well as children's books. The same is true on eBay. You can buy plenty of these books at garage sales, flea markets, and thrift stores, and resell them on eBay for markups as high as 100–500 percent.

The easiest books to sell are the large "coffee table" editions on art, photography, transportation (trains, boats, cars, etc.), and sports. I recently purchased a beautiful history of Porsche motor cars at a local thrift shop for $1.00. It sold on eBay for $29.00. I was browsing the closeout table at Barnes & Noble just after Christmas and bought a brand-new, marked-down *History of the Superbowl* for $5.99. The cover price was $29.95, and it sold on eBay for $17.50. I once purchased a set of Ansel Adams photography books at a garage sale for $15.00. I sold them individually on eBay for a total of more than $90.00.

Cookbooks can be excellent sellers. Look for cookbooks by big-name authors such as Julia Child, Emeril Lagasse, and Bobby Flay, as well as classics like *The Joy of Cooking* and *The Saucier's Apprentice.*

Children's books are great sellers, if they are in very good condition. Any pop-up book is highly sought after. If you are selling low-cost books, such as children's books, group them into sets of three-to-five books each so you are not running a lot of small, individual auctions and you save on listing fees.

Another great category is old law and medical books, especially anything pre-1950s. It is amazing how many of these turn up at garage sales. Some of them, such as an early edition of *Black's Law Dictionary*, can go for huge amounts of money on eBay.

Finally, look for books on fine woodworking, as well as woodworking magazines. And while I recommend that you stay away from general "how-to-fix-anything" books, books that contain plans for building objects tend to sell readily.

Stay away from book club editions and series books, such as the Time-Life books, unless you have a complete set in perfect condition. I once found the complete Time-Life Photography series at a used bookstore for $65. I sold it on eBay for $122. That was less than I hoped to get, but still a nice profit.

Only buy books in good condition, preferably with intact dust jackets. Never pay more than 30 percent of what you think the item will sell for, and no more than 25 percent of the cover price. You can find plenty of books at garage sales for less than $2 that will sell on eBay for $10 or more. Stay away from books that would sell for less than $10; otherwise, you will have to sell dozens of books every week to make a decent income.

A great way to find books to sell is to place a small classified ad in your local paper like the following:

> *Local dealer will pay top dollar*
> *for nonfiction books in good*
> *condition. Call Kathy, 666-555-1111*

CLOSEOUT MERCHANDISE

Closeout merchandise is new merchandise that a retailer couldn't sell, or surplus goods left over at the end of a season. You can make good money selling closeout goods, but beware of some pitfalls in this area. We will cover buying closeout merchandise in great detail in chapter 6. In the meantime, the following surplus items sell well on eBay and are worth considering if you want to go this route.

Clothing

Brand-name surplus clothing is readily available from a number of wholesale dealers. The key words in the last sentence are *brand name*. Non–brand-name clothing may sell on eBay, but it will not bring the prices you need to make a profit. We will show you how to find unlimited supplies of brand-name clothing in chapter 6.

Surplus Electronics

As noted earlier, it is both difficult and expensive to get *new* consumer electronics to sell. However, you can find tons of *surplus* electronics—goods that stores couldn't sell and must now unload to clear shelf space for new models—and these are strong sellers on eBay. Make sure you are buying surplus goods and not *returns*—products customers brought back because they didn't work or there was some other problem with them. For ideas on how to acquire this merchandise, see chapter 6.

Remanufactured Electronics and Consumer Goods

Manufacturers of almost all types of expensive electronic and mechanical merchandise offer "remanufactured" or "refurbished" goods. These run the gamut from computers and digital cameras to stereo and television equipment, and home appliances.

Remanufactured equipment and merchandise are typically goods that were returned by consumers and, although not used, could not be sold as new because the package had been opened or some of the items had been assembled. In some cases, refurbished items are warranty returns. Typically, the manufacturers run these items through their normal quality-control process and repackage them. These goods are almost always offered with a full warranty. In the case of subsequent warranty returns, the items are repaired and once again run through the quality-control process.

Some large manufacturers, such as Sony, actually have outlet stores where they sell this merchandise directly to the public. For example, I once bought a Sony digital camera at the company's outlet store in Dallas at one-third the cost of retail. I used it for almost a year and then sold it on eBay for almost double what I had paid for it. You can find a list of Sony's outlet stores on the company's Web site (www.sony.com).

These remanufactured goods can be great items to sell on eBay. How do you find them? The best way is to visit the manufacturer's Web site and see if there is a link to an outlet for these goods. If not, then e-mail the manufacturer and ask how and where the company sells its refurbished items. As a last resort, you can call the company and ask for the purchasing department; a representative will usually tell you how you can access these products. In chapter 6, we will discuss specific Web-based closeout dealers offering remanufactured goods.

CLIPPINGS

Do you have teenage or preteen children? If so, selling magazine clippings could be a great business for you. Go to eBay and type the word *clippings* into the search box. You will get hundreds of auctions listed that sell magazine clippings of famous sports, music, and Hollywood stars. Each auction represents dozens, or even hundreds, of clippings people have assembled from magazines and sold as a lot. Here are examples of recent sales on eBay:

Elizabeth Taylor	217 Clippings	$383.00
Natalie Wood	136 clippings	$353.00

Charlie's Angels (Farah Fawcett/Cheryl Ladd)	110 clippings	$323.00
Michael Jackson	149 clippings	$192.00

Clippings of more contemporary celebrities can also be profitable on eBay:

Cal Ripken	117 clippings	$121.00
Shania Twain	88 clippings	$94.00
Johnny Depp	77 clippings	$79.00
Mira Sorvino	80 clippings	$55.00
Jude Law	127 clippings	$41.00

The older the star, or the older the clippings, the greater the value.

You can find old magazines at garage sales, thrift shops, small-town auctions, and many more places. Just put your kids to work, clipping the magazines and arranging the pieces into file folders or envelopes. Pay them a penny or a nickel a clipping. Once you collect a large number of clippings for a specific celebrity, put them up for sale on eBay—you'll make about 1,000 percent on your investment. Your kids can even make money by paying their friends to find and collect clippings for them. There is one lady in South Carolina who has an entire neighborhood of children collecting clippings and selling them to her. One local kid brought her a pack of fifty Dale Earnhardt, Jr. clippings. She paid the young boy $5 and sold them on eBay for over $75.

I was attending a small, local auction recently, and a box of old magazines came up from the 1950s and 1960s. The box sold for $30. I spoke to the woman who bought it, and she told me she could turn these old magazines into over $1,000—just by selling the clippings on eBay.

COLLECTIBLES

There are all kinds of collectibles you can sell on eBay. Almost anything you can think of is collected by someone. Did you know, for example, that people collect and pay big money for old eyeglasses? "Great—where do I find old eyeglasses?" you may ask. You will probably never see them at a garage sale. However, if the people putting on the sale are over fifty, try asking them if they have any old eyeglasses or even old sunglasses lying around the house. You will be amazed how many people will come up with them. Antique or vintage eyeglasses, both prescription and nonprescription, sell on eBay in the $25–$200 range.

The same is true of many more collectibles. Everyone knows that Elvis and Beatles memorabilia is highly collectible. The trick is to find the lesser-known items that most people don't think of. I have a friend who sells nothing but old fishing equipment and lures on eBay. He brings in more than $2,000 a month. That doesn't sound like much money, but he usually gets a 500 percent to 1,500 percent markup. He can buy an old fishing reel at a garage sale for $5 and sell it on eBay for $75. Other sellers do the same thing with vintage stereo equipment, old computers and cameras, old golf clubs and tennis rackets, and so on. You just need to do the research to see what is selling.

EBAY MOTORS

eBay Motors is a huge marketplace. More vehicles are sold on eBay Motors than on all the other automobile sales Web sites combined. For example, according to eBay, a Ford Mustang sells every seventeen minutes. Selling cars may be problematic, because most states have regulations that prohibit you from selling more than three or four cars a year unless you have a dealer's license. But most states exempt vehicles under three thousand or four thousand pounds from that requirement. This covers motorcycles, motor scooters, Airstream trailers, pop-up camper trailers, boat trailers, car engines and parts, and all types of automotive accessories and after-market products.

The husband of the manager at my local Starbucks has developed a great business buying old cars, breaking them up, and selling the parts on eBay. For a few hundred dollars, he can buy an old Plymouth from the '50s or '60s that's in such bad shape it can't be profitably restored, and make several thousand dollars selling everything from the brake pads to the window winders on eBay. A single piece of interior hardware can be worth $50 to $100 to someone who is trying to restore an original car. A friend of mine had a British Triumph TR-7, one of the worst British cars ever made. He fully restored it and drove it for about a year and then tried to sell it. He had over $3,000 invested in the car and couldn't even get an offer of $2,000 for it. He ended up selling it for parts on eBay and made over $4,500.

Another prolific eBay seller scours the countryside for old Airstream trailers. If he finds one in good condition, he does some simple cosmetic repairs and can usually make 50–100 percent on his investment. If the trailer is in poor condition, he breaks it up and sells the parts, again always doubling his money.

One of the largest PowerSellers on eBay is a young man named Michael, who sells under the Store name "Urban Import." He started his business while he was a junior in high school, using his dad's eBay account. Michael started selling race car seats he got at a good discount from his local auto parts store. By the time he was a senior in high school, he was importing after-market car seats and performance parts from Asia and grossing over $20,000 a month on eBay. Today he is a Platinum PowerSeller, someone who averages minimum sales of $25,000 to $150,000 a month on eBay. Michael will not reveal his total sales, but he is obviously doing very well.

CONSIGNMENT SELLING

When you sell something on consignment, you are selling an item for someone else as a service. This is the perfect eBay business. You do not need to purchase any inventory so there is no risk involved (except for the small amount you must pay in eBay listing fees). Someone gives you something to sell. You photograph the item, write a description of the piece, and put it up for sale on eBay. If it sells, you earn a commission—sometimes as high as 40 percent. Since the buyer pays for the shipping, whatever commission you collect is pure profit. If it doesn't sell, you simply return it to the consignor and you are only out a couple of dollars for eBay listing fees.

eBay actually has a program for consignment sellers called Trading Assistant. If you become a registered trading assistant, eBay will list you in its directory and help you promote your business in your local community with flyers, letters, business cards, and a co-op advertising program. These materials are available from eBay as Microsoft Word downloads. Simply enter your personal information (name, phone number, and so forth), and have them printed at a local print store. To attract customers (consignors), distribute your business cards to appropriate contacts and post the flyers on any free community bulletin board.

How much can you make as a trading assistant? When I was working on the manuscript for this book, I got a call from someone who saw my name in the eBay Trading Assistant directory. He was trying to sell a vintage Indian motorcycle. I went to his house and took the photos, launched an auction that night, and within two days a buyer in San José, California, hit the Buy It Now button and bought the motorcycle for $13,500. My commission was 10 percent for about one hour's work.

We are going to cover eBay consignment selling in chapter 27 in great detail. But before you get too excited, this is a skill that takes some experience. You will want to have completed at least a couple hundred auctions before embarking on consignment selling. (Don't worry. I am going to show you how to do that within a month or two.) While getting a consignment business up and running may take longer than three weeks, it's important to understand how this technique works from the outset. If you decide that you're interested in consignment selling, you'll want to work this strategy into the overall business plan you will develop as you read this book.

The Business & Industrial Category

Take a look at the Business & Industrial category on eBay. Some of the subcategories include construction equipment, farm equipment, medical equipment and supplies, restaurant equipment, and much more. This is a great area for consignment selling. For example, you can contact doctors and hospitals looking to sell their used equipment, building contractors who are replacing tools and gear, and farmers looking to sell their farm equipment for top dollar rather than trading it in to a dealer for rock-bottom value. We will cover more of this in chapter 27 on consignment selling.

In this chapter, I only touched on a few of the categories of items that sell on eBay. As part of your research, I suggest that you spend a couple of hours surfing the various eBay categories and the many subcategories of products available on the site. Then look at the auctions in those subcategories to become familiar with all the items and services that sell on eBay. As you do this, you will see myriad possibilities and opportunities for areas to specialize in. In the next chapter, we are going to show you how to use eBay's powerful search engine to conduct product research.

POWER MOVES

❏ In your notebook, make a list of your hobbies and interests.

❏ Next, brainstorm all possible products that fall into those categories. Don't rule anything out at this point.

❏ After reading the next chapter on product research, search on eBay to determine if there is a market for these products.

CHAPTER 4

✦PRODUCT RESEARCH✦

I am often asked, "What is the secret to making lots of money on eBay?" It's not exactly a secret, but the answer to that question is simple: *selecting the right product to sell.* What makes something the right product? First of all, there must be a market for the product. You have to have something that other people want to buy. Second, you must find a product that you can buy for a price that allows you to make a profit reselling it. Last, the market for the product you're selling cannot be overly saturated. A moderate amount of competition is fine; you can always best your competition. Also, competition usually shows that there is a market for the product—otherwise, other sellers would not be selling it.

In chapter 3, we covered some of the popular selling categories on eBay. Here we'll explore how to dig into these and other categories to find products that are marketable on eBay and can earn you consistent profits as an eBay seller.

TYPES OF SEARCH TOOLS

There are three tools for searching out products on eBay:

> **EBAY ADVANCED SEARCH FEATURE**

> **ANDALE RESEARCH TOOL**

> **TERAPEAK RESEARCH**

The eBay search engine is very powerful and, best of all, it's free to eBay members. Andale (www.andale.com) sells an online research service for $7.95 a month. This service gives you access to important statistical data, such as a product's average selling price and the best day and time to list an auction for a specific item. Terapeak (www.terapeak.com) is by far the most sophisticated research tool and reveals the most information. Terapeak gives you everything Andale and eBay do, plus a wealth of additional data.

THE EBAY SEARCH ENGINE

If you want to know what something is selling for on eBay, you need to search completed auctions. Looking at an ongoing auction will only reveal what the current bid is—you want to know what an item actually sold for.

At the top of every eBay page is a *Search* link. If you click on this link, you will go to eBay's search function page. Once there, look for another tab that says *Advanced Search*. Here you will be presented with a list of options, including *Completed listings only* (see Figure 4.1). Check this box before beginning your search.

Figure 4.1 eBay Advanced Search Page

If you scroll to the bottom of the Advanced Search page, you will see two drop down menus. One of them says *Sort by*. This allows you to sort by *Time: ending soonest; Time: newly listed; Price: highest first;* and *Price: lowest first*. When I am searching for a product I want to sell on eBay, I usually sort by *Price: highest first*. Because you are trying to determine what an item sold for, this gives you the results you are looking for without having to look through several pages of auctions that failed to close. The next drop down menu is *View results*. The options in this menu are *Picture Gallery* and *Show item numbers*. You can just ignore these options, since they reveal nothing useful.

Another check box is *Search title **and** description*. Do not check this box: It will bring up every auction that includes any of your keywords in the description, which could be thousands, depending on your keyword. For example, if you searched for *old fountain pen*, selecting this option would bring up every auction with the word *old* or *fountain* or *pen* anywhere in the description.

Narrowing Your Search

Since using a single word for your search can return hundreds of auctions, you may want to narrow the search even further. For example, suppose you are looking specifically for Omega watches, as opposed to just any brand of watch. You can find exactly what you're looking for by using the *and* keyword function in your search. In the search field, simply enter *Omega and watch.* This will return a list of all results with both the words *Omega* and *watch* in them, and exclude all that do not contain both words.

To narrow your search even further, look for items that include certain phrases or words that go together in a specific order. For instance, if you are searching for teddy bears, you can use quotation marks: "teddy bear." This will return a listing of all auctions with the words *teddy bear* in them. The word *bear* must immediately follow the word *teddy* or the listing will not come up.

Finding Auctions with Multiple Search Terms

If you are searching for listings that include any of several words, you can use the *or* keyword function in your search, indicated by a combination of parentheses and commas in the search field. For example: If you wanted to find all auctions that have in their title listing the words *cat* or *kitten,* then you would enter *(cat,kitten)* in the search field. This returns all auctions that have the word *cat* or the word *kitten* in their listing. Make sure you type the parentheses and *do not* insert a space between the comma and either search term. You can also include other keyword functions. For example, *(cat,kitten) +crystal* will return all items that have *crystal* and either *cat* or *kitten* in the title, thereby narrowing your search to crystal figures of cats or kittens. (Note: There is a space between the parentheses and the plus sign, but not between the plus sign and the search term.)

Eliminating Words from Your Search

eBay's search engine also locates auctions that include one word in the title but not another. For example, if you are looking for watches, but are not interested in Casio watches, you can use the *and not* keyword function, represented by a minus sign in the search field: *watch -Casio.* This will return all results whose auction titles include the word *watch,* but exclude the word *Casio.* (Note: There is no space between the minus sign and the excluded word.)

Spend some time playing with eBay's search feature until you are an accomplished searcher. This talent will put money in your pocket.

Learning from Listings

Besides discovering what a given product is selling for on eBay, there is much more you can learn from the eBay search feature. If you are about to sell a new product, look at all the auctions for that product and related products, and analyze them. What could you have done better? Could you improve on their listing titles? How do the descriptions read—could you write a better one? What about the photographs? Were successful auctions RPAs (Reserve Price Auctions) or did they start with low or high bids? Compare two auctions for the same or similar products. Which one got the most bids? A little research at this point will pay huge dividends down the road.

Search and eBay Seller Central

More than 60 percent of all people looking for products on eBay use the search feature. As we have just seen, you find products by typing in keywords. If you know the most searched-for keywords on eBay in any given category, you'll have a pretty good idea of what people are looking for. Knowing what people are looking for can help you decide what to sell.

Sometimes you have a product to sell and you need to see if there is a market for your product on eBay. Other times, you may want to start your research by determining what hot products are selling on eBay, and then finding a product to fill a market niche. To do this, you need to know what other people are searching for.

Here's an easy way to find the most sought-after keywords on eBay. Visit eBay Seller Central at http://pages.ebay.com/sellercentral.

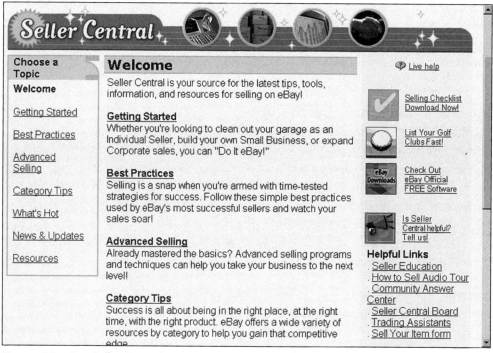

Figure 4.2 eBay Seller Central

On the Seller Central page (see Figure 4.2), you can find all sorts of valuable information, including teaching tutorials, the What's Hot report, and a monthly keyword research tool. If you look at the navigation bars on the left-hand side of the page, you will see two items related to research: *Category Tips* and *What's Hot.*

Click on Category Tips first. A list of the major eBay categories, accompanied by a category symbol, will come up when you click on this link. Select the category you are interested in and click on the link that says *In Demand.* This brings up a list of subcategories with the highest sell-through rates in the past month. Under that you will see a list of the top ten keywords for each subcategory.

Now let's click on What's Hot. Three options appear: *Merchandising Calendar, eBay Pulse,* and *Hot Items by Category.* Now, click on Hot Items by Category.

Clicking on this link will open up a report in Adobe Acrobat Reader that lists every category on eBay, followed by an associated "hot list" of the most searched-for keywords in that category. Take a few minutes to print out the report. It's a valuable research and marketing tool. If you don't have Adobe Acrobat Reader, eBay provides a link to download a free copy.

ANDALE RESEARCH TOOL

Andale (pronounced ON-da-lay, which is Spanish for "get going") is one of the oldest and largest Web-based auction management service companies. Andale provides the free hit counters that are used by almost every eBay seller. In addition to auction management services, Andale also offers several tools for auction sellers on a monthly subscription basis. (You do not have to use Andale's auction management tools to subscribe to the research service.) Andale's valuable tools include *Price Finder* and *What's Hot.* (Note that Andale and eBay both use the same terminology for their lists of best-selling items.) Andale charges $7.95 a month for its complete suite of research products.

What's Hot at Andale can help you find the best-selling items on eBay—both on the overall site and by category. Click on the main Research tab at the top of any Andale page once you have signed in. When the Research section opens, click on the What's Hot tab.

You will see a clickable box that says *Find out what's hot.* Just below this you will see the hottest item currently selling on eBay. *Hot* items are those with the highest number of successful auctions in a particular subcategory.

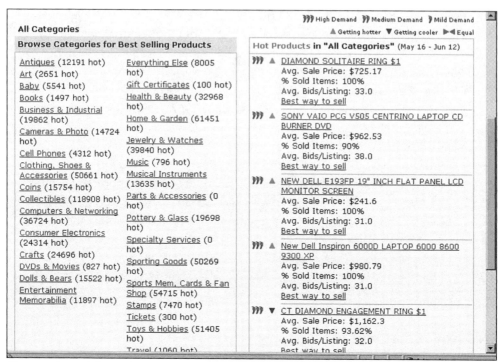

Figure 4.3 Andale's What's Hot Page

Click on the link and it will take you to Andale's What's Hot List (see Figure 4.3). On the right-hand side of the page, you will see a list of the current top five hottest-selling items across all of eBay. At the bottom of the list is a tab marked *More* that will expand the list to the top one hundred best-selling items.

On the left-hand side of the page is a list of eBay categories, each one followed by a number in parentheses. This is the number of "hot" items selling in each category. When you click on a category, it will take you to a further breakdown by product type or subcategory.

So how do you use this information?

If I were selling apparel on eBay, I could look at this list and learn several things. According to Andale's What's Hot rundown, in *Clothing, Shoes & Accessories* there are currently 50,661 hot items. That tells me I am in a good product category. When I click on that category link, it shows me which products are hot in that category. I can drill all the way down to specific products to get a list of how many are listed on eBay. I can use this data to evaluate if there is a market for my item, and if that market is "hot" or overly competitive.

The other tool on this page is Price Finder. When the page opens, you simply type in the name of the product you want to search for. In this case, let's search for *bird house.*

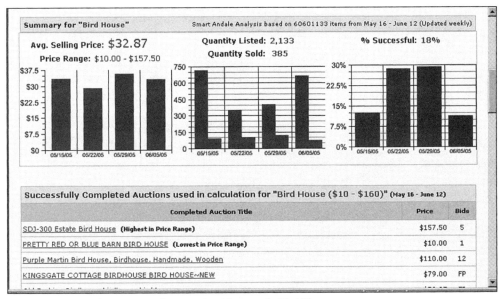

Figure 4.4 Andale Price Finder Results, Keywords Bird House

If you look at the results in Figure 4.4, you will see that the average bird house sold for $32.87. There were 2,133 items listed and 385 sold. That is an 18 percent sell-through rate. Eighteen percent is not very high, so let's refine our search further. Now type in *Martin Bird House.* This brings up new results. (See Figure 4.5 on page 54.)

The average selling price for a Martin bird house (a Martin is a type of bird, in case you're curious) is $63.79, a much higher price point. In addition, there were forty-four such bird houses listed, of which forty-four were sold. At 100 percent, the Martin bird house has a much better sell-through rate. This tells me that Martin bird houses would be a great item to sell on eBay.

You should perform this exercise for any product you're thinking about selling before deciding to buy inventory to stock.

Going back to the first results for *Bird Houses:* An 18 percent sell-through rate may not sound that high, but you have to evaluate the unsuccessful auctions in context. Many of them were priced wrong, some had poor photos and descriptions, others actually ended in the middle of the night when no one is awake, and, in some cases, the product being offered just didn't appear to be very good quality. When I looked at the

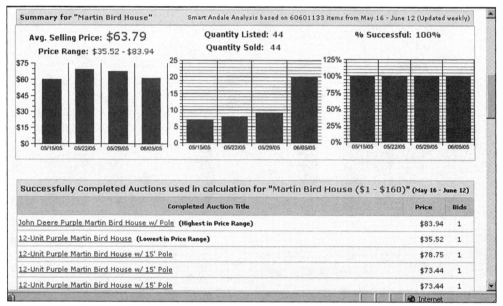

Summary for "Martin Bird House" — Smart Andale Analysis based on 60601133 items from May 16 - June 12 (Updated weekly)

Avg. Selling Price: **$63.79**

Price Range: $35.52 - $83.94

Quantity Listed: 44

Quantity Sold: 44

% Successful: 100%

Successfully Completed Auctions used in calculation for "Martin Bird House ($1 - $160)" (May 16 - June 12)		
Completed Auction Title	**Price**	**Bids**
John Deere Purple Martin Bird House w/ Pole **(Highest in Price Range)**	$83.94	1
12-Unit Purple Martin Bird House **(Lowest in Price Range)**	$35.52	1
12-Unit Purple Martin Bird House w/ 15' Pole	$78.75	1
12-Unit Purple Martin Bird House w/ 15' Pole	$73.44	1
12-Unit Purple Martin Bird House w/ 15' Pole	$73.44	1

Figure 4.5 Andale Price Finder Results, Keywords Martin Bird House

failed auctions, I estimated that about 30 percent of them did not sell due to poor listing techniques. Eliminating the listing errors, I'd place the real sell-through rate closer to 25 percent.

Another factor to consider is that the Andale Price Finder takes into account fixed-price eBay Store listings. This also skews the sell-through rate; since it only costs sellers two cents a month to list a Store item, a lot of merchandise gets parked there that moves very slowly.

To summarize: Sell-through rates are important to note when researching a product, but you need to consider them in the context of sellers' pricing and listing strategies. We will cover both of those factors in detail in chapter 10 to show you how to maximize your own personal sell-through rate.

TERAPEAK

Terapeak is the most powerful and sophisticated research tool available today. All this power comes at a price: Terapeak charges $16.95 a month—more than double Andale's price. Terapeak breaks its research reporting into four categories:

> **Basic**

> **Listings**

> **Sellers**

> **Trends**

Let's switch from *Bird House* to *Bird Feeder* and look at each report Terapeak offers.

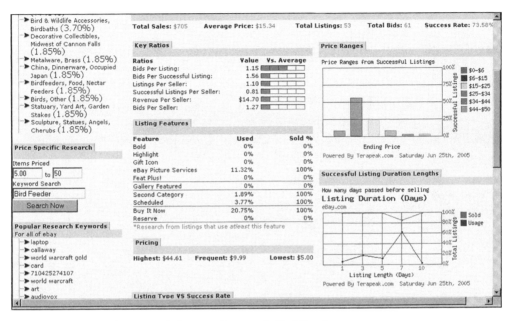

Figure 4.6 Terapeak Research Report, Keywords Bird Feeder

Basic Reports

Figure 4.6 shows Terapeak's Basic Research report. This report tells us quite a bit about how to sell bird feeders. This shot is only for one day; you can also pull a similar report for seven days, thirty days, or the current month-to-date. As you can see, there were fifty-three listings that received a total of sixty-one bids and a success rate of 73.58 percent. The total sales for all successful listings equaled $705.

Below these top-level statistics are the key ratios. Frankly, I don't find them that useful—with the exception of Successful Listings Per Seller. At .81 (81 percent), that tells me that almost any seller can sell a bird feeder if it is priced right.

Below the ratios are the Listing Features. These are special features that eBay charges extra for. (We will cover these in detail in chapter 16.) Because these features have additional costs associated with them, it pays to scrutinize this information closely to make sure these add-ons are a good investment. In this example, no one used the Bold, Highlight, or Gift Icon features. However, 11.32 percent used the eBay Picture Service (which rotates and supersizes your photos). These sellers had a 100 percent sell-through rate. Another small percentage used the Second Category add-on, which lists your item in two categories, and the Scheduler, which schedules your auction to launch at a specific time. These sellers also had a 100 percent sell-through rate.

You can also see the pricing various sellers used. The highest starting price was $44.61 and the lowest was $5.00. The most frequent starting price was $9.99.

Listings Reports

Let's switch to the Listings report format (Figure 4.7). This shows you the actual listings on eBay. This is useful because you can look at the listings that have bids and see what the sellers' strategies are. What prices are they starting their auctions at? What features are they using? Which models and types are selling and which are not?

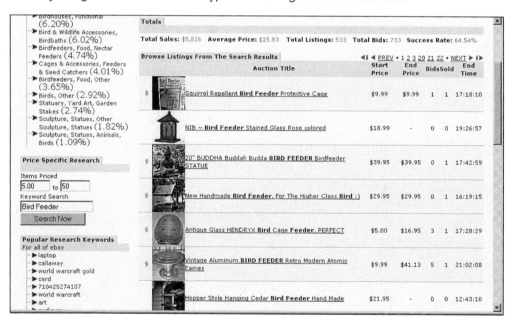

Figure 4.7 Terapeak Listings Report, Keywords Bird Feeder

Sellers Reports

Next is the Sellers Report. This shows you how the top sellers for a specific product are performing. Once again, you should examine their auctions to see which products are selling and which techniques work best. We will discuss various listing, pricing, and selling techniques in later chapters, but the key here is to help you find a product that will sell on eBay. Figure 4.8, a snapshot of a Sellers Report for bird feeders, reveals two things: First, bird feeders are big sellers. Second, judging from the number of auctions, the competition is not that great. For example, there were about five hundred auctions listed for bird feeders during the week of this report. If you did a search for digital cameras, you would see roughly eight thousand auctions listed. If you narrowed the search down to one manufacturer, such as Sony or Nikon, you would still see several hundred auctions for each one.

Figure 4.8 Terapeak Sellers Report, Keywords Bird Feeder

Trends

Finally, there is the Trends Report. This report shows you overall revenues and successful listings for a product over a specified period. Examine Figure 4.9, a snapshot of a Terapeak Trend Report for bird feeders (see page 58). The graph reveals that Sunday, Thursday, and Friday are the best days to end an auction for bird feeders.

As you can see, this is very useful data for helping you determine if a product you want to sell on eBay has a market. Once you begin listing your items on eBay, you can return to this report to click on the more successful (highest final value) auctions and determine which promotional features are most effective, and which days and times are best to list and end an auction for almost any product.

Figure 4.9 Terapeak Trend Report, Keywords Bird Feeder

As you narrow down the list of products you want to sell—and discover new products as your business grows—continually return to and verify your research. Here is a quick way to do this: Open a Word document and list the items you want to sell. Now open the Terapeak research page in another window. Copy and paste products from your list of items one at a time into the Terapeak research box and perform a search on each one. Print out the basic report for each item and study it offline.

Once you have your printouts, for each product ask yourself the questions discussed in the next chapter. This research and analysis should help you to make an informed decision about which items it would be best for you to sell.

POWER MOVES

❑ Go to Andale (www.andale.com) and Terapeak (www.terapeak.com), and read the features and benefits of each service. Determine if you would like to sign up for one of these services, and go through the necessary registration processes.

❑ Review your list of potential products to sell from chapter 3. For each product you are considering, use the eBay advanced search tool—as well as Andale or Terapeak, if you have signed up for either—to determine:

> Marketability

> Average selling price

> Effective promotional features

> The best days and times to list the product for sale

Be sure to keep detailed notes on your research, so that you can use this information when you begin listing items for sale.

❑ Based on your research, begin eliminating products from your list that do not appear to have a market, or whose average selling prices are lower than you are looking to charge per item. (You will narrow this list down further in the next chapter.)

CHAPTER 5

✦ WHAT SHOULD YOU SELL? ✦

You have now given some thought to products you would like to sell, and you've learned how to research whether a specific product has a market on eBay. The key words in the last sentence are *on eBay*. There are plenty of products that might sell well in a specialty store or at your local mall, but cannot get any traction on eBay. This is why it is so important to take the time to research a product thoroughly before committing to purchasing a large quantity of merchandise.

We're about to move on to one the most important topics in eBay selling: product acquisition (chapter 6). However, let's review in this chapter some final factors to consider before deciding which products and categories are right for you as a seller.

MARKET SIZE

First consider this: *Does the product you are thinking of selling have a viable market on eBay?* This question can best be answered by using the research tools we covered in the last chapter. If you searched for an item and found that only three items of its kind sold in the past month, that is not a large enough market to sustain a business.

COMPETITION

How much competition is there for the product you want to sell? Competition is a relative term. If thousands of items are selling in a given category, but there are only a handful of sellers, then the competition is low. On the other hand, when we were looking at bird feeders, we saw that only a few hundred of these items sold each week. It's crucial to examine the number of competitors very closely. A large number of sellers indicates a high level of competition. One clue as to level of competition is the average price the product is going for. If you are looking to sell an item, and you see that the average price for the item is ridiculously low, there is probably either too much supply or too many sellers.

PROFIT MARGIN

Can you source (buy) the product at a price where you can make money? We are going to cover in detail how and where to buy products to sell on eBay in chapter 6. However, in evaluating which products to sell, you need to understand basic pricing and margin strategies.

If you are buying a product for $9.00 and selling it for $13.00, it would seem that you are making $4.00 on each product you sell. Four dollars works out to a 31 percent margin. That may seem fine at first, but remember, eBay listing and selling fees and PayPal fees are going to eat up about $1.00 of your margin. That brings your profit down to $3.00 per item. At $3.00 per item sold, you have to sell one hundred items a week to make $300.00. That is an awful lot of work for $300.00. If you are selling a $75.00 item and making 33 percent profit, then you are grossing $24.75 on each auction before fees. Now you don't have to sell as many to make a decent amount of money. While there is no set rule for how much of a profit margin you should be aiming for, always keep in mind the following indisputable fact: The lower your selling price, the greater your margin must be to make a profit. If I am selling an item for less than $25.00, I want my margins to be much higher—closer to the 50–75 percent range.

INVENTORY

Do you have a reliable continuing source of supply for your product? If you are selling closeout-type products or buying your products from a range of vendors, your inventory may become depleted and you might not be able to restock. Unless you are selling a broad category of closeout products, such as apparel, where there is always a large supply, you may want to pick a product you can source from a manufacturer or distributor on a regular basis.

UPSELLING

Does your product lend itself to upselling? An *upsell* (some people call it a *cross-sell*) refers to attaching a second product or a multiple quantity to the first sale. Let's look at our bird feeders, for example. When someone buys a bird feeder, he also needs bird food. I could send the winning buyer an e-mail offering free shipping if he bought a package of bird feed, which I could ship with his order. If he agrees, I have only paid one set of fees to eBay, but I have made two sales.

Upselling is one of the keys to making huge profits on eBay. Whatever product you decide to sell, make sure there are compatible products that you can upsell the buyer at the time of sale. We will explain how to do this in detail in chapter 25.

EASE OF SHIPPING

Does this product present any shipping challenges? Shipping costs can be a big turnoff to your buyers. Large or unusually shaped products may require substantial shipping costs. I once had a great source of Australian didgeridoos. They weren't that expensive to ship, but a specialized box ended up costing me $11 each. The price I listed on eBay was attractive—until I tried to pass the extra $11 on to the customers.

LONG-TERM VIABILITY

Does your product have legs? The phrase *having legs* refers to staying power. Is this a fad product, or does it have either a lasting or an evolving market? Millions of people bought Beanie Babies at the height of the craze and are still stuck with them today. I know one seller who bought the contents of a video rental store that was going out of business. He now has thousands of videotapes at a time when the rest of the world has moved on to DVDs.

SIMILARITY TO YOUR OTHER PRODUCTS

Is this a niche product that complements your other products? Does this item fit into your current product niche, or will this represent a new direction for your business? If it's a new category, are there other products you can find to complement it?

If you ask yourself these questions before deciding which products to sell, you will avoid errors that many new sellers make. There is still no foolproof way to select a product. You may find a hot product, only to have a competitor come along and undercut you. This is why you should always be looking for new products and product categories. Both eBay and the Internet are highly competitive and fluid. If you are going to run even a small successful business, you must be on the lookout for new products and opportunities all the time.

POWER MOVES

For each item on your narrowed-down wish list of products, ask yourself the following questions:

- ❏ Is there a sufficient market for this product?
- ❏ How much competition is there for this product?
- ❏ What is the projected profit margin for this product?
- ❏ Is there a continuing, reliable source of supply?
- ❏ Does the product lend itself to upselling?
- ❏ Can this product be packaged and shipped easily?
- ❏ Does the product have a long-term market?

Based on the answers to these questions, eliminate any products from your list that do not appear viable at this time. You should now have a final list of products you would like to sell on eBay. In the next chapter, we will explore ways to source this merchandise quickly and economically.

CHAPTER 6

✦ PRODUCT ACQUISITION ✦

"Where can I find products at wholesale prices to sell on eBay?" is one of the most frequently asked questions by new eBay sellers. Learning how and where to acquire wholesale products can be intimidating. Yet it doesn't need to be. Successfully working with wholesalers is mostly a matter of learning their jargon and how the market works, as well as finding wholesale companies that will agree to work with small businesses.

In this chapter, we are going to learn just what *wholesale* means; in addition, we'll discuss the different types of wholesale suppliers, how to locate wholesale sources that will work with you, and how to deal with these suppliers once you are ready to buy. We will also introduce you to the specialized terminology of the wholesale world and some of the more common paperwork and forms used by wholesale suppliers.

DEFINITION OF *WHOLESALE*

First of all, you need to understand exactly what *wholesale* means. The term *wholesale* is a very fluid concept that loosely refers to the discounted amount at which you buy an item to resell at a (hopefully) higher price. Unfortunately, there is no such thing as a standard wholesale price or percentage. If I buy a pair of antique silver candlesticks at a local auction for $190 and sell them on eBay for $230, then $190 was my wholesale price. That is not a very large margin, but I did buy for less than I sold, so my purchase price could be considered a wholesale price.

To better understand wholesale pricing, it helps to understand the different types of pricing used by resellers.

- ✳ **RETAIL PRICE:** Retail stores have very high expenses that include employees, rent, utilities, and inventory carrying costs. Most retail stores need to have a 100 percent markup on merchandise to make a profit over time. Therefore, retailers consider a wholesale price to be 50 percent (or less) of the suggested retail price.

- ✳ **QUICK SALE PRICE:** The quick sale price is the price bargain hunters are looking for. You find these prices in wholesale clubs like Costco and Sam's Club, at outlet malls, and on the sale tables in retail stores. Because people go to eBay to find a bargain, the quick sale price is often comparable to the eBay price.

✳ **DISTRESS PRICE:** Manufacturers, distributors, and retail store owners cannot afford to sit on nonperforming inventory: Such items tie up their cash and monopolize shelf space needed for newer products that will sell for higher prices. Once merchandise reaches this point, it is often sold to closeout or surplus dealers and ends up in dollar stores, flea markets, and on eBay. Distress prices can be as low as ten cents on the retail dollar or half (or better) off the original wholesale price.

Retail stores typically buy from distributors, although some buy direct from manufacturers. When a retail store owner buys merchandise, he is looking to *keystone* the pricing, or set his retail price at twice what he pays for the item. So if you are negotiating with a wholesale distributor, she might say something like this: "Here are the retail prices. We give you the keystone discount on your first one hundred items and an additional 10 percent if you pay cash." If the retail price was $10.00, your price would be $5.00 each in quantities up to one hundred, and an additional 10 percent off the wholesale price ($5.00, minus 10 percent [$0.50], for a final per-piece cost to you of $4.50) if you paid cash as opposed to getting thirty-day credit terms.

TYPES OF WHOLESALERS

There are several types of wholesalers, and we will explain shortly how to find these sources of merchandise. But first you need to understand who you are dealing with.

Importers

Importers may be large or small. A large importer generally sells in very large quantities, such as container loads or quantities of five thousand to ten thousand at a time. There are, however, many small importers who buy large quantities and break them down into smaller lots. These importers may sell by the case, by the dozen, or may require a minimum dollar order, such as $500.

Look in your local Yellow Pages™ under *Importers*. If you live in a small town or in the middle of the country, get a Yellow Pages directory from any large port city—such as New York, Philadelphia, Baltimore, San Francisco, Seattle, or Los Angeles—where you'll find a higher concentration of importers. You can use www.yellowpages.com or www.smartpages.com to locate importers as well.

A new resource set up in cooperation with GlobalSources, Inc. and eBay is www.GlobalsourcesDirect.com. This is a Web site for large exporters from Asia who break up huge wholesale lots into smaller lots and sell them to eBay sellers. A typical order will be for twelve to forty-eight units, with prices running from a minimum of $100 to a maximum of about $500.

Manufacturers

Manufacturers come in all sizes. The largest manufacturers, such as Sony, General Electric, Liz Claiborne, Revlon, and Cuisinart, will rarely deal directly with a reseller or retail outlet unless you are the size of Wal-Mart or Sears. Instead, these manufacturers rely on distributors. There are however, thousands of small- and medium-sized manufacturers in the United States and overseas that will work directly with resellers. Some of them will even drop ship to your customers. (We'll discuss drop shipping in the next chapter.)

BIZ BUILDER
___

Whenever you buy from a manufacturer, you are as close to the source as you can get. This is always where the best pricing is.
___

Smaller manufacturers will often work directly with you, while others work through manufacturer's representatives, or *manufacturer's reps*. A manufacturer's rep is usually a one- or two-person business that represents both domestic and foreign manufacturers on a commission basis. If you are talking to a large manufacturer or foreign exporter, ask if the company has a manufacturer's rep. This person will often sell goods to you at a lower price and in smaller quantities than a distributor will. Later in this chapter we will show you how to locate and contact both manufacturers and manufacturer's reps.

Distributors

There are two types of distributors—*master distributors* and *general wholesale distributors*. A master distributor is usually a sizable company that only distributes for one or two large manufacturers, or only distributes one product line, such as computers, apparel, furniture, or the like. Typically, a master distributor will not carry competing brands of the same product. For example, a master computer distributor might carry one brand of computers, printers, and monitors.

A general wholesale distributor buys products from various American and foreign manufacturers, and resells them to retailers. Some specialize in certain products, while others can, and often do, sell virtually anything.

Closeout or Surplus Dealers

Closeout dealers go by several names—closeout, liquidation, surplus, and overstock dealers—but they all do roughly the same thing. These dealers either buy distressed goods outright and resell them, or they act as consignment dealers for companies seeking to sell distressed merchandise. Remember that distressed merchandise consists of goods and products that a manufacturer, distributor, or retailer needs to get rid of quickly. Because of the subsequent low cost to resellers, surplus or distressed merchandise represents the majority of new items sold on eBay. Buying from closeout dealers is an excellent way to find goods to sell on eBay that will allow you to make a healthy margin.

It is important, however, to understand some of the terms that closeout dealers use. *Surplus, overstock,* and *shelf pulls* refer to new merchandise that did not sell. These items will typically still carry the original store price tags. Be very careful that you are not buying *returns.* You want to avoid purchasing an item a customer returned because it was broken, didn't fit, or was the wrong color—or perhaps was an expensive dress someone bought to wear to a party one night and then returned to the store the next day. I generally do not buy returns unless I can physically inspect them, which is rare.

The other category of closeout merchandise to avoid is called *seconds.* These are goods that have some type of manufacturing defect. These can be real bargains if you know what you are getting. However, I recommend holding off on purchasing seconds until you have more buying experience, and can acquire and resell this merchandise effectively.

LOCATING WHOLESALE SOURCES

There are two basic ways to find the wholesale sources we've discussed so far:

> **The Internet:** As each year goes by, more and more companies are listed on the Web.

> **Offline:** It is also very easy to find sources close to you, using traditional methods, like the Yellow Pages and business directories, and by visiting local wholesale merchandise marts or trade shows in cities near you.

Finding Wholesale Sources on the Web

There are several well-known wholesale search engines where you can perform a search online by product or manufacturer:

* **THE THOMAS REGISTER** (www.thomasregister.com; see Figure 6.1) lists virtually every manufacturer in the United States. If you know who makes a certain product, you can find the manufacturer—and often, the distributor's e-mail address, phone number, and other contact information—by typing the manufacturer's name into the search box. You can also search by product, which will bring up a list of manufacturers. Just click on a manufacturer's name, and the Register will direct you to the company's Web site, if there is one, or display the company's contact information if there isn't.

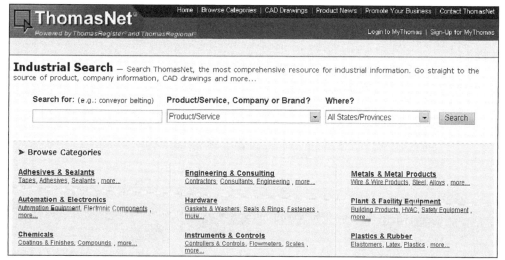

Figure 6.1 Thomas Register Homepage

✳ **GOWHOLESALE** (www.gowholesale.com; Figure 6.2) is one of the largest Web sites designed to help you locate dealers and distributors that sell to small resellers directly. You can search by individual products, such as shirts, cameras, or computers, or by brand name, such as Tommy Hilfiger, Nikon, or Dell. One minor shortcoming of goWholesale is that a search will often bring up retailers who sell at discounted prices and call themselves wholesale sellers. However, it is pretty easy to screen these retailers out by carefully reading the descriptions accompanying your search results.

Figure 6.2 The goWholesale Homepage

✳ **WHOLESALEGOPHER** (www.wholesalegopher.com) is another great search engine where you can locate wholesale sources. In addition to offering a search feature, WholesaleGopher can connect you to dozens of major wholesalers who advertise on the site. All of these advertisers are seeking eBay sellers to work with.

✳ **WHOLESALECENTRAL.COM** (www.wholesalecentral.com; Figure 6.3) lists several hundred wholesale vendors who pay to be hosted on this site. Its companion site, CloseoutCentral.com (www.closeoutcentral.com; Figure 6.4) hosts dozens of closeout and surplus dealers.

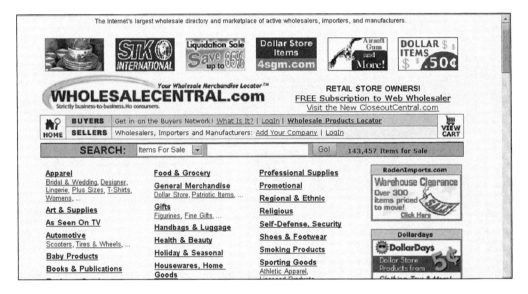

Figure 6.3 The WholesaleCentral.com Homepage

BIZ BUILDER

On the homepage of my Web site (www.skipmcgrath.com) is a link labeled *Web Wholesale Search*. This link will take you to a free wholesale search engine optimized for eBay resellers.

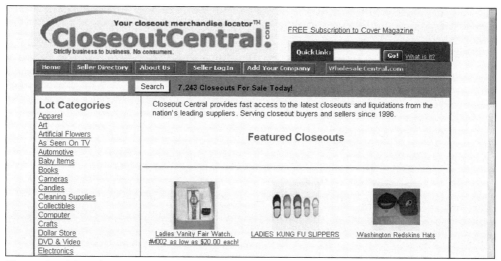

Figure 6.4 The CloseoutCentral.com Homepage

✳ **ALIBABA.COM** (www.alibaba.com; Figure 6.5) is a pay-per-click site where manufacturers from China, Taiwan, Korea, and other Asian countries list their products. (The manufacturers pay for each click or pay a monthly fee to be listed. It does not cost you anything to search this site.)

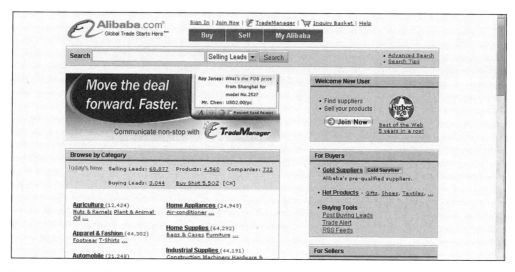

Figure 6.5 The Alibaba.com Homepage

Alibaba is a very powerful search engine, where you can find thousands of products. Many of the companies sell only in large volume, but if you are patient and keep searching, you can find plenty of sources that will sell in smaller quantities, suitable for the average eBay seller. One word of caution: *Anyone* can list products for sale on Alibaba, and there are many scam artists out there. If you look closely at the Alibaba site, you will see a link to Gold Suppliers. Alibaba has certified these suppliers and confirmed their identities. I recommend confining your search to these suppliers.

✳ **GLOBAL SOURCES** (www.globalsources.com; Figure 6.6) is a large international pay-per-click Web site similar to Alibaba. In fact, you will find many of the same companies listed on both sites. You can link to Global Sources directly from eBay. In 2005, eBay announced a strategic partnership with Global Sources, whereby the exporter works with several manufacturers to sell to eBay sellers in smaller quantities. These items will be placed for bid in lots in the eBay *Wholesale, Large Lots* category.

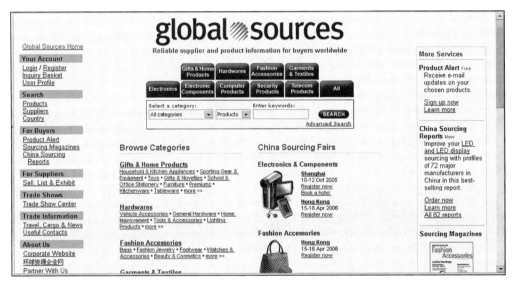

Figure 6.6 The Global Sources Homepage

✳ **BUYLINK** (www.buylink.com) is an online merchandise mart for gifts, collectibles, and household accessories. Once at the site, you have to fill out a form to register before you can view any pricing. It typically takes about two business days for BuyLink to e-mail you with a password and username. Once you are registered on the site, you can see prices and specifications, and purchase online from more than five hundred wholesale sources.

Merchandise Marts

Almost every large city in America has a *merchandise mart.* A merchandise mart is a building where various wholesalers—including small manufacturers, manufacturer's reps, and distributors—rent showroom space. (If you live in a small town or rural area, you will likely have to go to the nearest large city to locate one, although you can reach some by e-mail, telephone, and fax.)

These venues go by many names; some specialize in one kind of item, while others feature all sorts of general merchandise:

* A *merchandise mart* typically showcases a wide variety of products, but most tend toward the low end in price.

* A *gift mart* usually specializes in gifts, collectibles, and small decorator and household pieces.

* A *design center* sells furniture, rugs, lamps, and decorator items.

* Some cities, such as New York, Chicago and Los Angeles, have *fashion centers* and *jewelry centers* that specialize in items of personal adornment.

Whatever the name and the type of goods they carry, all these markets have one thing in common: They are not open to the general public. When you walk up to the information booth at a merchandise mart or design center, you will often see a sign that reads, "Admission to the trade only." The word *trade* refers to retail stores, eBay and Web site sellers, and interior decorators. Depending on the venue, it can be somewhat difficult to gain admission. Some even insist that you own a retail store, although this is changing, as more and more companies conduct business on the Web.

You can locate a merchandise mart by doing a Google search for the term you are looking for: *merchandise mart, jewelry mart, design center,* and so on. This will usually bring up a list of markets by city. Just look for the one nearest you. You can often find local results by adding "+ [name of city]" to the end of the search, for example: *jewelry mart + Chicago.*

When you approach the mart to go in, there will usually be a counter where officials are checking to see if you have a badge, which was issued in advance, or the qualifications to obtain one on site. To gain admission to most of these marts, you'll need to show proof of your business status, including a sales tax number, a registered business name, a commercial checking account, business cards, and company letterhead. Once the person at the front desk examines these, he will issue you a badge that you must wear while you are inside.

Once you gain entry, a whole new world of wholesale products opens up to you. Merchandise marts, gift marts, and wholesale trade shows (which we discuss next) are the best places to find new merchandise to sell. You will find dozens, even hundreds, of products that you will not come across on a Web search. Each dealer has a showroom that is much like a retail store, displaying all her products. Unlike a retail store, however, you can't walk out with the items. When you enter each showroom, ask for a catalog and price sheet. As you walk around the room, you can refer to the prices for any items you see.

Most dealers at merchandise marts have minimum-order requirements. Sometimes it will be a case or a dozen units; sometimes it will be a certain dollar amount, such as $250 or $500. Unless the dealers are selling expensive merchandise like jewelry, the minimums will rarely be more than $500.

When you decide what you want to buy, return to the front desk and fill out an order form. You can pay by check or sometimes by credit card. Once you place a few orders with the same dealer, he will usually ship on credit.

Trade Shows

Trade shows are just like merchandise marts, only larger. Trade shows move around the country, and there are different shows at various times of the year. Here in Seattle, where I live, the Seattle Gift Show is held every January and August. (If you go to the Web site for this book, www.skipmcgrath.com/3_weeks, I have posted links where you can find trade shows nearest your community.) Certain cities, such as Las Vegas, Los Angeles, Chicago, Dallas, Atlanta, and New York City, host dozens of specialized trade shows virtually year-round.

Getting into a trade show is much like gaining admission to a merchandise mart. The first time you register, the managers will want to see your business license or sales tax certificate, your business card, commercial checkbook, and so on. In many cities, once you register at the local merchandise mart, your name will be given to trade show companies coming into town, and you will automatically receive tickets in the mail.

You shop at a trade show the same way you do at a merchandise mart. Browse the merchandise and place an order when you see something you like. The goods will usually be delivered within a week or so, unless you are seeing samples of products that are not yet available. For example, shows that run from July to October will often showcase merchandise the vendor plans to release in time for Christmas. While you might place an order in August, the goods might not be shipped until early November.

Most trade shows have a computer kiosk in the lobby as a convenience for the attendees. If not, there may be a "hot zone" in the convention center or hotel where you can boot up your laptop and gain Internet access. If I see a product that interests me, I go out to the kiosk and do a search on eBay to see what it's selling for before deciding to buy.

Trade shows are an excellent way to see the newest merchandise on the market. When the Texas Hold'em poker fad was just getting started, I found a dealer selling complete Texas Hold'em poker kits, consisting of chips, cards, instructions, and the table covers you see in the casinos. I purchased a couple of cases and sold them quickly on eBay before everyone else jumped on the fad. They were so hot I was actually getting 50 percent over retail. Within a few months, everybody had them and the prices had fallen to 20 percent below retail. You could still make money at that price, but not nearly as much as when they were new.

Other Ways to Find Wholesalers

The final way to find local wholesale sources is through your local phone book or an online service such as SMARTpages (www.smartpages.com). If you look up a product in your local Yellow Pages, the product will usually be broken down by category. For example if you looked up *cameras*, you would see listings for *cameras, accessories; cameras, repair; cameras, retail;* and so on. Typically, at the end of each product listing, you will see an entry for *cameras, wholesale* or *cameras, wholesale distributor*. This is true for almost any product you can find in the Yellow Pages. If you live in a large city, there is often a special directory for the business community called the Commercial Directory or sometimes the B2B Yellow Pages.

SMARTpages is an online method for finding local wholesale companies. In Figure 6.7 (see page 76), I selected the button that said *Business Type* and entered a city and state into the search box. For Business Type, I entered the word *wholesale*.

In this scenario, if you hit search, you'll see a list that is several pages long, as illustrated in Figure 6.8 (see page 76).

This list shows virtually every type of wholesale manufacturer and distributor for the entire Pittsburgh region. When you click on one of the links, you'll get a list of companies. Click on an individual company's name to find its contact information and a list of the goods the company sells.

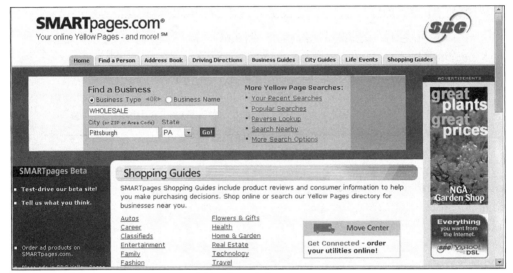

Figure 6.7 The SMARTpages.com Main Search Page

Figure 6.8 SMARTpages.com Results for Wholesale Suppliers in Pittsburgh

Wholesale on eBay

The final place to find products to sell on eBay is on eBay itself. Almost every category on eBay has a subcategory called *Wholesale, Large Lots*. Here you'll find companies (usually overstock companies) selling wholesale lots to the highest bidder. Make sure the seller has a good feedback rating, that the company is located in the United States (goods from overseas are often knockoffs, and it can be difficult to get your money back from an overseas vendor), and that you get a thorough and accurate description of the products being sold.

I once bought a pallet load of 7 for All Mankind jeans and made a ton of money reselling them individually on eBay. But then a few weeks later I bought a shipment of Burberry golf caps that turned out to be fake. I did eventually get my money back, but it was a lot of trouble and I was still out the return shipping.

A final piece of advice: Don't be an impulse buyer. Whether you are shopping on eBay, on a wholesale Web site, or strolling through a merchandise mart or trade show, take the time to do some basic research to make sure there is a market for the product you are considering before placing a bid or an order.

POWER MOVES

❏ Once you select a product or product category that interests you, visit the various search engines mentioned in this chapter and run product searches to locate suppliers.

❏ Make a list of potential suppliers and begin contacting them to see if they work with small accounts. If so, ask about pricing and minimum-order requirements.

❏ If you live in a city with a merchandise mart or design center, visit it and register for admission.

❏ Call the convention bureau in your city (or the nearest large city) and find out if and when any wholesale trade shows are coming to town. Register to attend them.

CHAPTER 7

✦ WINNING WITH DROP SHIPPING ✦

Drop shipping is an interesting and potentially profitable business concept. In the drop-shipping business model, you locate a wholesale vendor who will agree to ship his products directly to your customer. In the models we've discussed so far, you purchase an item and then resell it on eBay. With drop shipping, you first list the item on eBay, at a price that is higher than the drop shipper's wholesale price. Once you make a sale and collect the payment and shipping fee, you then send a payment to the drop shipper, who in turn ships the item directly to your customer.

The advantage of this business model is obvious. You do not have to risk any money buying products until the merchandise actually sells and you receive payment. Theoretically, if you found a vendor with hundreds of products to sell, you could list hundreds of auctions on eBay and, each time an auction closed with a winner, simply collect the money and send the payment and shipping instructions to the drop shipper. At first blush it sounds easy—a sort of unstoppable money machine. It can work, and it does work for many people. But like many things in life, it is not as simple as it sounds.

EBAY DROP-SHIP SUPPLIERS

If you do a search on Google for the term *drop shipper,* you will get several hundred results. There are dozens of companies that purport to have warehouses full of merchandise you can list on eBay—and then just sit back and collect the money, allowing them to drop ship for you. When you visit their Web sites, you will usually see a sales pitch to sign up for a membership, although some of the sites offer free memberships if you register with them. The problems arise when you start examining the merchandise and the pricing.

Disadvantages of Drop-Ship Suppliers

True wholesale companies can only sell at low wholesale prices when they sell in bulk. Because their margins are much lower than a retailer's, they have to make a larger average sale to make a profit. Most drop-shipping companies buy from wholesalers and then mark the price up somewhere between wholesale and typical retail. On top of this amount, they will usually charge a special drop-ship fee of anywhere from $2 to $5 per item, plus the shipping charge. When you compare their shipping charges to those of UPS, you will often see that they are making another few dollars on the shipping as well.

Once you determine the final price (including all the special fees), search for the same product on eBay. You will often see the product selling for the same price or even less. This is because other eBay sellers are purchasing the same products from the actual wholesalers, and therefore can sell them at much lower prices than you can using a drop shipper.

There are other drawbacks when dealing with a drop shipper, even if you can find items to sell at a profit. The primary one is customer service. Unfortunately, you are at the mercy of the drop-shipping company. If the drop shipper sends out the product late, ships the wrong product, or packs the product poorly and it arrives damaged, you are stuck with an angry customer who may leave you negative feedback. So even if you find a drop shipper with products that allow you to make a profit, you must still manage the relationship very carefully to ensure that the drop shipper is giving your customers the same customer service that you would.

Working with Drop-Ship Suppliers

Does all this mean you cannot make money drop shipping? No, you certainly can, and many eBay sellers do.

Out of the dozens of companies offering to drop ship goods for eBay sellers, I have only found one that is both fairly reliable and actually has a good selection of products you can sell on eBay. The company started out as Wholesale Marketer and later bought and merged with other drop-ship companies. It recently changed its name to DOBA, the name of Wholesale Marketer's original parent company. You can find DOBA at www.doba.com.

DOBA charges a monthly fee; however, the company does offer a one-week free trial membership (and a three-week free trial for readers of this book; see the Web site for the book). This would allow you enough time to find and research products and even to run a few trial auctions on eBay. If you do decide to join, you can sign up for a month-to-month membership, so you are not locked in for a full year. Currently, DOBA charges $29.95 a month for access to its fifteen warehouses arranged by product category, and an additional $14.95 per month if you use its eBay launching tool (called the "Push eBay Wizard"). With this tool, you simply click on a product, and the photo and description are automatically exported to eBay's auction selling form. DOBA also offers an Elite Seller's report that focuses on the top one hundred best-selling products on eBay.

Although DOBA is now the largest eBay drop-ship supplier, I should point out that it is still not a perfect solution. Not all the products you see in the DOBA ware-houses can be sold profitably on eBay. You will still have to hunt for products that can deliver an acceptable profit margin. Another issue is competition: Hundreds—if not thousands—of eBay sellers are using the same drop-ship companies and selling the same products. This tends to drive down the prices, making it even harder to derive a profit from drop shipping.

BIZ BUILDER

Use the eBay search engine and research tools and methods we discussed in chapter 4 to determine which drop-ship products will sell and what price points are realistic.

The fastest-selling and most popular products will be the hardest ones to profit from because everyone else is selling them, too. The key is to look for those small niche or specialty products that very few people are selling. Instead of trying to sell digital cameras, for example, look for accessories, such as camera cases, batteries, flash cards, tripods, and so on. You will be far more likely to make money if you work around the margins than if you try to compete directly by offering top-brand consumer products.

I don't want to imply that there are no other drop-ship companies from which you can make a profit. It is just that I haven't tried them all, and traditionally this industry has been plagued by upstart companies that don't last very long, as well as by a number of scams.

In addition to general drop-shipping companies, there are also specialty companies that will often drop ship. Again, the best way to find these are with a Google search—but you want to add the product name to the search term *drop shipping*. For example: *Drop ship books, drop ship Christian, drop ship china, drop ship art supplies,* etc. This will usually bring up a list of companies that specialize in those products.

DROP-SHIP MANUFACTURERS

You can also find thousands of small- and medium-sized manufacturers that will agree to drop ship goods for you. There are two ways to locate them: You can go through the Thomas Register (www.thomasregister.com) and contact the companies to determine if they will drop ship, or you can pay someone to do this for you.

Worldwide Brands (www.worldwidebrands.com; Figure 7.1 on page 82), an eBay-certified solutions provider, offers an online service that costs $69.95 for life and locates manufacturers that will drop ship. The listings in its online directory are updated weekly by a staff, who research the manufacturers and actually call them on the phone to confirm if they will drop ship and if they will work with eBay sellers. Visit the Web site for this book (www.skipmcgrath.com/3_weeks) to find a link to a special offer for the Worldwide Brands Drop-ship Source Directory.

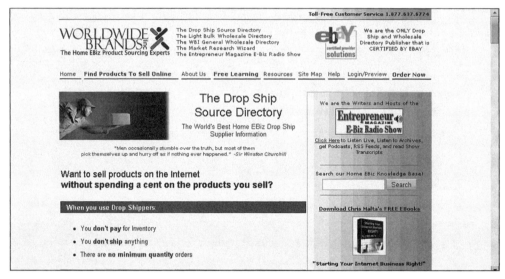

Figure 7.1 Worldwide Brands

I have personally used this service and can attest to the quality of the information. In just one hour of working with the directory, I was able to locate three manufacturers that would agree to drop ship for me. I tried out all three of them. One manufacturer's product just wouldn't sell on eBay; another one sold sporadically (but at a nice profit margin); and the third product, a handmade steel barbecue grill, has been a steady producer of profits. We make about $90 on each one we sell and have sold as many as thirty in a single month. I have since found a line of digital photography lighting systems and accessories that are selling quite well. In this case, the small manufacturer readily agreed to drop ship and he also gave me a semi-exclusive deal, so I would not face too much competition.

I am not going to kid you: Setting up these relationships can take a lot of research, testing, and hard work. But if you can make it work, drop shipping really can be a money machine. Keep in mind, however, that in the long run you're much more likely to be successful with drop shipping if you specialize.

POWER MOVES

❏ If you are interested in drop shipping, sign up with DOBA for a one-week free trial offered to readers of this book at www.skipmcgrath.com/3_weeks. Find products that interest you and then see what they are selling for on eBay, using the *Completed listings only* search option.

❏ Use the Thomas Register to find manufacturers of products that interest you. Contact the manufacturers and ask if they will drop ship for you.

❏ As you explore Wholesale Marketer and other potential drop shippers, maintain a list of products they offer that you believe you can sell for a profit. Once you are ready to begin selling, come back to this list and try listing a few of these items.

❏ Once you begin working with drop shippers, evaluate each one in terms of competitive pricing, reliability of delivery, customer satisfaction, and ease of dealing with returns and other customer service issues.

CHAPTER 8

✦ TYPES OF AUCTIONS ✦

When eBay first started, there was only one type of auction. All auctions ran for a specified period and ended at a specified time. The highest bidder at the last possible moment was the winner.

Now eBay offers several auction formats, as well as Buy It Now and Fixed Price listings. Before you begin to sell, it is important for you to understand all the different formats available to you—and to familiarize yourself with the unique advantages and disadvantages of each one. Most sellers use several formats, depending on what they are selling. For example, if you are selling a high-priced antique or collectible, you may want to use a Reserve Price Auction (RPA). Alternatively, if you purchased a wholesale lot of inexpensive toys just before Christmas, there are advantages to using a Fixed Price sale. In this chapter, we'll explore each of the selling formats in detail.

STANDARD AUCTIONS

A typical auction-style listing works this way:

* The seller offers one or more items and sets a starting price.

* Buyers visit the listing and bid on the item during the online auction's duration.

* When the auction-style listing ends, the high bidder or bidders buy the item from the seller for the high bid.

eBay uses a system of *proxy bidding*. Let's say a seller started an item at $1.00 and it's now been bid up to $9.00. eBay sets the minimum incremental bid at fifty cents. Now assume that you are a bidder and you decide you would be willing to pay as high as $14.50 for the item being offered. You enter a bid of $14.50 and hit the button that says *Place Bid*. eBay now adds fifty cents to the current bid of $9.00, and displays the item's price as $9.50. No one else knows the top value of your bid—others can only see the current bid. Now another bidder comes along and bids $10.00. The bid price rises to $10.50 (her bid plus a fifty cent incremental bid from you), and she gets an immediate message that she has been outbid. If no one else bids, you will win the item for $10.50. As long as no one bids more than your $14.50 maximum, you are still in the running.

If someone bids more than your maximum, you will receive an automated e-mail from eBay that you have been outbid. You can let it go, or you can go back in and place a higher bid if you still want the item at a higher price.

RESERVE PRICE AUCTIONS

Some auctions have a *reserve price*—a hidden minimum price—for the item. This is done to allow a seller to start an item at a low price that is sure to attract attention, yet protect him from selling it at too low a price. A few points to keep in mind when it comes to Reserve Price Auctions:

* Buyers are not shown the reserve price, only whether or not the reserve has been met.

* The seller is not obligated to sell the item if the reserve price is not met.

* The winning bidder must meet or exceed the reserve price *and* have the highest bid.

When you're bidding in a Reserve Price Auction, bid as usual, entering the maximum amount you're willing to pay for the item. Watch the label next to the current price to see whether the reserve price has been met. Until you see that the reserve price has been met, there have been no successful bids in the auction. Once the reserve has been met, the item will sell to the highest bidder when the auction closes.

If your maximum bid is the first to meet or exceed the reserve price, the bid displayed will automatically be raised to the reserve price.

BUY IT NOW AND FIXED PRICE LISTINGS

Buy It Now (BIN) is an option eBay created for people who don't want to wait for an auction to end to purchase an item. The BIN option allows you as the seller to set a price at which you are willing to end the auction immediately and sell the item to the buyer. One thing you need to know about the BIN option is that it disappears once an auction bid is placed. When you choose the Buy It Now option on a traditional auction listing (available for single quantity only), your item has two ways to sell:

* If a buyer is willing to meet your Buy It Now price before the first bid comes in, your item sells instantly and your auction ends.

* Or, if a bid comes in first, the Buy It Now option disappears. Then your auction proceeds normally. (In Reserve Price Auctions, Buy It Now disappears after the first bid that meets the reserve.)

The purpose of Buy It Now (BIN) is to make immediate sales. You set your BIN price at the upper end of what you would like the item to sell for. For example, say you are selling a pair of cowboy boots (yes, these are big sellers on eBay) in a standard auction with a starting bid of $49 and you hope to get at least $75 for them. You could set your BIN price at $79 (or even higher). Now if someone comes along and really wants those boots and doesn't want to take a chance on getting outbid, she simply clicks the BIN button in your auction. The auction ends and she is taken to a page where eBay calculates the shipping and insurance and your buyer pays instantly with PayPal.

Another variation on Buy It Now is the *Fixed Price listing*. You list an auction with a starting price and a BIN price that are identical. In this case you are simply putting an item up for sale at a fixed price. If someone bids the starting price, eBay will realize that it is identical to the BIN price and will end the auction and declare that buyer the winner.

SELLING MULTIPLE ITEMS

Depending on the type of merchandise you sell, you may want to use one of the formats allowing you to sell multiple, identical items. If you sell art, antiques, collectibles, or used books, this format generally won't work for you, because each item is different. However, if you bought a pallet of toys or games from a closeout dealer, you might find yourself with several or even dozens of identical items to sell.

There are three ways to sell multiple items on eBay:

* **MULTIPLE ITEM LISTING (DUTCH AUCTION)**
* **FIXED PRICE LISTING**
* **LOT LISTING**

Using these methods can save you time and simplify the auction process. Let's explore how each one works.

Dutch Auctions

eBay calls this type of auction a *multiple-item listing*, but almost every eBayer knows it as a *Dutch Auction*. This format is used when you have multiple, identical items to sell. Instead of running ten different auctions, you can run one auction and sell all ten items individually to ten different buyers, or some buyers can buy more than one item.

The winning bid in a Dutch Auction is based on the *lowest successful bid by quantity*. I know this sounds confusing, but stay with me. Here is an example:

Suppose you have twenty flashlights, all the same, that you'd like to sell for at least $5.99 each. You would list them as a quantity of twenty, and a starting price of $5.99. Here's how the auction works:

✳ Bidders specify both their offered price per unit, and the number of items they want to buy. A bidder can bid on just one flashlight or any quantity up to twenty.

✳ Winning bids are selected in order of bid price per item—that is, a bid for five units at $12 per unit is ranked above a bid for ten units at $11 per unit.

✳ If two bids have the same price per item, the earlier bid is given priority. Winning bidders pay a price equal to the *lowest winning bid.*

Table 8.1: Sample Dutch Auction Results

BIDDER	A	B	C	D	E	F	G	H
QUANTITY BID ON	5	3	10	1	1	2	3	1
BID AMOUNT	12.00	11.00	9.50	9.00	8.00	7.00	5.99	5.99

In this example (see Table 8.1), there are twenty flashlights for sale at a starting bid of $5.99. Remember: Everyone gets the number of flashlights they bid on at the price of the lowest successful bidder *by quantity*. Starting with the highest bid (bidder A) count the quantity bid on until you get to twenty. That would bring you to Bidder E, who bid on one flashlight with a bid of $8.00. Therefore bidders A through E each get the quantity of flashlights they bid on for the price of the *lowest successful bid by quantity*—which is the $8.00 bid placed by bidder E.

Some additional points to keep in mind with this type of auction:

✳ Bidders cannot lower their "total bid value" (the bid price per item times the number of items on which they're bidding) when they raise their bid in this type of auction listing. For example, if you bid $10 on ten of the same flashlights (a total bid value of $100), you couldn't raise your bid to $15 on just five flashlights (a lower total bid value of $75).

✳ Winning bidders have the right to refuse partial quantities. This means that if you win some, but not all, of the quantity you bid for, you don't have to buy *any* of the items. In the example shown in Table 8.1, imagine that Bidder E had bid on two flashlights, but won only one of them. Bidder E can refuse to complete the purchase, because Bidder E did not win the quantity he bid on.

* Bids are displayed when the buyer or the seller clicks on the link reading *Bidders list*. Bid prices on non-winning bids are displayed, but winning bids show only the price that these bidders would pay if the auction ended immediately. So in the Bid History, all winning bids show the same price per unit—the lowest winning bid. To place a winning bid (a bid that wins at least some units), a bidder would need to exceed this price.

Fixed Price Listings

In a *Fixed Price listing* you list multiple, identical items in one listing with a fixed price for each item. Buyers can choose the quantity they want and pay the set price.

For example: Suppose you have fifty flashlights that you'd like to sell for $9.99 each. You would list them as with a *quantity* of fifty and a *price* of $9.99. Buyers could purchase any available quantity of your item at any time, without waiting for an auction to end.

In both Dutch Auctions and Fixed Price listings, eBay only permits multi-item listings in which the price times the quantity is less than $100,000. In order to sell with this format, you must:

* Be ID verified

Or
* Have a feedback rating of thirty or above and be registered on eBay for at least fourteen days

Or
* Have a feedback rating of fifteen if you have a PayPal account, and accept PayPal as a payment method on the listing.

Lot Listings

In a *Lot listing* you sell similar items together in one listing to one buyer (such as a record collection, a lot of same-size clothing, and the like).

For example, suppose you have fifty baseball cards that you'd like to sell together to one buyer for an average price of $1.99 each. To list the cards as a *lot*, you would first click the Lot tab in the Quantity section of the Sell Your Item form, and enter *1* in the Number of Lots box and *50* in the Number of Items Per Lot box. You would set the price at $99.50. The winning bidder will win all fifty cards.

PRIVATE AUCTIONS

When a seller creates a private listing, a buyer's Username does not appear in the listing or in the listing's bid history. Only the seller is authorized to view the buyers'

Usernames associated with that listing. This type of auction is typically used for items of an adult or sexual nature. Sometimes it's also used for expensive art and antiques to help protect the identity of wealthy bidders.

EBAY STORES

The final type of listing is the *eBay Store*. An eBay Store is essentially a Fixed Price Auction, except that you can list items for 30 days or create a Good 'Til Canceled listing, which renews automatically every thirty days. The eBay Store listing fees are lower than auction listings. We cover eBay Stores in detail in chapter 26.

I suggest that you stick with the regular auction format for your first few dozen auctions. Then, after you have read chapter 10 on listing and pricing strategies, I would start adding Buy It Now to your auctions and even putting up some Fixed Price Auctions.

Keep in mind that Dutch Auctions can be somewhat complicated. Although they can also be highly profitable when properly run, you may want to get some more experience before delving into them. I tried a few Dutch Auctions early on in my eBay career and ended up losing quite a bit of money because I didn't structure or price them right.

POWER MOVES

❏ Spend some time on eBay looking at the various types of auctions. Analyze which types of auctions seem to be most popular/successful for different products.

❏ Think about the products you plan to sell, and which type of listing is right for each one. In your notebook, note which formats your competitors used, and which appear to have been successful.

❏ If you plan on selling multiple, identical items, study various multiple-item listings until you become comfortable with Dutch Auctions, Fixed Price listings, and Lot listings. Make a list of what worked and what failed for other sellers.

CHAPTER 9

✦ LAUNCHING YOUR FIRST AUCTIONS ✦

You've gone through the process of bidding and buying on eBay, you've figured out how feedback works, you've seen how to pay and get paid, and how different sellers package and ship their goods. Now it's time to try selling. You are going to learn a lot more about selling techniques in the following chapters, but try launching a few auctions to get your feet wet. Throughout this chapter, I point out that we are going to cover some tasks, such as writing headlines, in greater detail later on. You may wonder, "Why don't we do that first?" Here's why: I have found that actually going through the selling process a few times, even if you don't fully understand all the techniques, makes these methods easier to understand when you study them in detail. These first few auctions are like learning to ride a bike with the training wheels on. When you take the training wheels off, you will be glad you had the experience.

FINDING SOMETHING TO SELL

If you've been following my system, you have researched products to sell and are well on your way to sourcing and/or ordering those items. However, for the purpose of this exercise, walk around your house, look in your garage and attic, and find a few items to sell that you don't need anymore. If you cannot find anything to sell around your house, then stop by a few garage sales this weekend.

Look for old golf clubs, nonfiction books in good condition, and small working appliances such as espresso machines, coffee machines, bread makers, pasta machines, and so on. Try to find machines that are still in the box and have the instructions with them. These sorts of products are reliable sellers on eBay.

If you have small children, you probably have some clothes that no longer fit them. Assemble the clothes into a set of the same size and gender—for example, two pairs of trousers, a jacket, and two shirts in Boys' size 3; or two dresses, two pairs of trousers, and two sweaters in Girls' size 4. Sets of used children's clothing sell extremely well on eBay, and you can realize a far greater profit on eBay than you would at a garage sale. Make certain the clothing is clean and in good condition. Don't sell clothing with rips, tears, or excessive wear. Generally, name-brand items such as Children's GAP or Old Navy outsell house-brand clothing.

Another good category is used sporting, hunting, camping, and fishing equipment. For now, avoid large items like skis or hockey sticks that could be difficult to ship.

PREPARING YOUR ITEMS FOR SALE

The next step is to take some digital photos of your items, and upload them to your computer's hard drive. Make sure you take sharp, properly exposed photos, and that you shoot the objects without a lot of background clutter. (See chapter 15, on taking effective auction photos, if you need some help in this area.)

Whenever you are selling something used, be sure to inspect it carefully and clean it. People know they are buying a used item, but they don't want it to arrive all covered in greasy fingerprints or caked with dust and grime.

Once you have your items assembled, you need to weigh them and pre-calculate the postage. Forget UPS for now; instead, visit www.usps.gov and look for the U.S. Postal Service's postage calculator. Type in the weight and a zip code that is at least halfway across the country (four zones away). Whatever cost you come up with, add 20 percent to cover the cost of your handling, shipping, and packing materials. If the postage comes to $3.90, you would add $0.78 (3.90 X .20) for a total of $4.68. When you enter your shipping amount into eBay, you might want to round up to $4.70. (We will deal with calculated shipping and other shipping methods, such as UPS, later on.)

The reason we chose four zones is that there are eight postal zones in the United States. If you live in the middle of the country, you will seldom ship farther than four zones from your current location. If you live on either coast, you will sometimes ship close to your zone—so you will make a few cents—and you will often ship more than four zones away, thereby losing a few cents. Overall, it will average out. Fixed shipping (as opposed to calculated shipping) is much easier for both the buyer and seller to deal with, so let's stick with that for now.

LAUNCHING YOUR FIRST AUCTION

Now, go to any eBay page and click on *Sell* at the top of the page (see Figure 9.1).

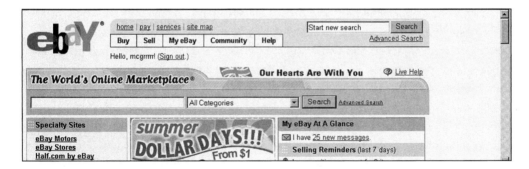

Figure 9.1 The eBay Homepage

The first question you are asked when the Sell page loads is this:

How would you like to sell your item?

> Sell item at online auction

> Sell at a fixed price

> Creat an ad format listing

> Sell your items in your own eBay Store

You want to select the first option, *Online Auction*. We will talk about Fixed Price sales and eBay Stores in detail later on. An ad format listing is useful for selling real estate and other expensive items, but it is unlikely you will use this option at this point in your eBay selling career.

Step 1: Selecting a Category

Once you opt for an online auction and hit Continue, a page will come up (Figure 9.2) requiring you to select the category you are going to sell in. You will have to scroll down to see all the categories.

Main category	
○ Click to select	
○ Antiques	Antique silver, furniture, ceramics, textiles & other décor
○ Art	Paintings, prints, photos, posters, folk art & sculpture
○ eBay Motors	Cars, boats, aircraft, motorcycles, parts & accessories
○ Baby	Feeding, gear, nursery furniture, strollers & more
○ Books	Books, textbooks, collectible books, children's books, magazines & more
○ Business & Industrial	Equipment & Supplies for Construction, Farm, Food Service, Retail, Healthcare, Manufacturing, Office and much more
○ Cameras & Photo	Cameras, camcorders, lenses, memory, accessories & more
○ Cell Phones	Cell phones, pre paid cell phones and cell phone accessories such as headsets, batteries, chargers, faceplates and more
○ Clothing, Shoes & Accessories	Apparel, footwear & accessories
○ Coins	Coins, paper money & numismatic supplies
○ Collectibles	Decorative Collectibles, Coin-Op & Casino, Comics, Militaria, Advertising and more

Figure 9.2 eBay Category Selection Page

Select the category that most closely fits the item you are selling. In this example, I am going to sell a Starbucks coffee mug that I picked up at the Pike Place market in Seattle. Seattle is the home of Starbucks and the Pike Place Market store is where Starbucks first started. These mugs are highly sought-after. I paid $9.95 for this particular mug, which has been discontinued and is no longer sold.

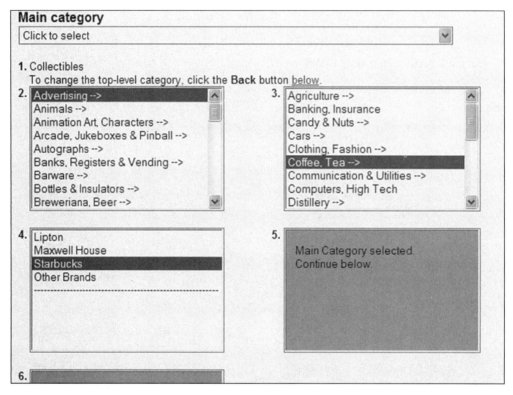

Figure 9.3 Category: Collectibles –> Advertising –>Coffee, Tea –> Starbucks

When you select a main category, eBay will then present you with a list of secondary categories, as in Figure 9.3. I have selected the secondary category of *Coffee & Tea*, and the final subcategory of *Starbucks*.

BIZ BUILDER

If you are having trouble finding a category, at the top of the page, eBay provides a category suggestion tool (see Figure 9.4). Type in the name of the product you are selling, and eBay will bring up a list of appropriate categories.

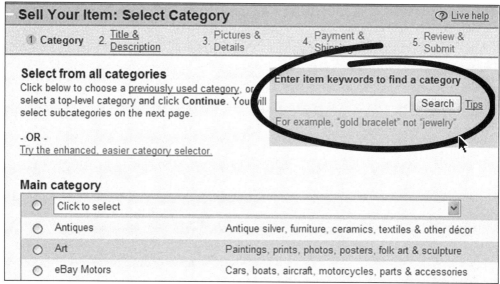

Figure 9.4 Category Suggestion Tool

You will also be given the opportunity to list in two categories. This is a special feature that costs a little extra. There are some situations where you will want to use this option, but let's ignore it for now. (We will cover this feature in detail in chapter 13.)

Step 2: Title and Description

After you hit Continue, you will be directed to the Describe Your Item page (Figure 9.5).

Figure 9.5 Describe Your Item

First, you must write a headline for your listing. Writing effective eBay headlines is a real art, and one that we are going to spend some time on in detail in chapter 14. But for now, let's just go with a straightforward description: STARBUCKS PIKE PLACE, FIRST STARBUCKS STORE MUG. Write a headline that simply and accurately describes what you are selling. If the product has a brand name, be sure to include it. And keep in mind that you only get fifty-five characters. Here are some examples:

LOT OF SIZE 6 GIRLS' TOMMY HILFIGER CLOTHES

HAMILTON BEACH BREAD MACHINE IN GOOD CONDITION

PEG PEREGO DUETTE, DOUBLE TWIN STROLLER, Excellent Cond

PAIR OF HARLEY DAVIDSON ROAD KING SADDLEBAGS

COMPLETE SET OF OLD WOODEN WILSON GOLF CLUBS WITH BAG

Punctuation marks, like commas and long dashes, may be used in these headlines as well. Just remember that punctuation marks count as characters in each headline's fifty-five-character maximum.

BIZ BUILDER

I like to use all caps in my headlines, because it helps them to stand out from the other auction listings. Using all caps in eBay headlines is not considered "shouting," as it is in Internet parlance. However, adding a few words in lowercase letters to an otherwise all-caps headline can help that information to stand out.

Right below the headline you will see a box that says *Subtitle ($0.50)*. This is another eBay option, and a somewhat expensive one at that. I only use subtitles for very expensive items.

Now that we have our headline, scroll down the page to the Item Description box.

If you look at Figure 9.6, you will see a box where you can enter text. Above it is a toolbar that looks similar to a Word document toolbar. Here you can select font and type size, as well as special formatting, such as bold, italics, underline, bullets, and numbered lists. This box is an HTML generator: You type in normal text, and it generates the HTML code necessary to present your text as you wish it to appear on the Internet. (While you don't need to know HTML in order to change paragraphs or format text, there are times it may come in handy. See Appendix D for a brief HTML tutorial.)

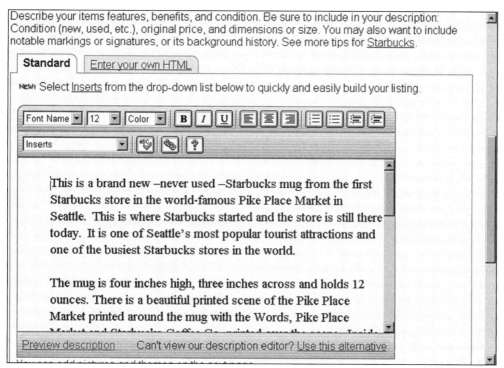

Figure 9.6 Sample Item Description

Type your description into the box. Use a series of short paragraphs instead of one long one, since that's easier for customers to read. If you have specifications to list, then use the bulleted list or numbered list feature. Although eBay's *Sell Your Item* form has an HTML editor that works like a Microsoft Word document, I prefer first to create my listing in Word, and then to copy and paste the description into the editor. This way I have a backup should anything go wrong, as well as a record I can use again in future auctions.

When you're selling a collectible or a used item, your description should contain as many specifics as possible. These might include:

* The year and provenance of the item

* Item size (length, width, height, weight)

* Brand (such as John Deere, Coca-Cola, or Hard Rock)

* Name of series set, special edition, or collection (for example, Coca-Cola Holiday Collection)

* The condition (new in box, mint, etc.), including possible flaws or scratches

* Material (such as porcelain, wood, or tin)

* Product type (sign, bottle, box, etc.)

So let's take a stab at describing my Starbucks mug.

> *This is a brand new—never used—Starbucks mug from the first Starbucks store in the world-famous Pike Place Market in Seattle. This is where Starbucks started and the store is still there today. It is one of Seattle's most popular tourist attractions and one of the busiest Starbucks stores in the world.*
>
> *The mug is four inches high, three inches across and holds 12 ounces. There is a beautiful printed scene of the Pike Place Market printed around the mug with the words, Pike Place Market and Starbucks Coffee Co. printed over the scene. Inside the rim of the mug is the legend: The Birthplace of Starbucks Coffee.*
>
> *This mug is from the Skyline Series, the most collected series of Starbucks mugs since they were introduced in 1995. This mug was introduced in 2002 and discontinued in 2004. This mug is very hard to find and has sold for as much as $75 on eBay.*
>
> *These mugs do not come up on eBay very often. Don't lose out to a last-minute sniper. Place your best bid now.*
>
> *Shipping and handling is $4.90 via priority mail to any US destination. Please e-mail me for shipping costs to Canada and overseas.*
>
> *I accept PayPal, personal checks and money orders. If your feedback is less than 20, I hold personal checks for one week until they clear. I guarantee this item to be exactly as described or you can return it for a full refund. I will post positive feedback for all buyers as soon as payment is received.*
>
> *Thank you for looking at my item. Please e-mail me with any questions.*

Notice that at the end of the description I specify my shipping cost, payment options, return policy, and feedback terms. The Sell Your Item process provides other opportunities to enter this data, but I always like to place it in the description as well.

Step 3: Picture and Item Details

Hitting *Continue* will take you to a new page, where you will be required to enter the starting price and duration of your auction.

Enter your starting price. As you can see in Figure 9.7, I have entered $9.99, which is what I paid for the mug. If you are selling a used item, make a low estimate of the value and use that as a starting price. In general, the lower your starting price, the more bids you will attract. Brand-name items usually attract a lot of attention and bids.

Pricing and duration

Price your item competitively to increase your chance of a successful sale.

NEW! Get ideas about pricing by searching completed items...

Starting price *	Reserve price (fee varies)
$ 9.99	No reserve price. Add

A lower starting price can encourage more bids.

Buy It Now price (Fee Varies)

$ [   ]

Sell to the first buyer who meets your Buy It Now price.

NEW! **Donate percentage of sale**

| No nonprofit selected ▼ | Select % ▼ | Remove |

Figure 9.7 Price Your Item

If you are selling something obscure that has a high value, you have two options: You can set a low starting price and use a reserve, or you can set the starting price at the minimum you will accept for the item. We are going to cover listing and pricing strategies in great detail in the next chapter, so if you are unsure about what starting price to set, you may want to read ahead a little. Remember, however, that for now you are simply trying to gain some experience—not necessarily make a ton of money. You should be selling relatively low-cost items from your garage or attic. So I would suggest that you just go with a low starting price in hopes of attracting bids.

Looking again at Figure 9.7, you'll see that eBay offers two additional options: selecting a Buy It Now (BIN) price and donating a portion of your proceeds to charity. Again, let's ignore these features for now; we will cover them in greater detail later on.

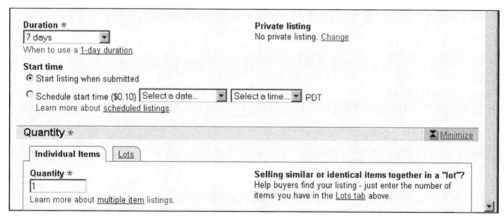

Figure 9.8 Set Your Auction Duration and Item Quantity

Next you are asked to set the duration for your auction (see Figure 9.8). A drop down menu offers several choices: one, three, five, seven, or ten days. We will use a seven-day auction for this example. Below this box is a place to enter your item quantity. Our quantity is *1*. If we had several identical items to sell, we could list the quantity here and it would become a multiple-item auction, or what is generally known on eBay as a Dutch Auction. For now we will stick with one item.

Next you are presented with Item Location (see Figure 9.9). You can either type in your zip code, and eBay will display your city and state, or you can enter a short custom message, such as "Proud Seller from the Show Me State."

Figure 9.9 Specify Your Item Location

Continuing down the page, we now come to an area where you can upload your own pictures. eBay gives you the option to use your own Web host. In this method, you type in the URL of a photograph you have hosted on a Web page. This is free. If you use eBay's picture hosting service, the first picture is free and subsequent photos are fifteen cents each. Later I am going to show you a way to avoid these charges, but for now let's just use eBay's Basic Picture Service (or the Advanced Picture Service, which I prefer, since it's easier to see what you're posting).

Start by clicking on the first *Browse* or *Add Pictures* button; this will bring up your document folders on your hard drive (see Figure 9.10). Navigate to the folder where your photos are stored and select the first photo you want to use by double-clicking on it. This will add your photo to your listing (see Figure 9.11). Repeat this process with any other photos you have. I always suggest including at least two and up to four photos of an item. The more you can show a prospective bidder the better. Below your photos you will see options for Standard Photos or a Picture Pack. Again these are expensive add-ons I only use when selling high-priced items.

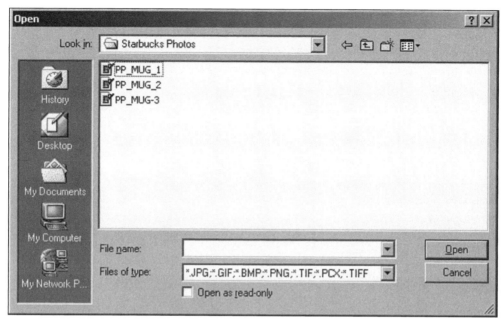

Figure 9.10 Choose a Photo from a Document Folder on Your Hard Drive

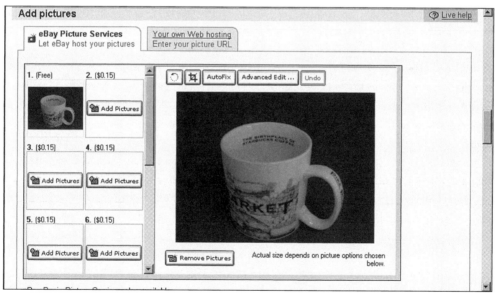

Figure 9.11 eBay Enhanced Picture Services

Next you'll encounter eBay's *Listing Designer* feature (Figure 9.12). This is a template that can add borders and background art to your auction listings. Since this only costs ten cents, let's use it. As you can see, I have selected an antique black frame for my listing. You can scroll down the list and select a frame that complements the category where you are selling.

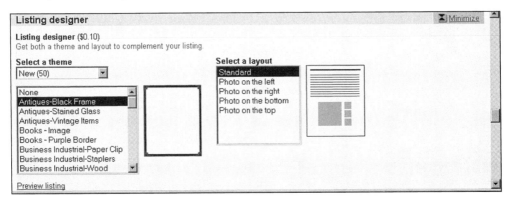

Figure 9.12 Listing Designer

Next you are given the opportunity to select from one of several eBay promotional options under the heading *Increase Your Item's Visibility*. Some of these options can get very expensive. We are going to cover all the eBay promotional features in chapter 16, but for now let's look at just two: *Gallery* and *Bold*.

The gallery option costs thirty-five cents and places a thumbnail photo next to your item description in the auction listing page and in bidders' search results. I have always found this to be an important option because many bidders will not click on an auction listing if they don't see a picture right next to it. The other feature I use regularly is Bold, which costs $1. When you select this option, your listing's title appears in boldface in bidders' search results pages. eBay offers strong statistical evidence that using the Bold feature increases the number of hits a listing receives, the number of bids submitted, and the final price the item commands. If you are auctioning something likely to sell for $15 or more, this option will usually pay for itself. If you're anticipating less than that amount, I would not use it.

Finally, at the bottom of the page, you can select the design of the hit counter you want to use. The hit counter will appear at the bottom of your listing and will tell you how many people have opened your auction. You should always select a hit counter, because this information is very useful when you are testing headlines and auction listing strategies.

Step 4: Payment and Shipping

The next page addresses the Payment Methods you will accept (see Figure 9.13).

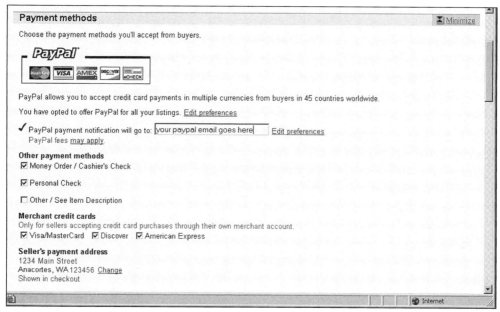

Figure 9.13 Select which Payment Methods You'll Accept

If you have signed up for PayPal (and you should have by now), you will want to check PayPal and money orders as accepted forms of payment. I also accept personal checks under $100 from an eBay seller with a feedback rating of at least twenty (with a good positive score). For items over $100, or if a bidder has a low feedback rating, I state that I will hold an item until the check clears.

BIZ BUILDER

A lot of people worry about taking personal checks on eBay. I don't. I have accepted personal checks in amounts as high as $600 without running into trouble. I did receive one check that bounced, but the buyer rectified the situation and reimbursed me for the $20 bounced-check fee my bank charges. If you are selling high-priced goods, you should ask for a certified check—or at least wait until a personal check clears before shipping the merchandise.

AN UNEXPECTED VISITOR

I used to list my home address in my auctions. A few years ago, one morning at about 7:00 a.m., my doorbell rang. I looked out to see a well-dressed woman standing on my porch. I was still in my bathrobe having coffee, so, keeping the chain on the door, I opened it a few inches and said, "Good morning, can I help you?"

"Hello," she replied. "I'm so sorry to bother you so early in the morning, but I won a Bearington teddy bear from your auction on eBay last night. I live nearby and was on my way to work, and I wondered if I could pay you now and take it with me. I want to send it to my grandson today."

Since my wife was already dressed, I called her down and let her handle the transaction. Later that afternoon I got a post office box.

If you are set up to take credit cards offline, you can check off the type of credit cards you accept. You can also enter the address where people can mail you checks. If you don't want to use your home address, you can rent a post office box from your local post office or a mailbox from a store like Mail Boxes, Etc.

The next choice on this page is *Ship-to locations* (see Figure 9.14). Check the box next to each location to which you will agree to ship. There are several issues involved in international shipping, which we will explore later on. For the time being, I suggest that you stick to the United States and Canada.

Figure 9.14 *Enter Shipping Information for Your Item*

This is also where you enter the shipping amount. As you can see, you may also select calculated shipping. There are times when I use this option, but most eBay PowerSellers prefer to use fixed shipping amounts for reasons of economy and convenience, both for the buyer and the seller.

BIZ BUILDER

If you select *calculated shipping,* eBay inserts a box in your auction where a bidder can enter her zip code, and eBay will calculate the shipping cost to her location. If you select *fixed shipping,* you set the shipping price and enter that amount into your listing.

Next you may enter sales tax information. If you do not yet have a sales tax number, you can leave this blank. Once you are set up to collect and pay sales tax, enter the sales tax amount for your state. Remember: You only have to collect and pay sales tax on merchandise shipped to an address in the state where you are selling.

Below the sales tax field, you're given the opportunity to add your return policy and payment instructions (see Figure 9.15). Once you enter data in these fields, this information will be saved for all future auctions. So if you are selling something that will follow a different policy, be sure to change your standard return and payment policies before launching the next auction.

Figure 9.15 *Specify Your Sales Tax Amount and Return Policy*

The last item on this page refers to buyer requirements (see Figure 9.16). I suggest that you check off the following options eBay offers here, blocking buyers who:

❋ Are registered in countries to which you don't ship

❋ Have a feedback score of −1 or lower

❋ Have received two Unpaid Item strikes in the last thirty days

❋ Don't have a PayPal account

Checking these boxes reduces the likelihood of dealing with nonpaying bidders or newcomers who don't yet understand the eBay process.

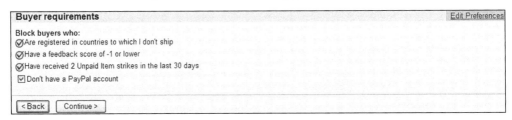

Figure 9.16 Establish Your Buyer Requirements

Step 5: Review and Submit Your Listing

After you have launched dozens of auctions, you will be able to review your listings very quickly. For now, take your time as you review each part of your auction for accuracy (see Figure 9.17). Read your description carefully for any errors.

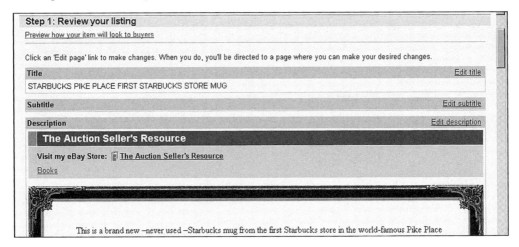

Figure 9.17 Review Your Listing

Be sure to examine the fees eBay will charge you. In this auction, my fees came to $2.10. If you recall, the cost of this mug was $9.95; if I add $2.10 to that, I get my true cost for launching this auction on eBay: $12.05. If the mug sells, there will also be a final value fee of 5.25 percent. Because I expect this mug to sell for at least $25, the final value fee should be somewhere around $1.31. This brings my total cost to $13.36. If the mug sells for $25, my profit will be $11.64. It took about ten minutes to create and launch the auction, and it will take another fifteen minutes or so to communicate with the seller about payment and pack and ship the box.

If this were an item you always carried in stock and were selling repeatedly, we would show you how to store your auction so you could launch identical auctions in less than a minute. In chapter 23, we are going to show you how to use outside services to automate your auctions and lower your eBay fees.

As you scroll down the page, you will come to an area where you can edit any part of your listing (see Figure 9.18). If you see something you wish to change, simply click on the appropriate link, make your changes and hit *Continue* to return to this page.

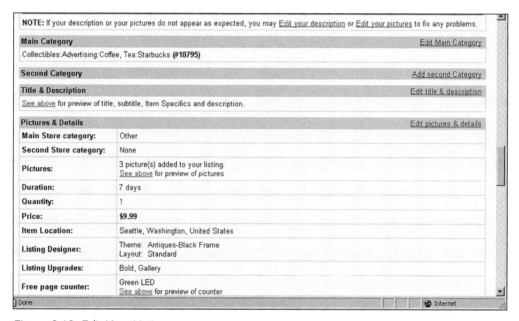

Figure 9.18 Edit Your Listing

Once you are satisfied, hit the *Submit Listing* button and give yourself a pat on the back. Now the fun starts.

THE LIFE OF YOUR AUCTION

Don't be surprised if your auction receives few bids—or even no bids at all—the first few days. This is normal. Most auctions see the heaviest activity in their final four hours, with furious bidding in the last few minutes. The advantage of having your auction up for seven days is that a lot of people will have a chance to consider your merchandise. Those who are interested will bookmark the auction and watch it, waiting until the right moment to place their bid. Other sellers use automated programs, called sniping software, which will not place their bids until thirty seconds before the end of the auction.

Don't be surprised if your used household items bring far more money than you would have expected. If you are selling an old pasta machine at a garage sale, you might have thirty or forty people look at it during the day. On eBay, the keyword *pasta machine* is searched more than two thousand times a day. I was cleaning out some old boxes in the attic last year, and I came across an RCA transistor radio from the early '70s. I think it cost about $25 when it was new, which was pretty expensive in those days. I put fresh batteries in it and it worked! I know people collect old radios, and I thought I might be able to get $30 or $40 for it on eBay. I placed it on eBay in a seven-day auction. It received over fifty bids and sold for $212!

And the Starbucks Pike Place Mug? It sold one week later for $28.90.

POWER MOVES

- ❏ Locate a few items from your attic or garage that you can use for your first listings. Make sure to clean them so that they're in good shape for selling.

- ❏ Take some digital photographs of your items. See chapter 15 if you need advice on how to do this effectively.

- ❏ Determine a price point for your merchandise. Do some research on eBay to determine the average selling price for your products.

- ❏ Follow the steps outlined in this chapter to launch your first auctions. Take note of any questions that arise regarding headlines, descriptions, pricing, and so forth. We'll cover these topics in greater detail later on in the book.

CHAPTER 10

✦ LISTING AND PRICING STRATEGIES ✦

Here's an indisputable fact about eBay: Low starting prices attract more bidders. The typical eBay bidder scans the category and search results pages for two things: low prices and items that already have bids. So getting that first bid is all-important, because it drives more traffic—and, therefore, more bids—to your auction. (We'll discuss the reasons why in a moment.) Therefore, where you set your starting bid is a critical decision, fraught with anguish and uncertainty. In this chapter, we'll go over different pricing strategies for different types of auctions, as well as the best days and times to begin and end your auctions.

GENERAL PRICING STRATEGIES

The risk in setting your bid price too low is that, if you don't get many bidders, you may end up giving your treasure away for a song. Conversely, if you set the price too high, you may not attract any bids. Setting the opening bid price is something of a black art. This is a decision that takes some experience and research. If you are selling hot or popular items that routinely attract a lot of bids, it is usually safe to set a low minimum bid. If you are spending money on eBay's optional features to attract attention to your listings (we will cover these features in the next section), it is probably safer to set a low starting price, so that your auction will receive more hits.

The problem arises when you are selling an item that is not well known or does not have a popular brand name.

Remember: The starting bid is only important to attract those first few bidders. Once the bidding starts, the current bid price will appear next to your headline on the category page. eBay's research shows that a sizable percentage of sellers will scan the search results page looking for items that already have bids on them. For some reason, buyers feel more secure bidding on an item that has already received at least one bid. In response to this buyer behavior, some unscrupulous sellers will have a friend place a bid on their item, just to record that first bid. This is a prohibited practice called *shilling*, and can get you kicked off eBay permanently.

One school of thought holds that you should start all items at $1, with no reserve. In theory, this practice works well most of the time, although you can get burned occasionally. Many experienced PowerSellers list their items at cost. Their reasoning goes like this: Their cost is lower than the item's value, and therefore will attract bids. At worst, they will recover what they paid for the item and only lose out on the eBay listing fees.

Other sellers argue that you should set the opening bid at the minimum price you will accept for the item. However, this strategy has a drawback: A smaller percentage of your auctions will actually receive bids. You'll eventually get killed by eBay's listing fees, which can add up pretty quickly.

Personally, I set a ninety-nine cent starting price, with no reserve, only when listing popular, name-brand items that I know will sell. The low starting price minimizes my eBay listing fees. However, unless the item is very popular and a sure seller, I usually use my cost as the starting price.

RESERVE PRICE STRATEGIES

We covered the basics of Reserve Price Auctions (RPAs) in chapter 8. An RPA is an auction where you start the bidding at a low price but establish a hidden reserve price— the minimum amount for which you are willing to sell the item. eBay charges special fees for RPAs. However, the RPA fee is fully refunded if your item sells. Table 10.1 presents a summary of these fees.

Table 10.1: Reserve Listing Fees

RESERVE PRICE (US$)	$0.01—$49.99	$50.00—$199.99	$200.00 and up
FEE	$1.00	$2.00	1% of Reserve Price (up to $50)

I rarely use RPAs for items under $50. But I almost always use them when listing an expensive item (over $200)—unless I'm selling an extremely popular product like an Apple iPod, which is likely to attract many bids and reach the desired price without a reserve.

When you use a reserve, be sure to place your starting bid very low; otherwise, you are paying an unnecessarily high listing fee. Listing fees increase as the listing price increases (as seen in Table 10.1).

Reserves are controversial on eBay. If you visit the message boards, you will see plenty of negative comments about them, mostly from buyers who have no experience with selling. While no one keeps official statistics on things like this, there is plenty of anecdotal evidence suggesting that a large percentage of eBay members will not bid on an item with a reserve.

Personally, I have not run up against this kind of resistance in my auctions. In fact, I sell several items in the $200–$500 price range, and I have actually garnered more sales with reserves—not fewer.

DUTCH AUCTION PRICING

Pricing for Dutch (multiple-item) Auctions can also be a challenge. As you'll remember from chapter 8, in a Dutch Auction, the lowest successful bidder by quantity determines the final price for all items.

In some respects, setting a low starting price can be a great strategy in a Dutch Auction, provided that two requirements are met: First, the product must be popular and in demand. Second, the supply must be limited. Just as with single-item auctions, if a product is a continual best-seller with a recognized brand name, it will attract plenty of bids until it reaches its value. If the supply is short, the bids will be higher. If, however, the bidders consider the supply to be plentiful, they will be reluctant to place high bids.

Therefore, when determining the starting price for your Dutch Auction, you must take into account your supply. If you have one hundred identical items and place them in one auction with a low starting price, and there is only a market for seventy-five of the items, then everyone will win an item at the starting price. If, however, you only put twenty-five items in the auction, it is likely that the price will climb well above the starting price, because seventy-five bidders will be clamoring for just twenty-five items.

BUY IT NOW PRICING

Buy It Now (BIN) is an eBay feature that allows a bidder to end an auction immediately by bidding at a fixed BIN price. The Buy It Now price is only displayed until the first bid is placed, and then it disappears. On Reserve Price Auctions, the BIN price is available until the reserve is met. BIN auctions exist to attract impulse bidders or to capture that one bidder who must have exactly what you are selling and cannot risk losing it to a higher bidder.

Table 10.2 specifies the special fees to use the BIN option.

Table 10.2: Buy It Now Fee Schedule

BUY IT NOW PRICE (US$)	$0.01–$9.99	$10.00–$24.99	$25.00–$49.99	$50.00 or more
FEE (US$)	$0.05	$0.10	$0.20	$0.25

BIN fees are only charged if an item sells, and are in addition to the final value fees. If you list a BIN price, avoid starting the auction too low. Otherwise, someone will simply bid a very low price, and the BIN option will disappear. When I use BIN, I like to start my items at slightly above the item's value. One benefit of BIN is that it works to establish a value in a bidder's mind. If I start an item at $19.99 that I think will sell for $29.00, I usually set the BIN price a little higher, say, at $33.00.

Another way to use Buy It Now is to create a Fixed Price Auction. You do this by listing a starting price that is the same as the BIN price. Here's how it works:

Let's say you have two identical items, and you launch one at $19.99 without a BIN price and the other at $33.00 with a Fixed BIN listing—both within a minute of each other. They will appear together, or very near each other, in the listings and search results. The BIN auction will run for the same period as your regular auction unless or until someone buys it at that price. There are two benefits to this technique: First, the BIN auction is subtly setting a value in the minds of bidders who see it, thereby attracting bids to the regular auction, which seems cheaper by comparison. (Remember: On the search results pages, bidders can't tell that the two auctions are listed by the same seller unless they open both of them.) Second, as the first item rises in price close to the BIN price of the other auction, some bidders will be attracted to the BIN item, lest they lose out to a last-minute sniper. When you use this strategy, always launch the BIN auction a minute or so later than the regular auction. That way, if someone does lose out in the regular auction, she can go back to the listing and buy the second item from your BIN auction.

THE SECOND CHANCE OFFER

eBay offers another useful feature that can really add to your profits. It is called the *Second Chance Offer* (SCO). Whenever an auction ends with a winner, if you look at your auction listing, you will see a link to *Send a Second Chance Offer*. This feature allows you to offer identical items to losing bidders after your auction ends, either because the winning bidder was unable to complete the transaction, or because you have more than one of a specific item available for sale.

Consider the following example: I've successfully sold a fire pit for $255. That is $36 over my target price of $219, the minimum price at which I will make a profit on this item. I have plenty of these fire pits. (Actually I have none of them, as they are all drop shipped from the manufacturer—but he has plenty of them and can make more if he runs out.)

If you click on the link to Second Chance Offer, it takes you to a page that lists all the losing bidders for your item.

Figure 10.1 Second Chance Offer Bids

If you look at the first two underbids in Figure 10.1, they were for $240 and $250, both of which are higher than my target of $219. The third bid, at $89, is too low, as are all the other bids. To make second chance offers, I simply check the boxes next to the two highest bidders, and hit the *Continue* button at the bottom of the page. eBay will send the next two highest bidders automated e-mails making the offer. They will have three days to respond. The e-mail that goes out from eBay will have a PayPal button embedded into it. All the bidders have to do to accept is hit the PayPal button, and I will receive both a notice of acceptance and a payment deposited into my PayPal account.

eBay will charge me a final value fee on each item sold, but I have sold a total of three items for one listing fee. This works out to $745 in sales from one auction.

THE BEST TIMES TO LIST AND END AUCTIONS

eBay offers five choices of auction duration: one, three, five, seven, and ten days. How long should your auction last? This is an area where many PowerSellers disagree, and there isn't really a hard-and-fast rule.

One theory is that the shorter the auction the better, because people don't like to bid on auctions that have a long waiting period until they end. Auctions attract impulse buyers. These types of bidders will definitely seek out shorter auctions. This is especially true if you are selling common products that are always available on eBay, such as diet pills, information products, low-cost jewelry, leather jackets, digital cameras, mp3 players, designer brand-name goods, and the like.

If you are selling something of a collectible nature, as opposed to a readily available product, you will want to expose your auction to as many people as possible over the longest period of time. Collectors tend to be more careful and will shop diligently for specific items for their collections. For rare collectibles, then, I recommend the ten-day auction.

The more important decision is this: *On what day should my auction end?* Different types of people shop at different times. The most popular prime-time shows are on Monday, Tuesday, and Wednesday evenings, meaning fewer people may be shopping on eBay at those times. Young people are usually out Friday and Saturday nights. Older folks who stay home spend a lot of time on eBay during the day and on Saturday evening, because it's usually a lousy TV night. Table 10.3 spells out the best and worst days to end an auction.

Table 10.3: Best Days and Times to End an Auction

DAY	RATING	COMMENT
Monday	Good	A lot of people surf eBay at work. After the weekend, they need their "eBay fix."
Tuesday	Worst	Tuesday statistically receives the lowest number of bids on eBay.
Wednesday	Poor	According to studies, Wednesday is not quite as bad as Tuesday, although still not a great day to end an auction.
Thursday	Fair	Thursday is not a bad day to end an auction in the spring and summer, because people going away for the weekend may place bids on Thursday before they leave.
Friday	Fair	Ending your auction Friday before 6:00 p.m. may attract bids from students and young people who are not usually home on Friday and Saturday evenings.
Saturday	Good	Weekend days are usually more profitable than weekdays, probably because more people have time to shop.
Sunday	Excellent	Sunday evening is the period of highest bidding activity on eBay. If your auction ends at about 11:00 p.m. Eastern time, you will maximize your bidding activity.

The auction duration you select determines which day your auction will end. I personally prefer to launch my three-day and ten-day auctions on Thursday evenings, so they end on Sunday evening. Between 6:00 and 8:00 p.m. PST (9:00–11:00 EST) seems to work best for me, but you should experiment, based on the types of products you are selling. Remember: eBay time is Pacific standard time, so you have to add three hours to calculate the time on the East Coast. Forty-four percent of the U.S. population lives in the Eastern time zone, and 69 percent live in the Eastern and Central time zones combined. So be careful not to allow your auctions to end too late in the evening in the Central and Eastern time zones.

Another factor to consider when choosing which day to end your auction is *where* your auction will appear.

When bidders perform a search or go to the listings page for a category, they are given several choices of how to view the auctions, including *New Today* and *Ending Today*. With the Ending Today view, auctions are displayed in order according to which are ending soonest.

If you place a three-day auction on a Friday, it will appear in a prominent location several times over the weekend, which is the time of highest bidding activity. On Friday it will show up under *New Today* and on Sunday it will show up in *Ending Today*.

Having said all of this, once you have settled on a product or category of products to sell, you will want to run your own tests to determine the best time to list and end auctions for the products you are selling.

POWER MOVES

❑ Go to http://pages.ebay.com/help/sell/fees.html and become familiar with the complete eBay fee schedule. Bookmark this link and be sure to check it before listing an item (or consult Appendix E at the end of this book). This will help you understand your potential costs when deciding on your pricing strategy.

❑ Do a completed items search for the product you plan to sell. Select the *Price: highest first* as the default to display the search results. Look at the items that sold for the most money, and open the auctions to see on what days and at which times they ended.

CHAPTER 11

✦ BUILDING GREAT FEEDBACK ✦

I have heard some eBay users remark that feedback isn't all that important, commenting that "No one reads that stuff." Nothing could be farther from the truth. While eBay novices often overlook the feedback factor because they don't understand it, veteran buyers will almost always check your feedback before placing a bid. If they see comments like "Product not delivered," "This guy is a fraud," or "Terrible seller," they will never purchase your merchandise. Once you have hundreds of feedback posts, you can survive the occasional negative feedback comment. As a new seller, you need to have an outstanding feedback rating, brimming with positive comments, to quickly grow your eBay business.

To attain that outstanding feedback rating, you'll need to provide impeccable customer service. In business circles, there's an old saying that, if you want to keep your customers happy and coming back, "You should not just service your customers, you should delight your customers."

Customer service encompasses each interaction with everyone from potential bidders to those who win your auctions or buy from your Store. Always answer a bidder's and/or buyer's e-mail as quickly as possible. Whether the customer is praising your product or complaining, whether he is offering his input or asking a question, he deserves an answer—especially on eBay, where feedback really counts!

THE VALUE OF FEEDBACK

In the first chapter, we introduced you to the concept of feedback on eBay by comparing it to a shopping mall where, outside each store, customers could post comments about the store's products and customer service on a large board. And store personnel were not allowed to remove or change the comments—they were there for all to see before entering the store. Would you look at the messages before shopping at the store? Of course you would. Well, this is the role feedback plays on eBay. Everyone gets to see a review of your customer service and integrity *before* placing a bid on your item.

How do you get an excellent feedback rating? By delivering quality products quickly, efficiently, and honestly. If you are looking to make a quick buck or stage a "hit-and-run" action, eBay is not the place for you. You can build a hugely profitable and legitimate business on eBay without cheating or misleading anyone. I know—I have done it.

There will always be a few rogue customers who claim they never received their product, or you were too slow to deliver it, or they were unhappy with what they received. We all know the customer is not *always* right.

My recommendation for dealing with such problem buyers is simply to offer a thirty-day, no-questions-asked refund. Offering a bidder a refund can head off negative feedback posts.

Once you have a high feedback rating (over 100) you can tolerate the occasional negative feedback comment. But, until then, you should take the long view and remember that you are trying to build a long-term business that can generate thousands of dollars in income. Don't take issue with a $9.00 item that someone was unhappy with. Just refund the buyer's money and move on.

HOW TO BUILD FEEDBACK QUICKLY

Here are some tips to build your feedback rating quickly:

* Sell low-cost items, such as baseball cards, stamps, or inexpensive pieces of costume jewelry for $1 each. You won't make much money, but you can sell dozens, even hundreds, of items in a short time and quickly build your feedback numbers.

* When your auction ends, send the winning bidder a confirming e-mail. Offer to exchange positive feedback with each buyer who pays quickly, and provide buyers with a link they can easily click to leave feedback. This will help build your feedback rating and your customers will appreciate it as well.

* Your e-mail signature to buyers should contain the current *Leave Feedback* link. As of this writing it is:

  http://cgi2.eBay.com/aw-cgi/eBayISAPI.dll?LeaveFeedbackShow

  (Note that eBay often changes its links. See eBay's site map for the most current link.)

* Here is an interesting statistic from eBay: Only 45 percent of buyers bother to leave feedback. Many sellers add a personal touch by including a handwritten thank-you note when they fulfill an order. Such notes should thank buyers for their business, encourage them to contact you with any questions or concerns, and remind them that you left positive feedback for them. I include the following preprinted note in all my packages:

  Thank you for your business. I have posted positive feedback for this transaction. If there is anything wrong with your order, please contact me immediately and I will do my very best to correct the problem or make it right.

I include my e-mail address and phone number after the message, and then sign each note. These notes are printed on four-by-five-inch colored stock. I have them sitting next to my shipping station (see chapter 17), so that it is easy for me to grab one, sign it, fold it in half, and insert it into the box.

Create a little giveaway of some kind. We print out the USPS postage zone chart and include it in the box when we send out our products. The buyer sees this as a little "gift." When someone buys an item over $50, I include an eBay pen. They cost me thirty cents each from the eBay shop. If this is too expensive, eBay also has little packets of mints that come in an eBay wrapper and only cost a few cents each. One woman I know who sells autographs and other paper memorabilia wrote a short article on how to spot fakes. She inserts a copy of the article in each shipment she sends out. Just use your imagination and you can probably come up with several ways to surprise and "delight" your customers.

Customers sometimes forget to leave feedback after they receive the product, because it has been a week or so since your last e-mail and your message is buried in their e-mail files. To combat this "out of sight, out of mind" effect, calculate the average shipping time to you customers. If the customer hasn't posted feedback on the transaction by the time you figure that he's received the merchandise, send an e-mail that includes your *Leave Feedback* link. Your e-mail could say something like this:

By now you should have received our unique baseball batting glove.

I hope you have had a chance to try it out. If you have any questions, or if there are any problems with your order, please e-mail me immediately.

I enjoyed doing business with you and I have left positive feedback for this transaction.

Best regards,

Sammy Sosa

P.S. If you would like to leave feedback about our eBay transaction, please go to:

http://cgi2.eBay.com/aw-cgi/eBayISAPI.dll?LeaveFeedbackShow

An e-mail like this reminds your customer to leave feedback. I have tested this type of e-mail, and it has increased my feedback response by at least 20 percent.

Another way to increase your positive feedback quickly is to be overly generous in posting your feedback. If a check didn't arrive until fifteen days after the auction ended, so what? I still post a nice feedback notice. If someone cancels or doesn't follow through, I rarely bother leaving feedback, unless the person was really a crook or a jerk (although I do file a nonpaying bidder request to recover my fees).

Ask yourself: How many times have I misplaced an e-mail, forgotten to send out that check, or been unable to get to the post office to buy a money order? Not all slow payers are nonpayers. Sometimes, people really do forget. Why make an enemy?

I remember the story of one poor lady who had a heart attack. Before this incident, her feedback rating was over 500, with a 100 percent positive rating. While she was recuperating from her heart attack, several winning bidders who hadn't heard from her left brutal negative feedback comments. A week or so later, her daughter sent all of them e-mails explaining the situation. Surprisingly, several of the buyers didn't believe her. They continued to send abusive e-mails and complaints to eBay. It took copies of her surgery report and a letter from her doctor to get the negative feedback comments removed.

CUSTOMER SERVICE DOS AND DON'TS

Always respond quickly and clearly to questions from eBay bidders and buyers. If I have auctions running, I check my eBay messages at least three times a day, and always a few minutes before the auction closes, in case bidders have any last-minute questions. If you fail to answer e-mails quickly, you may receive negative comments, such as "Unresponsive seller" or "Ignored my repeated inquiries," in your feedback file.

Keep your answers short, courteous, and to the point. Provide all relevant information and be friendly; however, don't get bogged down in long e-mail conversations or let the customer lead you on an irrelevant tangent. Your time is money.

All your business policies as they relate to shipping, payment, feedback, and so forth should be written in a clear, personable style, and specified at the end of each of your item descriptions. You want to convey your policies without listing a set of rules that turn people off. It is also helpful to explain why you have certain policies. For example, if you only ship with Priority Mail, you might want to say something like:

> *We use Priority Mail for all shipments under five pounds. Priority Mail costs less than UPS and includes free boxes and shipping materials so we don't have to charge you for those or build in a hefty handling fee.*

SHORTCUTS TO SUPERIOR SERVICE

When it comes to customer service, you need to balance time, efficiency, and courteousness to maximize your working potential. One way to save time is to create a folder in your e-mail program called "prewritten messages," in which you store template messages for answering common questions like these:

* When was my item shipped?
* Did you receive my payment?
* How long does shipping take?

You'll create additional prewritten messages customized to fit your particular product, as you continue to receive similar questions and comments from customers.

It is much easier to send out a prewritten e-mail than to write a specific answer to each inquiry. However, to prevent your e-mails from sounding like form letters, add a personal touch whenever possible. Use the person's name if you know it, or her eBay username if you don't. Always "sign" your name at the bottom.

BIZ BUILDER

Amazingly, giving out your telephone number can actually save you time. I've started listing my phone number in my e-mail signature. Sometimes a phone call can clear up an issue in much less time than it takes to send several e-mails back and forth. Also, the fact that you list your phone number enhances your credibility and reduces suspicion.

NEGATIVE FEEDBACK

While you are still a new seller trying to build up your feedback rating, *be very careful about leaving neutral or negative feedback for others.* Most of the time, it is better not to leave any feedback at all than to leave negative feedback.

True, eBay is a community. If someone is a crook or taking advantage of people, then you have a responsibility to leave appropriate feedback. However, you don't want to start a "feedback war" over something that was poorly shipped unless the seller is being really unreasonable. There are, unfortunately, some "crazies" out there. If your feedback angers someone, she could potentially bid on your auctions, not pay you, and then leave negative feedback for you as revenge.

If you suspect that someone is violating the community guidelines, you may be better off reporting it via e-mail to the eBay Safe Harbor Team. (Click on the link to *Security Center* at the bottom of any eBay page). If eBay suspends the violator, he will not be able to leave you negative feedback.

Once your feedback is over 100, the occasional negative feedback won't hurt you that badly. Until then, I would suggest that you not leave negative feedback for someone else unless her actions are truly egregious.

FEEDBACK REMOVAL

Getting eBay to remove a negative feedback comment is extremely difficult. There is, however, one way that works most of the time if you really did not deserve the feedback. SquareTrade (www.squaretrade.com) is an eBay partner that offers the SquareTrade seal of approval to sellers. If you are a member, you can use the SquareTrade seal in your auctions and you can apply for SquareTrade's dispute resolution service. For a $20 annual fee, SquareTrade will attempt to resolve a dispute between a buyer and seller. If both parties agree to the resolution, then SquareTrade will notify eBay and eBay will remove your negative feedback.

BUYING VERSUS SELLING FEEDBACK

eBay recently implemented a very important change to the feedback system, whereby there are separate tabs for feedback left by buyers and feedback left by sellers. This is valuable for the following reason: Suppose you're interested in bidding on an item, and you see that the seller has a feedback rating of 35. When you look more closely, however, you notice that most of the feedback comments are from *sellers*, for merchandise the seller *purchased*. His feedback for items he's *sold* may be quite low or even nonexistent. Therefore, you, as a buyer, may be wary of purchasing from this seller. I know this will hamper new sellers—but all of us were new at one time. Most PowerSellers worked very hard to build their rating over a long period.

You can also view the feedback a member has left for others, on the tab *Left for Others*. I like to see what kind of feedback sellers leave for other people. Someone who leaves a lot of negative feedback is less likely to get bids from me. Why take the risk?

In the end, building positive feedback is all about honesty and customer service. If you are honest in your descriptions and provide good customer service, your feedback rating will climb rapidly.

POWER MOVES

❏ Go to the eBay site map and click on the links under the heading *Feedback*.

❏ Bookmark (add to Favorites) the links you will use most often, such as:
> Follow Up to Feedback You Left for Others
> Leave Feedback for a Member
> Leave Feedback for a Transaction

❏ For the auctions you launched in chapter 9, send winning bidders confirmation e-mails and encourage them to leave feedback. Make sure you leave positive feedback for them as well.

❏ Sell a series of inexpensive items for the purpose of quickly building your feedback rating. Include a personal note in each package, thanking the customer for his order and stating that you have left positive feedback for the transaction.

❏ Consider sending a follow-up e-mail to buyers who have not left feedback. Always include the Leave Feedback link in your e-mails to buyers.

❏ Visit the SquareTrade Web site (www.squaretrade.com) and consider applying for SquareTrade's sellers program, so that you have recourse should someone leave you negative feedback.

❏ Set up a folder in your e-mail program for prewritten messages. Create template messages for answering common questions you receive.

CHAPTER 12

✦ WRITING YOUR SUCCESS PLAN ✦

In the introduction, I asked you to evaluate your personal definition of success. This is an important concept. Now that you understand some of the basics involved in running an eBay business, it is a good idea to ask yourself the following questions: What are my goals? How much time do I want to devote to eBay? And how much money can I make, given the time and resources I have to commit?

Most people starting a business write a plan and establish their goals before they start. However, before you attempted that, I wanted you to have a better understanding of how eBay works and what is involved in selecting a product to sell. Now that you understand the work and costs involved, you're ready to put together your business plan.

In the business world, almost every company has a business plan that its executives continually revise and update as the business develops. For selling on eBay, you don't need a full-blown business plan with financial statistics and detailed marketing strategies, but you do need to set some basic goals and map out a series of steps to help you reach those goals. As we conclude Week 1 of this three-week program, we will focus on the basics of setting some realistic objectives and writing a success plan to guide you through the next stages of developing your eBay business.

EVALUATING YOUR EARNING POTENTIAL

The first question you have to answer is how big you want to be, or, put another way, how much money you want to make. If you already know what you want to sell on eBay, this is a much easier question to answer—your anticipated revenue depends on the price point or the final value of what you will be selling. Let's do some simple math to demonstrate this point.

If you are selling a product with an average selling price (ASP) of $50, and the item costs you $30, you will make an average of $20 on each successful auction. So if your goal were to make $3,000 a month on eBay, you would have to close 150 auctions a month. Experienced sellers will successfully close (or convert) as many as 70 percent of all their auctions. So, you would have to launch about 215 auctions a month—or just over 50 auctions a week—in order to close 150 auctions. Alternatively, if you were selling a $100 item for an ASP of $160, you would make $60 an auction. Now you would only have to convert 50 auctions a month to make the same amount of money.

If you focus on selling higher-value merchandise, you will make more money for the same amount of work. The key to moving "up market" is to thoroughly research a product to make sure there is a market for it, and that you can buy it at a price where you can make money selling it on eBay. Remember—you make money when you *buy*, not when you sell.

So if you haven't yet researched and selected a product or products to sell on eBay, now is the time to complete these tasks. You first must determine what you are going to sell and what your average price points will be before you can start setting concrete goals and crafting a business plan.

SETTING GOALS

I know plenty of people who are successful in life and in business who do not create formal, written goals. But I know far more who *do*—and, on average, they tend to be much more successful.

Written goals serve several purposes. Long-term goals give you a vision of where you want to be in the future; short-term ones provide the stepping-stones to get there.

To be useful, your goals should be both specific and achievable. A goal "to become a millionaire within three years" is both vague and difficult to achieve, unless you already have $500,000 in assets. A better goal would be, "I want to achieve Gold PowerSeller status within one year and Platinum PowerSeller status within two years."

.... BEST PRACTICES ....

POWERSELLERS

PowerSellers are top eBay sellers who average consistently high volumes of sales from month-to-month, maintain a high percentage of positive feedback, and comply with eBay's policies. PowerSellers are divided into five tiers, based upon sellers' average monthly sales totals. Certain benefits and services vary with each tier. eBay automatically calculates sellers' eligibility each month; if you qualify, you will be notified of your status via e-mail. The following are sales criteria for each PowerSeller tier:

Bronze	Silver	Gold	Platinum	Titanium
$1,000	$3,000	$10,000	$25,000	$150,000

If you want to relate your goals to income, you could set up steps like these:

1. Earn $1,000 a month by (date)
2. Earn $3,000 a month by (date)
3. Earn $5,000 a month by (date)

Once you establish your primary business goals, you should set subgoals, or a list of tasks that have to be completed to get you there.

Your first set of tasks should be a list of all the things you have to do to set up and organize your business—we covered these in chapter 1. These might include getting your state sales tax number, opening your business checking account, verifying your PayPal account, and so on. You should make a complete list of all these tasks and treat them like individual goals.

Next, you will want to set specific business goals. This will involve determining how many auctions you will run and how often. You should also set your goals for reaching certain metrics such as conversions, sell-through rates, and average selling price.

.... BEST PRACTICES ....

DEFINING METRICS

Metrics is a term that means "measure." There is an old saying in business that goes like this: "If you can't measure something, you can't control it." Some of the more important metrics in eBay selling are:

Conversion or Sell-through Rate: This is the percentage of auctions you close versus the number you listed. If you listed one hundred auctions and successfully closed sixty-five with a sale, your sell-through rate would be 65 percent—or you might say you "converted" 65 percent of your auctions.

Average Selling Price (ASP): This is the average price of all the items you listed that sold (ASP does not include listings that did not sell).

Gross Merchandise Sales (GMS): GMS is the total dollar value of your sales for the month (or week, or year, and so on).

Gross Margin: This is the amount you made on your sales after taking into account the cost of the items you sold and your eBay listing and selling fees.

There are many other, more detailed metrics that eBay sellers track on a daily, weekly, and monthly basis; however, they are all variations or extensions of the ones specified above.

The purpose of establishing goals is twofold: First, you want to set targets to achieve. Second, you want your progress in reaching these targets to be measurable.

Remember that goals can have a numerical value, such as "dollars earned," and/or an accomplishment value, such as "Completed Phase I of my product research." But all goals must have a time value (the date by which they are to be accomplished) to be meaningful.

Here are some points to help you set and achieve your goals:

* **KEEP MOVING FORWARD.** Never look back, except to learn from your mistakes.

* **FOCUS YOUR ENERGY.** Don't be distracted by other issues and businesses.

* **HONE YOUR SKILLS.** Practice and experiment for success.

* **INCREASE YOUR KNOWLEDGE.** Read everything you can find that relates to your business and your goals.

* **MANAGE YOUR TIME AND YOUR ENERGY.** Set aside some time for yourself, your family, and your friends. Otherwise, you're likely to burn out.

* **SURROUND YOURSELF WITH POSITIVE PEOPLE.** Don't listen to those who say you can't be successful.

* **MOST OF ALL, HAVE FUN!** If you enjoy what you're doing, you're more likely to work hard and be successful.

YOUR BUSINESS PLAN

Now that you have your goals specified, it's time to write your business plan—or, as I like to call it, your *success plan*. You have already done most of the work by establishing your goals. Your business plan is nothing more than a statement formalizing these goals in writing:

* What business you are in

* Where you want to go with this business

* What resources you will need to get there

* What will determine your success

You might be tempted to skip this step—or take mental notes rather than write down the details. That would be a mistake. The act of writing this information down in an organized fashion will help clarify your thinking. If you are starting a business with your spouse, you should create this plan together and discuss each of the points. If you are married or living with someone and are doing this alone, you should still discuss your plan with your significant other to get his feedback and to make him part of your success plan.

My wife and I have been running a successful eBay business for over seven years, and I am good friends with several of the top PowerSellers on eBay. We know—and they know—that there is no "quick fix" to success on eBay. If someone tells you she has the "instant secret to success on eBay," and that you can make $5,000 a month by working only a few minutes a day, she is trying to sell you something. Furthermore, she has probably never actually sold anything on eBay. Yes, you can make $5,000 a month on eBay (and even more), but you cannot accomplish this with just a few minutes of work a day. Now that you know what is involved in launching auctions, part of setting your goals is assessing the amount of time and resources you can devote to the business. If your plan is realistic and you see progress week after week, you will be encouraged to keep pursuing your goals.

I am doing my best to reveal all the tips and tricks I have learned over the last six years to help you succeed. However, none of these take the place of planning, research, and hard work. Now that you understand the basics of selling on eBay and how the system works, take the time to set your goals, write a plan, and create a schedule for success. In Week 2, we are going to delve into the advanced systems and techniques that will save you time, reduce your costs, and help you launch professional-looking auctions to ensure that you build a long-term profitable business.

POWER MOVES

- ❏ In your eBay binder, write down short- and long-term goals for your business. Determine how much money you are looking to make and how much time you can realistically devote to achieving your goals on eBay.

- ❏ Review your research and estimate the average selling price of your product(s). Using the formula discussed in this chapter, calculate how many auctions a week you would need to launch to reach your monthly goals.

- ❏ If the number of auctions you need to launch to reach your goal will take more time than you can realistically devote to your business, reassess your product selection. Do additional research, if necessary, to come up with alternative products to sell.

- ❏ Either with your partner or alone, turn your goals into a formal business plan. Keep updating and revising this plan as your business develops.

PUTTING YOUR AUCTIONS TO WORK

By now you have organized your business, completed your product research and determined what you want to sell, and even taken steps to acquire the products. You have launched your first eBay auctions and worked through the steps of getting paid, communicating with customers, and delivering the product. You may even have earned a few feedback comments. Now it's time to start building and refining your skills, to make your fledgling business a success.

In Week 2, we're going to focus on specific ways to improve your auctions and grow your profits on eBay, including driving customers to your auctions by using strategic category selection, writing auction headlines and item descriptions that sell, improving the effectiveness of your auction photos, and using listing upgrades to promote your auctions across eBay. In addition, we'll discuss how to increase profits by selling internationally, and how to minimize your costs and maximize your buyers' confidence by choosing wisely from various shipping, payment, and insurance options. Finally, we'll explore how to monitor and revise your auctions so they are as successful as possible, and review the steps you need to get paid in full and in a timely fashion.

You have already encountered some of these choices and tasks as an eBay seller. We'll now discuss these topics in greater detail, and reveal how to set up processes and systems so you can run your business like a pro, saving you both time and money—and boosting your profits.

CHAPTER 13

✦ CATEGORY SELECTION ✦

Category selection is important for several reasons. While 60 percent or more of eBay buyers find items by *searching,* that still leaves about 40 percent who locate products by *browsing.* Browsers are usually looking for particular kinds of items, so they tend to browse by category, and they're generally impulse buyers (as opposed to searchers, who come to eBay looking to buy something specific). This impulsiveness can prompt unexpected sales or increased bidding activity, which, as we discussed in Week 1, can generate more interest from *all* potential bidders.

In this chapter, we'll discuss how to drive more traffic to your auction by choosing the most strategic category for your item, as well as when to list in more than one category and how to take advantage of pre-filled information.

THE MANY CATEGORIES OF EBAY

To date, eBay has thirty-four main categories and more than twenty thousand subcategories. Table 13.1 spells out the main eBay categories.

Table 13.1: Main eBay Categories

Antiques	Computers & Networking	Musical Instruments
Art	Consumer Electronics	Pottery & Glass
Baby	Crafts	Real Estate
Books	Dolls & Bears	Specialty Services
Business & Industrial	DVDs & Movies	Sporting Goods
Cameras & Photo	Entertainment Memorabilia	Sports Memorabilia, Cards & Fan Shop
Cars, Parts & Vehicles		
Cell Phones	Gift Certificates	Stamps
Clothing, Shoes & Accessories	Health & Beauty	Tickets
	Home & Garden	Toys & Hobbies
Coins	Jewelry & Watches	Travel
Collectibles	Music	Video Games
		Everything Else

eBay gives you some flexibility in choosing categories, but your item must somehow be related to the category in which you are selling. Selecting the optimal category and subcategory (for simplicity's sake, going forward we'll refer to both collectively as "categories") for your item is important because you want your item to be listed where other similar items can be found. Remember: You are trying to reach browsers and impulse buyers, so you need to list your goods where they are looking.

Before you list your item, do some research. Search for items on eBay that are similar to yours, and pay attention to which categories they are listed in. Try several different keyword searches and see if you find particularly active categories (those with more than five thousand auctions). Think creatively about your item. For example, maybe the hand-thrown potter's lamp you first thought belonged in Antiques/Decorative Arts is better suited for Home & Garden/Home Décor. (To see which category an item is listed in, just look at the top of the auction listing, as illustrated in Figure 13.1.) Look at the page-view counters and numbers of bids for similar items listed in different categories. Select categories where other sellers are conducting successful auctions.

If you're stumped for category ideas, try entering some descriptive keywords into the *Search for Categories* box when setting up your auction with the *Sell Your Item* form. This tool helps you find matching categories based on keywords you might use in your item title. You can then choose the best category for your item, or conduct additional research, based on eBay's suggestions.

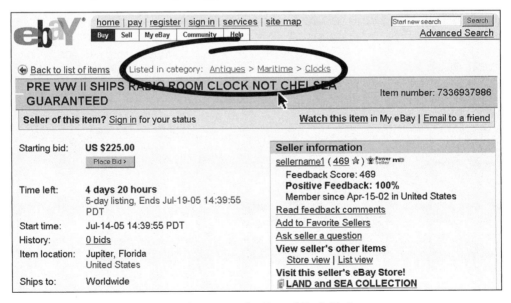

Figure 13.1 Auction Categories Appear at the Top of Each Listing

Before listing your item in any category, follow these simple steps: First, browse through all of eBay's categories, and write down which ones you feel are relevant to your product. You should be able to find at least three to five possible fits. Next, write down the number of auctions currently under way in each of those categories (this information will appear next to the category name). If there are fewer than five thousand auctions under way when you check a category out, you may consider it *inactive*.

I consider categories with over 5,000 auctions to be *popular* and those with over 20,000 to be the *most popular*. Some categories have over 100,000 auctions going at any one time. Using this ranking system, rate the categories you have chosen for your product.

I recommend listing in the most active categories because they get the most traffic. If you put your product in an inactive section of eBay, you may get few or no bids, even if you feature it. Avoid categories with less than one thousand auctions, unless your product is highly specialized to that category.

LISTING IN TWO CATEGORIES

eBay has another feature called *Listing in Two Categories*. Listing in a second category is a great way to reach more eyeballs and generate more bids for your item.

For example, an old tray table from China could fit in both Asian Antiques and Antique Furniture. By listing in both locations, you can attract browsers in each category.

Listing in two categories incurs an additional expense, and I only use it for items that I expect to sell for over $50. When you list in two categories, eBay doubles your insertion fee, as well as the fees for most listing upgrades (bold, gallery, and so on). Scheduled listing and homepage featured fees are not doubled; similarly, final value fees are unaffected. eBay claims to have research proving that listing in two categories will, on average, increase final values by 17 percent. If you are selling an expensive item, this can be quite profitable. When you select that second category, be sure to select a highly active one with plenty of auctions. This will get you more bang for the extra buck you are spending.

PRE-FILLED ITEM INFORMATION

For certain categories, such as Books, CDs, DVDs, and Video Games, eBay offers a useful feature called *Pre-filled Item Information*. When you list in those categories, the pre-filled information form comes up automatically. Simply enter the title, author, director, artist, ISBN, or UPC code into the form, and this handy tool will automatically fill in your listing with a title, item specifics, a stock photo, and a short description of the item you are selling. You may customize the item information further with additional item details or use a photo of your own.

This feature is a huge time-saver. I once had a large lot of books to sell on consignment for a friend. I was able to open an auction listing for one of the books, type in the ISBN, add a couple of lines about the original cost and the condition of the book, and launch the auction in less than ninety seconds. In fact, using the pre-filled information, I was able to launch thirty auctions in about forty-five minutes.

When you use the pre-filled item tool, you must list in the category eBay selects for that item, but you can still select a second category. While this feature may not be a determining factor in selecting a category for your item, it's a potentially valuable tool that you should try to take advantage of as your business grows.

POWER MOVES

- ❏ Take some time to go through any categories relating to the products you plan to sell. Explore the various subcategory listings, including the number of auctions in each one.

- ❏ If you are going to sell books, music, or movies, go to the eBay Help tab at the top of any eBay page and type in *pre-filled information*. This will bring up a link to an excellent tutorial on how to use this feature.

CHAPTER 14

✦ WRITING AUCTION HEADLINES ✦ AND DESCRIPTIONS THAT SELL

The two most important factors in attracting bidders to your auctions and closing the sale are your *title* and your *item description*. The title, usually referred to as the *headline*, is what potential bidders see when they perform a search or browse through the categories. The item description is your sales pitch—a description of what you are selling and why the person reading it should bid on it or buy it. In this chapter, we will look at what constitutes a good headline, how to use keywords to win search results, and how to write a benefit-rich item description that closes the sale.

YOUR HEADLINE

The headline is the single most important item in your listing. An arresting headline has the power to "get the eyeballs" (eBay slang for getting people to view your item). Your headline should immediately attract potential buyers to your listing—if you get someone to click on your headline, your odds of getting a bid or making a sale have just gone up by about 100 percent.

When a buyer performs a search or clicks on a category, she is presented with a page listing about forty auction titles. The potential buyer scans the list, looking for something that catches her attention. Making your headline stand out in this list is critical to your success.

Viewed this way, a headline is nothing more than a collection of words designed to stop your potential buyer's eyes from scanning the page, and instead linger long enough for him to eventually click on your listing. To accomplish this, the headline must first contain a keyword that describes the item the buyer is looking for. It should also be compelling, right to the point, and state or imply a benefit to the buyer.

Keywords

The single most important criterion for headlines is the use of relevant keywords. According to eBay, over 60 percent of bidders find items on eBay by using the search feature. Therefore, your headline should be as precise as possible—yet also contain specific keywords that will make it come up in the greatest number of searches. Look at this headline:

JERRY RICE SIGNED FOOTBALL JERSEY FROM 1982 SEASON –NR

This is an excellent headline for several reasons. First it exactly describes what is being offered. Second it is rich in keywords. It would come up in a search for the following terms:

* Jerry Rice

* Football

* Football jersey

* Jerry Rice signed

eBay allows fifty-five characters (including spaces) in an auction title. This one uses fifty-four. (Note that, to remain under this character count, the seller has used the abbreviation "NR" for "no reserve." See Table 14.1 for a list of abbreviations frequently used in auction titles.) Here is another example of a keyword-rich headline:

TRUE RELIGION DESIGNER BLUE JEANS, SIZE MEDIUM 30 WAIST
(55 characters)

A woman searching for designer blue jeans might type in several combinations of keywords such as: *blue jeans, designer blue jeans, true religion* (a popular trademarked brand name), *blue jeans medium, blue jeans 30, True Religion jeans*, etc. Any of those keyword combinations would bring this auction up in a search. This headline also uses all fifty-five characters.

Sometimes you need to describe the condition of an item:

STEINBECK SIGNED 1ST EDITION ~ OF MICE AND MEN, MINT

The word "mint" tells the buyer this book is in perfect, like-new condition—something every book collector searches for.

Notice that I use all caps in my headlines. Experience has shown that all-caps headlines will generally stand out better in a list of auctions than will those with a combination of upper- and lowercase letters.

Because people are searching for products by keyword, it is extremely important that you use correct spelling. If you are selling a Staffordshire plate and spell it *Stafordshire*, your auction will not come up when bidders use the eBay search feature to find items.

Table 14.1: Common Abbreviations Used in Auction Titles

In order not to exceed eBay's strict character limit for headlines, eBay sellers often use the following well-known abbreviations* in their auction titles:

NR	No reserve	OOP	Out of Print
NIB	New in box	VG	Very Good
NWT	New with tag	NM	Near Mint
FS	Free Shipping	MIB	Mint In Box

* You can find more abbreviations in the glossary at the end of the book.

Hot Button Words

Years of research by direct marketers have proven that certain words have the power to make people act. If you have room in your title, after including all the relevant key-words, you should try to include *hot button* words in your title. These are words that motivate people and increase interest. Table 14.2 lists some of the best-performing hot button words, according to the Direct Marketing Association.

Table 14.2: Hot Button Words

RARE	NEW	LIKE NEW
SECRET	VINTAGE	BEST VALUE
TOP SELLER/SELLING	UNIQUE	UNBELIEVABLE
BEST SELLER/SELLING	SEXY	LOVE
FREE	SUPER DEAL	HARD-TO-FIND
UNUSUAL	AWESOME	BEST ____ ON EBAY
LOOK BETTER	GUARANTEED	RELIABLE

Be reasonable and accurate with your choice of words. Your credibility is on the line. If a headline makes a buyer click on your auction and it's immediately obvious that the bidder is being misled, you have just written a check that you can't cash. Potential bidders will just hit the *Back* button on their browser and move on.

Remember that eBay gives you fifty-five characters to get your point across. Use every one of them as if it were a valuable piece of real estate.

ITEM DESCRIPTIONS

Once a person clicks on your auction, you have the opportunity to sell to her—and your description is your best sales pitch. The first goal of your item description is credibility. Your auction description must inspire trust, so forget about making irresponsible, wild claims. If your item descriptions are too far-fetched, overuse adjectives, or make unfounded claims, you will sow doubt in prospective bidders' minds. Although the item description is basically a sales letter, it is important to strike a balance between compelling copy and silly or outrageous claims.

One way to inspire trust is to accurately describe your product, including any shortcomings. If a product has a flaw, mention it. If the product is new, but the box is damaged, be sure to inform prospective buyers about this. If a product is perfect except for a small scratch, tell bidders and show them a photo of the scratch.

Just the Facts, Please

The first part of your description should be no more than an accurate portrayal of the product. Describe what you are offering before you start to *sell* it. You want to be very specific. Include model number, size, weight, color, and any attachments or accessories—any information that will help bidders understand exactly what they are about to bid on or buy. There should be no confusion about the product.

It is critical that this information be contained in the first paragraph of the description. If bidders have to scroll through the entire page to find out exactly what is included in the auction, you risk them clicking away.

Know Your Audience

Before you start writing your description, decide who you are writing to. If you are selling baby clothes to stay-at-home moms, your item description will be quite different than if you are selling software to computer users. Look at your niche market and try and picture your customers. What are their likes and dislikes? What are they looking for? How old are they and what sorts of jobs do they generally hold? What are their hobbies and interests? What makes them tick? Do they have plenty of disposable income? Are they seeking quality—or a bargain? The tone of your description should reflect all the facts and benefits you emphasize.

What's the Benefit?

Next I like to talk about the product's *benefits*. Words mean something. Use their power to convey the benefits readers will enjoy when they buy your item.

To do this, first list all your item's benefits on a sheet of paper. Then arrange them in order of priority (for your target customer), and place this list next to your computer. Now, start describing the first benefit on paper—and move down your list until you've exhausted every benefit of your product. Keep these sheets of paper in the binder by your computer for easy reference.

Be sure here to write about the product's *benefits*—not its *features*. For example, "This barbecue grill has two height settings" is a feature. Compare it to this statement: "This barbecue grill has two height settings, an upper setting to cook slowly so your food doesn't burn and a lower setting to sear your meat instantly for the best taste." The benefits here are *so your food doesn't burn* and *sear your meat instantly for the best taste*.

A successful sales pitch appeals to the base desires and self-interest of the customer. When composing a sales pitch, attention to psychology counts more than attention to writing style. What do people want? They want to be loved or liked. They want to be rich. They want to look better. They want to be successful. They want to feel that they have just scored an incredible bargain. They want to believe they are doing some good in the world. These are the factors that Madison Avenue advertisers consider when conceiving big-budget ad campaigns. However, you don't need all their talent and experience to write great item descriptions. You just have to keep in mind who you are selling to and what stimulates people to buy.

I once bought a wholesale lot of Tommy Hilfiger polo shirts from an overstock dealer. I thought I was getting a mixed lot of shirts. When they arrived, they were all large and extra large, and all of them were black. I was really annoyed; however, I now owned the shirts and had to make the most of them. I reasoned that men who wore large and extra large shirts were probably a little thick around the waist. So I wrote an item description that first described what I was selling. In the second paragraph I said:

> *I love these black polo shirts. They have the classic "Tommy" look—rich and elegant, and the black tends to hide my middle age paunch. When I wear my Tommy Hilfiger black polo shirt, my wife says I look thinner.*

Now I wasn't lying. It is well known by fashion designers that black is slimming. In fact, my wife did say I looked good in the shirt. I got top dollar for the entire lot—several customers bought two or three shirts at a time. (I offered free shipping to anyone who bought two or more.)

Potential buyers want to know what your product will do for them, and do not need a lot of useless distraction. Again, your item description must appeal to the profile of the buyer, display your professionalism, and promote a feeling of trust in you as the seller.

All the romancing you can do with a product is based on the product's real or perceived benefits. If I can't come up with enough benefits, I will often do a Web search for the product to review the advertising that others have done. You don't want to plagiarize the consumer advertising copy, but you can certainly get ideas from it.

White Space and Boldface

I'm constantly frustrated on eBay by auction descriptions that appear in small type and go on and on in one long paragraph. See Figure 14.1 for an example. This is a screenshot from an actual auction. The description is fairly well written, but because it's all run together in one long paragraph, it is somewhat hard to read. Breaking the description into three paragraphs with white space separating them would dramatically improve this description's readability.

Description

This LUCY COLA CLUB SODA SIGN is GUARANTEED 100% ORIGINAL and very OLD. Circa 1940's. This is a **VERY RARE** and outstanding **Early soda fountain/country store sign.** Sign is in **Near Mint Condition**. This Sign was **NEVER USED** as seen by no holes were ever punched for mounting. This is a "tacker" sign which means the first time it was mounted the sign had to be "tacked" in placed by driving a tack and creating the holes. Sign is made of Painted Metal. This sign has outstanding Artwork with highly detailed graphics. The Colors are Excellent as from day one. This sign has light wear only due to its age but the sign still displays great in an outstanding way. Excellent size for easy display. Measures 27" X 10". Please add $17.75 Shipping and Insurance. Please read payment instructions Before you bid. Please do NOT ask me to end this auction early. I will ship within the USA Only. Thanks for your bids.

Figure 14.1 Sample Item Description

People tend to scan a Web page looking for something that grabs their attention. Instead of one long paragraph, I recommend using a series of short paragraphs of three or four sentences each. Make lists, use bullets, and highlight important information with boldface type. (Just don't overdo it. If every other word is in bold or all caps, you lose the impact.)

By using short paragraphs and lists, you create *white space* in your auction. This makes it easier for people to scan the page to find the information they want.

The other major auction killer is *reverse* or *drop-out* type. This refers to featuring white or light-colored type against a dark background. It may look artistic, but it can be difficult to read. If you are selling anything to people over forty-five, this factor is very important. As people age, their eyes require more light and greater contrast to see well. An older person will have a difficult time reading yellow type on a black background.

Type size is another factor. If you are selling body jewelry to teens, they probably won't have difficulty reading eBay's small, default type size. But if you are selling products that older customers might want to buy, remember that many people over forty need bifocals, or reading glasses, to read. Therefore, a larger type size may be more effective. To increase the type size in your auctions, in the Sell Your Item form, select the larger type size in the HTML editor, or start your auction description with the HTML command <font size +1>. Inserting this command before the first word in your description will increase the font size in your entire auction description.

Increase Bids with a Call to Action

Salespeople have an old saying: "If you want to make the sale, you have to ask for the order." I have worked in sales and sales management, and I can tell you that statement is 1,000 percent correct. I cannot tell you how many times I have seen a salesperson go through a perfect product presentation and then conclude with a weak statement, such as "Well, what do you think?" You don't want to take the time to write a terrific auction description, only to water it down with an ineffective final statement. Instead, ask for the sale: "Don't be knocked out by a sniper. Place your best bid now so you can enjoy a sizzling steak on your new barbecue this weekend."

I always end my auctions by asking for the bid. This is known as a *call to action*. Think of all the direct marketing pieces you've received in the mail over the years. Didn't all of them end with something like this: "Don't let this once-in-a-lifetime opportunity pass you by. Call now!" You need to end your auction with a similar punch.

THREE QUICK WAYS TO DISCOURAGE BIDDERS

There are three common errors that eBay sellers make, all of which discourage bidders:

* They threaten the bidder with negative feedback.
* They don't take PayPal.
* They write payment, shipping, and return policies that sound like jailhouse rules.

At least once or twice a day I will surf eBay and come across an auction that includes a statement like this: "If you don't pay right away I will report you to eBay and give you negative feedback." Who would want to do business with this kind of seller?

Over 70 percent of regular eBay members use PayPal. Yet I always see auctions with big, all-caps statements, declaring: "I DON'T TAKE PAYPAL. DO NOT BID ON THIS AUCTION UNLESS YOU CAN SEND CASH OR A MONEY ORDER." Apparently, these sellers don't want to pay PayPal's fees. This makes little sense. By refusing to accept PayPal, they do save PayPal's 2.9 percent processing fee, but over half their auctions close without a bidder, costing them much more in eBay listing fees for items that didn't sell.

Last is the drill sergeant mentality. This refers to people who spell out their shipping, payment, and return policies in harsh language, often in all caps. Here is one I saw recently:

> I SHIP ON TUESDAYS AND THURSDAYS SO GET YOUR PAYMENT IN BY THOSE DAYS OR WAIT UNTIL THE FOLLOWING WEEK. I ACCEPT PAYPAL AND MONEY ORDERS ONLY. DO NOT SEND A CHECK. IF YOU DO I WILL THROW IT AWAY AND RELIST THE ITEM.

It is important to spell out your payment, shipping, and return policies. However, the policies should be realistic, and they should be written in friendly language that *explains* instead of *dictates* your policies.

Here is another example from an actual auction. This seller had a feedback rating of just over 50 percent with twelve negative comments (no wonder):

> I ship everything by priority mail on Monday and Friday. I charge the priority mail rate plus $2.00 to pay for box and packing material. I don't guarantee anything. If you want insurance the extra cost is $5.00. I know it doesn't cost that much to insure a package but I have to wait in line and fill out forms at the post office and keep the forms until a claim is made and that is a big pain but I will do it for $5.00.

This seller is doing everything he can to tell me he doesn't want my business. If the tone of his e-mails to customers is anything like his policy statement, it is no wonder he has poor feedback. If someone pays on a Monday night, he won't ship until Friday and the parcel likely won't arrive until the following Tuesday or Wednesday. The whole point of paying for Priority Mail is to get something quickly.

In contrast, the following is an auction description we use to sell a line of expensive decorative fire pits. Others are selling similar items much cheaper, yet we tend to outsell our competition. Notice how we appeal to the prospective bidder's desire for quality and how we communicate the product's benefits. Also note the use of white space, the call to action, and the inclusion of shipping and payment details.

YOU ARE BIDDING ON THE WORLD'S BEST SOLID-STEEL, HAND FORGED, FIRE PIT AND GRILL

Perfect for barbecues, gatherings, camping, or a quiet evening at home. Our fire pits are handcrafted from durable cold-rolled steel and include a FREE BBQ grill, a poker for stirring coals, and a spark-arresting screen to let the fire die down safely.

Unique flame cutout Santa Fe–style designs provide ventilation and add to its unique charm. Creating the perfect complement to your backyard couldn't be easier. Natural rust patina finish, no assembly required. Made in the USA—by hand. This is not a mass-produced product.

These fire pits are normally only sold in high-end mail order catalogs and expensive gift shops out west. The normal retail price is $399. We are starting the bidding at $1. I have placed a reserve at my cost.

Limited time offer: If you buy this fire pit from my eBay Store or at the Buy It Now price, I will give you a FREE $29-value custom cover.

You can click on the group photo to see the other designs available from our other auctions and eBay Store.

The fire pit is 31" x 31" x 17" and weighs 56 lbs. Just think how good steaks would taste cooked on this grill, grilled over some real mesquite wood.

It is not just a fire pit—it comes with a free removable grill top so you can cook steaks, burgers, hotdogs, and more on it.

THIS IS THE BEST FIRE PIT I HAVE EVER OWNED.

I have owned several fire pits of different designs and have always been disappointed. When I found this fire pit, I bought one for myself. The very first evening we had friends over, I sold two of them on the spot.

This is absolutely the best fire pit on the market—bar none. The top cover is a very fine mesh so large sparks don't fly out and burn your clothes. THE CUTOUTS IN THE SIDE PROVIDE PERFECT UPWARD VENTILATION. The smoke really goes UP. It doesn't blow around sideways, so you can sit close to it and get all the warmth without being bothered by smoke and sparks.

Also, if you live in an area where open fires are banned, you can still use this model, because it qualifies as a COVERED GRILL.

We also have this model and other designs in our eBay Store for immediate purchase. The other themes include Chinese Symbols, Grape Vines, Bear & Moose, Santa Fe, Kokopeli Indian, Western Broncos (in photo w/cowboy) and Moon & Stars.

Shipping and handling is $55. I am sorry but we cannot ship to Alaska,

Hawaii, or Canada. Please Note: We do not stock these because of the size and weight. They are drop shipped directly from the forge. Shipping can take as long as 5-7 days to the East Coast. Sorry but we cannot ship this item overseas. Insurance is $4.90 and is REQUIRED.

Don't lose out to a sniper. Place your best bid now. Or, buy it from our eBay Store and get a free $29 cover.

I am going to go out on a limb and offer a money back guarantee on the cost of the pit and the outbound shipping. Keep it for 30 days and use it for a few fires. If you are not completely satisfied, send it back (at your expense) and I will refund all of your money including the $55 shipping cost. Your only risk is the return shipping cost. I know you will love this grill and I don't really expect to get any back, but I will stand behind my guarantee if I do.

This transaction is insured against fraud. Please note the buySAFE Seal on this page. This means that every auction is insured against fraud by buySAFE and by a $25,000 bond from The Liberty Mutual Insurance Company. Please click on the buySAFE Seal to get more information.

We have an excellent feedback rating and strive to keep it that way. Your complete satisfaction is our first priority. Please visit our About Me Page to learn more about our company and our feedback, and to see our other auctions.

Thank you for looking.

After reading all this, you may worry that writing successful auction descriptions is difficult or a lot of work. It's not, once you get the hang of it. Take your time crafting effective auction descriptions as you are getting started, and after a while you will find that it becomes second nature.

POWER MOVES

HEADLINES:

❏ Sit down with a notebook and a pen, and write out as many keywords as you can think of for your product.

❏ Now do a search on eBay for those keywords. Write down the headlines that appeal to you. Open those auctions and look at the corresponding hit counters. Determine which headlines appear to get the most hits.

❏ Using the above information as a guide, begin creating your own attention-grabbing headlines.

DESCRIPTIONS:

❏ In your binder, list every benefit of your product. Now write a sentence about each benefit and how it relates to a buyer. Remember to "romance" your item a little; however, don't go overboard.

❏ Once you have done this, list your item for sale. In the description field, first include all the facts about the product that you are selling. Fill in the rest of the description with the benefit statements you created.

CHAPTER 15

✦ MASTERING AUCTION ✦ PHOTOGRAPHY

As an eBay seller, you need to take sharp, attractive photographs. Photography is one of those skills that can take years to learn well. Fortunately, digital cameras—with all their automated features—have made this task much simpler. In this chapter, we will look at the equipment and software you will need to take digital photographs and upload them to your auctions. We'll also discuss powerful techniques for taking photographs that sell, and the most efficient ways to host and upload your pictures.

DIGITAL CAMERA SELECTION

Your first task is to select a good digital camera with all the features you will need. There are hundreds of digital cameras on the market, and new models are coming out every week. The trend today is toward higher and higher image quality. This is expressed in the number of pixels or megapixels a camera can resolve. The higher this number (or the greater the resolution), the more expensive the camera.

Luckily, you do not need extremely high resolution for your auction photography. In fact, high-resolution photos are undesirable because they take a long time to download when someone opens an auction.

eBay recommends limiting photo file sizes to fifty kilobytes. Actually, you can go as high as sixty-four kilobytes without a problem. Sixty-four kilobytes (64 KB) is the typical size of the *e-mail setting* on most digital cameras. So this is one of the first features you should look for when buying a camera—make sure it has a low-resolution or e-mail setting. (Most digital cameras include this feature.) The e-mail setting is fine for most digital photos—provided you are not going to resize them, causing you to lose detail. If you are selling a product where detail is important, then you will want to shoot at a higher resolution, at least one or two megapixels, and crop or resize the photo with software such as Adobe Photoshop to get the file size down to 64 KB. Shooting at this higher resolution will preserve the detail when you crop or resize.

Features you will need in a camera used for auction photography include:

✳ **TRIPOD:** Almost all cameras include a standard tripod screw mount at the bottom. It is very important to use a tripod when taking auction photographs, to avoid the blurred images that occur when you hold a camera by hand.

✳ **MACRO SETTING:** *Macro* is the photographic term for the ability to focus very close to an object. Typically the macro feature will allow you to focus as close as three or four inches (8 or 10cm) from the subject. This is important for photographing small objects or showing details, such as the original manufacturer's price tag or a maker's mark on pottery or silver.

✳ **WHITE BALANCE ADJUSTMENT:** We will talk about *white balance* in detail shortly. Basically, this is how you adjust a camera to account for the different "color temperatures" of light. (The color reflected from an object will vary subtly depending on the type of lighting.) Almost all cameras have an automatic white balance adjustment feature, but you want to make sure you get one that allows you to manually choose between daylight, fluorescent, halogen, and incandescent settings.

✳ **MANUAL FOCUS:** The ability to manually focus on an object or part of an object is very important, because oftentimes the autofocus feature will not provide the exact image quality you are looking for.

✳ **EXPOSURE ADJUSTMENT:** The light meter in a camera can be fooled by bright backgrounds. Since you'll often be shooting against a white background, especially when using a light tent (see page 154 for more about this), you need a camera that can adjust for this exposure.

✳ **OPTICAL ZOOM:** Digital cameras come with *optical zoom* and/or *digital zoom*. Digital zoom is restrictive and difficult to work with; therefore, make sure your camera has a basic optical zoom feature. You can tell if it does by pushing the zoom button and seeing if the lens actually moves in and out. If not, the camera is using digital zoom.

✳ **APERTURE PRIORITY SETTING:** The ability to select a small lens opening (aperture) allows you to achieve what is called *depth of field*. This means that objects close to you and far away will both be in focus.

Nikon, Sony, and Canon all make fairly low-cost cameras that fit these criteria. Having said this, I have found that the Nikon 2100 (which I own) and the Nikon 3100 work well for auction purposes. They are both available in the $100–$200 range.

The Canon PowerShot A70, A75, and A95 all take great product shots for the Web. The A75 sells for as little as $200, and the A95 sells for about $250.

Sony offers several cameras in its Cyber-shot line that have all the features outlined above, if you go up to its midrange models. These cost upwards of $300.

The cameras mentioned here are by no means the only ones suitable for product photography. There are lots of great cameras on the market. However, these cameras all have the features specified above.

TAKING PHOTOGRAPHS THAT SELL

A complete course on digital photography is a subject for another book. Instead, I have organized the most important information as a series of tips. If you want to learn more about digital photography, there are several books on the market that run the gamut from beginner to advanced. For a handy, basic book aimed at the auction photographer, check out David Steiner's great little e-book, *Snappy Auction Photos,* available through my Web site (www.skipmcgrath.com). Another easy-to-follow primer is Nick Vandome's *Digital Photography in Easy Steps* (Barnes & Noble Books, $9.95).

Use a Tripod

Unless you are shooting outdoors or using a flash, digital cameras tend to use a very slow shutter speed. With a slow shutter speed, typically under 1/125th of a second, most people cannot hold a camera steady enough to prevent blurring. Using a sturdy tripod will allow you to shoot all the way down to 1/30th of a second with good results. Make sure your tripod has an adjustable head that will rotate the camera both horizontally and vertically. A quality tripod can cost as much as $100, but I have found that most large photo stores often have good—even professional-quality—secondhand tripods for as little as $20–$30.

Focus Carefully and Correctly

I see out-of-focus pictures on eBay every day. One reason for this is autofocus malfunction. Most digital cameras project a laser or infrared beam onto the object being photographed and measure the reflection to determine the focus. Problems may occur when large objects allow the beam to spread out, or when something reflective on the object itself "fools" the autofocus feature.

The other issue is depth of field. Have you ever looked at a photograph where the subject is in focus and the background is all fuzzy? Depth of field is the focal distance, from near to far, in which a camera can focus. The aperture, or lens opening, on a camera adjusts to allow more or less light into the camera. When the lens opening is large, the camera has a very narrow range of focus. When the opening is small, the focal length is longer. This effect is magnified when you are shooting very close up, such as when you are photographing small objects.

The aperture can be set manually on most of the digital cameras listed earlier, and on many others. Lens openings are marked as a series of numbers that range from 3.5 to 16. The higher the number, the greater the depth of field you will have. This is critical when shooting up close with the macro function, because the macro function also limits the depth of field (for technical reasons I won't get into here). If I am shooting an object close up, I typically use an aperture of 8 or higher. With automatic digital cameras, when you set the aperture at a high number, the camera compensates for the reduction in light by slowing down the shutter speed. This is why you need a tripod. If you try to handhold a camera at a slow shutter speed, you will almost always get a blurry photo.

Finally, using your camera's Aperture Priority mode to narrow the lens opening can improve the performance of your autofocus, if you are using that feature, by improving your depth of field.

Use Soft Lighting

Sunlight or direct light from a bulb or a flash may create hot spots and reflections in your photos. If you are shooting outside, you should shoot in bright shade or on a cloudy day. If you have a north-facing window, this can often produce very nice, diffuse light. If you are using lights, you can either purchase white plastic light covers to diffuse the light or use a light tent like the EZ Cube pictured in Figure 15.1.

The EZ Cube is widely used by eBay sellers. It makes taking great photographs easy. You simply place an object inside the light tent, shine the lights, and shoot. This eliminates glare and reflection from shiny objects. Place colored paper or cloth in the background to create different effects. You can purchase EZ Cube light tents at a dis-

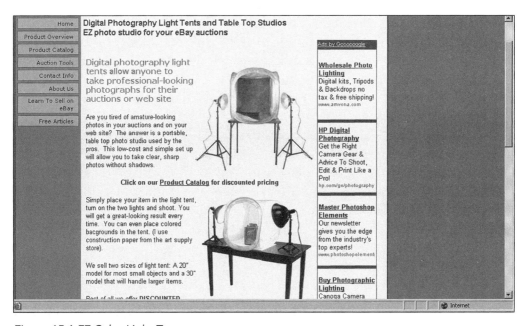

Figure 15.1 EZ Cube Light Tent

count from one of our Web sites, www.EZAuctionTools.com. They start at around $50 and go up to just over $100 for the larger sizes.

Avoid Clutter

Try to photograph only the object you are shooting. Placing an object on a table with other stuff in the background will distract from your subject. If you use a system like the EZ Cube, this should be easy. However, you will sometimes have to photograph large objects that do not fit in the cube. In this case, be sure to clean up the background as much as possible. If you are shooting a computer, for example, remove everything from the desk it's on and hide the wires or any other distracting objects. If you are shooting a car, drive the car to a park where you can shoot it with grass and trees in the background, instead of in your garage or driveway.

If you are shooting apparel, you should invest in a dress form or mannequin. Place the mannequin against a wall draped with cloth to contrast the color and diffuse any shadows.

Avoid Underexposure

If you are shooting against a white or bright background, or shooting outside in bright light, you camera's automatic light meter may "read" the surrounding light instead of your object, underexposing the image. Most good digital cameras include an over/underexposure compensation adjustment feature. If you are shooting against a white background, such as in an EZ Cube light tent, try adjusting your camera's exposure setting to +1 or even +1.5. This will prevent the subject of your picture from appearing too dark, as your camera adjusts to the white background (a case of underexposure). One way you can tell whether you are underexposing your pictures is if white backgrounds appear gray in the photographs. If this happens, or if your objects are just too dark, then try adjusting the exposure compensation until the white looks truly white.

Use the Correct White Balance

Different types of light have different wavelengths. Without getting into a discussion of optical physics, this means that you have to adjust your camera for the type of light you are using. If your camera is set on *daylight* and you shoot with an ordinary household light bulb, your photos will appear yellow. If you shoot with a fluorescent light, your photos will appear blue-gray. You can purchase daylight bulbs—ordinary light bulbs with the same wavelength as daylight—at most large camera stores. All the digital cameras mentioned here have a white balance setting. If you are using halogen, indoor light bulbs, or fluorescent lights, just set your camera for the type of light you are using.

Get Close

Getting close to your subject will produce a better photo. It is easier to focus accurately when you are close, and you'll capture more of the object without the distracting clutter.

The best way to learn to take good photos is to practice. Read your camera's instruction manual from cover to cover, and experiment with all the controls and functions until you are comfortable with them. Fortunately, with digital cameras you don't have to spend a fortune on film and developing to learn how best to use your camera.

BIZ BUILDER

When shooting a colorful item, try placing a piece of colored cloth or craft paper behind the object. Pick a color that matches one of the minor colors—not the main color. For example, if you were shooting a blue teapot with a gray or yellow trim, you would use a gray or yellow background paper. This is a trick used by professional photographers that will give your photo an image of greater depth and allow the main color to "pop" in the photograph.

MANAGING YOUR PHOTOS

Image management is the term used by eBay sellers for editing, storing, and uploading photos.

Editing Software

Most digital cameras come with photo editing software. I happen to like Nikon's the best. You can set it so whenever you plug your camera into the computer, the program automatically opens and you can import your photos with one click. If you own an Apple computer, you are lucky. All Macs come with iPhoto, which is one of the best all-around photo editing and management programs on the market.

There are also a number of software programs you can buy to perform these functions. There are some very advanced (and expensive) programs available, such as Adobe Photoshop; however, there are functional (and less expensive) programs available as well. If you go to www.shareware.com or www.tucows.com, you'll find a number of free image and photo management programs you can download (just type *photo software* into the search box). One of the best is PhotoPlus. The download is free; the company makes money selling the support and training tools, which cost far less than most expensive programs and are excellent.

Whichever program you use, you should be able to easily plug your camera into your computer, import the photos, give them file names so you can organize them, and then edit and crop the images. Most software programs allow you to adjust the brightness and contrast of your photographs. This is a real time-saver because you don't have to reshoot your product.

Storing and Uploading Your Images

Once you have your photos edited and named, you need to create a folder on your hard drive called *Auction Photos* (or something similar). Within this folder, you should create subfolders for the various product categories you are selling. Simply file your photos in the appropriate folders, so you can easily find them when you are ready to upload them to your auctions.

Once you have your photographs stored on your hard drive, you need to import them into your auctions. eBay offers two ways to manage your images. You can insert images one at a time from your computer's hard drive as you launch auctions. The first photo is free and each additional image costs fifteen cents. So, if you use four photos in an auction, you're spending forty-five cents (on top of eBay's other fees), whether the item sells or not. This is obviously too expensive if you are running dozens of auctions a week. eBay also offers a subscription hosting program based on the amount of storage space you require (a function of the number and size of photos you host). The service starts at $9.99 a month for 50 MB, and increases to $14.99 a month for 250 MB and $24.99 a month for 1 GB. The basic plan (50 MB) will allow you to store over 500 average-size images. This service is also expensive, although eBay does give you free editing software when you subscribe to this service.

Another way to host your photos is with a Web site. If you already have a Web site, you can simply upload your photos to your site, labeling each one with a separate URL (Uniform Resource Locator, or the "address" of the photo) and then insert the URL of the specific photo into each auction. I don't recommend this option. Not only is it is time consuming, but you also have to pay for the Web space and need FTP (file transfer protocol) software to upload your photos.

Managing Photos with Auction Management Services

In chapter 23, we are going to cover auction management services. My favorite is Mpire.com. Other popular services are Vendio, Andale, and Marketworks. All these companies will host your images as part of their service. The money you'll save by forgoing eBay's hosting service will easily pay for all or most of an auction management service's monthly fee. In addition to photo hosting, you'll get numerous features so you can automate your auctions as well. In my opinion, this is the best option if you plan to launch fifteen or more auctions a week.

Here's how it works: You simply upload your images to the Web site of the auction management service, where they are subsequently stored (you can also organize them into folders). When choosing an image for your auction, simply double-click or check the appropriate photo. The auction management service inserts the URL of the particular image into your auction. When the auction launches, eBay looks for those images at the named URL, and they are displayed in your auction every time someone clicks on it. If you select a gallery image, the URL is fed constantly to eBay, so the image is always visible when members are searching or browsing through the gallery.

Once you start using an auction management service, you will appreciate the speed—and therefore the time-saving aspects—of hosting your photos this way. You will also enjoy the additional benefits, such as templates, automated customer e-mails, shipping calculators, and inventory management tools that come with the service—usually for what you would be paying eBay to host photos individually.

POWER MOVES

❏ After selecting the camera you are going to use for your auction photography, spend some time familiarizing yourself with the instruction manual. Pay special attention to the size settings, white balance, macro (close-up) feature, manual focus, and aperture priority settings.

❏ Once you understand how all the features work, take some practice shots. Upload them to your computer and use whatever imaging software you have to crop, rotate, and resize the photos.

❏ Compare the costs and benefits of importing your photographs into your auctions using:

> eBay's Picture Services (Basic or Enhanced) to individually upload images

> eBay's subscription hosting program

> A third-party auction management service

CHAPTER 16

✦ PROMOTING YOUR AUCTIONS ✦

eBay offers several optional features to help you drive potential buyers to your auctions. While a few of them are free, most come with a fee. The key to using these features effectively is to make sure they are appropriate to the type and value of the auction you are running, and that the cost provides a good return on investment (ROI).

Now that you have enhanced your listings with photographs, descriptions, and headlines that sell, the next step is to attract more buyers to your listings. In this chapter we will explore how to take advantage of various free promotional tools and evaluate the performance and ROI of those that are fee-based.

FREE PROMOTIONAL TOOLS

Obviously, free tools provide the best ROI. A free opportunity worth exploring is promoting your auction on eBay's homepage. eBay's homepage is the third most visited page on the Internet, receiving over 5 million hits a day. eBay creates several boxes on the homepage dedicated to promoting your auctions. If you look at Figure 16.1, a screenshot of the eBay homepage, you will see a seasonal promotional box, called "Summer Dollar Days From $1." This box lists items by category that started at $1 with no reserve. How do you get your auction included in this type of special promotion?

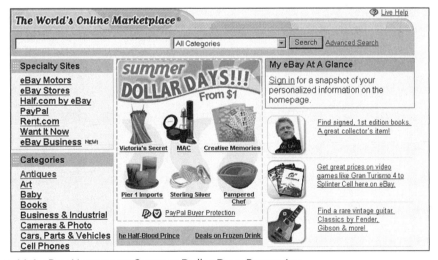

Figure 16.1 eBay Homepage Summer Dollar Days Promotion

If you visit Seller Central, there is a link to *What's Hot* (see Figure 16.2). When you click on this link, you are taken to a page offering various options (see Figure 16.3).

Figure 16.2 Seller Central: What's Hot Link

Figure 16.3 eBay's What's Hot Page

The first option is *Merchandising Calendar* (Figure 16.4). This is a list of all of the upcoming promotions and features that eBay is planning for the homepage in the coming three-month period. eBay updates this page every week.

Figure 16.4 *Merchandising Calendar*

You should get in the habit of checking this page periodically to look for promotions that could benefit you. Let's continue with the Summer Dollar Days promotion as an example. If you sell items in any of the categories listed, you want to make sure to start several of your auctions at $1, with no reserve. When the promotion begins, eBay's search engine will seek out auctions in the listed categories that start at $1. When someone clicks on the box on the front page, your auctions will come up. This is a powerful promotion. Every summer my wife and I sell barbecue grills. My grill auctions normally receive about four hundred hits each over a seven-day period. During one week, when my auctions were linked to the eBay homepage, I averaged over fifteen hundred hits per auction, and my bids and final values rose significantly. One barbecue that usually goes for between $225 and $240 sold for $292!

Other free promotions offered by eBay include free listing days, where you may list as many auctions as you like with no listing fees. You can learn about these and other opportunities on the General Announcements page, accessible from the bottom of any eBay page. All announcements from the past two weeks are posted in chronological order, with the most recent at the top. You should check this list first thing every morning, since free listings and listing discounts are always offered on very short notice—usually one day or less.

In addition to free listing days, eBay occasionally offers free bold and highlight features, one-penny listing days, and free gallery listings. And, as we discussed in chapter 14, it costs nothing to create keyword-rich titles for your auctions. Remember: Over

60 percent of eBay bidders find items by searching. The more searchable keywords your headlines contain, the more often your auctions will be viewed.

EBAY PAID PROMOTIONS

eBay offers you various listing upgrades, each for an additional fee. Let's take a look at each one. (Remember that fees are subject to change; consult eBay for the most recent fee schedules.)

eBay Subtitles (Fee: $0.50)

A subtitle is just that, a second title that appears in slightly smaller print just below your auction title on the eBay search results page. A subtitle can provide descriptive information about your item that buyers will see when browsing through categories or viewing search results. (Words included in the subtitle do not come up when buyers perform a basic search.) Subtitles are limited to sixty-five characters—ten more than the auction title. Because of the cost (fifty cents), you only want to use a subtitle for items where you expect the profit margin to easily cover the expense. For example, if you were selling a product with a projected profit margin of less than $5.00, the subtitle would represent 10 percent or more of your profits. If you anticipate that the cost of the subtitle will equal more than 10 percent of your profit margin, the feature may not be worth its cost.

A subtitle allows you to spotlight features or benefits that may not fit in the title field, but would be of interest to potential buyers viewing a list of items. It may contain additional information about what you are selling, such as accessories included, outstanding benefits, special offers and so on. I find that subtitles make your listing stand out somewhat from the other listings around it. Here is an example of how I use a subtitle:

COWBOY STYLE, SOLID STEEL FIRE PIT & BARBECUE – NR
Free poker, grill & spark arrestor. Free Shipping with Buy It Now

Bold (Fee: $1.00)

This feature presents your auction title in boldface type, making it stand out from other listings. This is one of my favorite options because it's a proven producer. eBay's own research has shown this feature to increase final values by an average of 21 percent. At a cost of $1, as long as you are listing an item that will sell for over $15 this is the single best promotional tool in terms of ROI. I use the bold option in almost all my auctions.

Highlight (Fee: $5.00)

Highlight is similar to bold, in that it makes your auctions stand out. When you select this option, it places your auction title within a pink-colored highlight band. Highlight costs

$5. However, if you use highlight without bold, it can be somewhat difficult for the bidder to read your title. So, in effect, this option costs $6 when you add the bold feature.

I am not a big fan of highlight. eBay hasn't announced any research statistics on this feature, which suggests that it probably doesn't work that well. At $5, I would probably not use it unless I were selling an item I expected to reach at least $100 and that had a high conversion rate.

eBay Gallery (Fee: $0.35)

This option allows you to place a small thumbnail photo next to your auction title on the search results and browse pages. At $0.35, this is eBay's least expensive promotional tool. Almost everyone uses the gallery and many eBay bidders will not click on a listing unless they see this photo—so I consider it mandatory. Plus, eBay's research shows that a gallery photo increases an item's final value by an average of 12 percent.

Featured Plus (Fee: $19.95)

Whenever an eBay user performs a search or browses through a category, the first thing he sees is a list of items featured in that category. This is the function of the Featured Plus tool. This is high-performing tool; unfortunately, it's also a bit pricey at $19.95.

I only use this tool for high-priced items, to make sure they get the visibility they need. Featured Plus is also useful for Dutch Auctions, where you may be selling a lower-priced item, but have a large enough quantity to offset the cost. The performance of this tool is impressive—eBay reports that Featured Plus items are 28 percent more likely to sell and have an average 12 percent higher final value.

Homepage Featured (Fee: $39.95 and $79.95)

The Homepage Featured auction is eBay's most expensive promotional tool, costing $39.95 for a single-item listing and $79.95 for a Dutch (multiple-item) Auction listing. Homepage Featured listings may rotate onto the eBay homepage; however, eBay does not guarantee when or if this will happen. While Homepage Featured is a bit of a crapshoot, it does work most of the time.

I once had an auction ending on a Thursday night for a pair of antique silver candlesticks. The listing rotated onto the homepage about one hour before the auction ended. My auction received over five hundred hits in that last hour, and the candlesticks sold for almost double what I was expecting.

Other Features

eBay offers two additional listing upgrades: ten-day duration and Gallery Featured. The ten-day duration option costs ten cents. I always use this option if I am paying for any of the other features (except bold and gallery), because I want to extend the life of the auction to amortize the cost of the other upgrades, such as Homepage Featured or Featured Plus, over a longer period.

The Gallery Featured option is an option to have your image featured in the gallery section of the homepage. If you select this option, your item will periodically appear in the special featured section above the general gallery. Your picture will be almost double the size of nonfeatured gallery pictures, and will also appear in the general gallery. At $19.95, I have never used this option and eBay has never released any research statistics on it. The only use I can think of for this feature is to showcase a visually stunning product, such as a valuable painting, an expensive antique, or a beautiful Persian rug.

BIZ BUILDER

As of February 2006, eBay began offering two bundles of listing features. For sixty-five cents, you can purchase a *Value Pack,* which includes the gallery, listing designer, and subtitle features. The Pro Pack offers the bold, border, highlight, Featured Plus and Gallery Featured upgrades for $29.95.

Despite what eBay says about the performance of its various promotional tools, you should test each one yourself on your own auctions. eBay's numbers are averages over all types of products in all price ranges. You need to see what works for you and your product(s).

Set up a spreadsheet that lists your auction items and which, if any, promotional features you used. Now, create columns for hits, bids, final values, total fees, and net profits. Try running auctions with various combinations of options, in order to gather a variety of data. In no time at all, you will be able to determine the optimal combination for your particular product(s). Keep this spreadsheet in your reference binder so that you may access it when you are considering using these features.

POWER MOVES

❏ Visit the eBay fees page at: http://pages.ebay.com/help/sell/fees.html. Expand the listing to show all the fees and print out a copy to keep by your computer. (You can also review Appendix E in this book.) Having this information at the ready when you are deciding on which promotional items to use will save you time and help you make better decisions.

❏ Create a spreadsheet for market testing. After every auction, record the options used, the number of hits and bids the auction received, and the final outcome—no sale or the final value. Use this information to assess the performance of your auctions with and without various upgrade combinations.

CHAPTER 17

✦ SHIPPING, HANDLING, ✦ AND INSURANCE

Poor shipping practices are a leading cause of negative feedback on eBay. eBay buyers have come to expect that they will receive their purchases intact and professionally packaged. What you charge buyers for shipping is also important, because that influences their expectations and feedback. Therefore, your challenge as a seller is to provide quality packaging and shipping at a low enough cost that it will be attractive to buyers.

In this chapter, we'll discuss the advantages of the various shipping carriers; ways to save on shipping costs, supplies, and insurance; and how to automate the process and set up a convenient and efficient shipping station.

SHIPPING WITH THE U.S. POSTAL SERVICE (USPS)

More and more eBay sellers are using Priority Mail to ship their items. For items that weigh less than six pounds, Priority Mail is competitive with UPS. (For heavier items, sellers don't seem to mind the extra charge of UPS, because they get their items much faster.)

USPS provides free boxes, envelopes, tape, and labels for Priority Mail. When you add on the cost of shipping materials, Priority Mail is not that much more expensive than regular first-class mail—and it's a lot cheaper than UPS for small packages, where you have to provide your own boxes. Even purchased in large quantities, twelve-by-twelve-by-twelve-inch (30cm) boxes can cost as much as ninety cents each. When you buy them in small quantities, they can cost as much as $1.50 each.

Priority Mail used to have a simple flat rate scale, but USPS recently changed to a zoned system. To find a shipping rate, go to http://www.usps.com and type in your package's weight and the zip code you're shipping it to. You can order free shipping supplies online at http://shop.usps.com. There is also a special link for eBay sellers where you can order Priority Mail boxes with the eBay Logo imprinted on them: http://ebaysupplies.usps.com.

DELIVERY CONFIRMATION

The USPS offers a service called *delivery confirmation* for fifty cents a package. The postal service will place a bar code sticker on your package that is tracked all the way through the postal system. You or your buyer can go onto the USPS Web site (www.usps.gov), enter the delivery confirmation number, and see where the package is in the system (or if it has been delivered). Private carriers, such as UPS and FedEx, provide delivery confirmation automatically as part of their standard service. Additionally, these services give you the option of requiring signature delivery confirmation—which can be useful if you need to prove that a package was received.

ENDICIA

If you are using the U.S. Postal Service for most of your shipping, I strongly recommend signing up with Endicia, Inc. (www.endicia.com). Endicia is an online postal solution. Once you have an account with the company, you can download software (both Mac- and PC-compatible) that allows you to calculate postage and print out a label with delivery confirmation. There are two advantages to using this system: First, you save fifty cents on the cost of delivery confirmation; and second, you can drop your packages off at the back door of the post office without having to stand in line and purchase postage and delivery confirmations individually.

Of all the online postal solutions, Endicia offers the most features and is the easiest to use. In addition, it offers more options than Stamps.com and other similar services. One of Endicia's greatest features is *Stealth Postage*. With this tool, you can print a postage label that does not show the actual cost of the postage. It has a bar code that post office computers can recognize, but there is no postage amount printed on the label. So if your postage is $3.90 and you charge $4.90 for shipping and handling, your buyer will not be able to see this disparity when the package arrives. When you use Endicia, you can also purchase insurance (see next page) from a private insurance company that costs less than that offered by the U.S. Postal Service.

USPS and eBay launched a new feature in 2005 called Click & Ship, allowing you to print postage directly from the eBay site. The service is free, whereas Endicia has a monthly service charge. However, I have found the USPS site to be cumbersome and slow, and the service ties up the printer. Besides, the money you save on insurance should easily pay for Endicia's services.

INSURANCE

Insurance can be a great money maker for eBay sellers. The truth about insurance is that very few packages are ever lost. We have been selling on eBay for six years. In that time, we have only lost two packages out of the thousands we have shipped—and one of them eventually turned up. There are, however, three benefits to insuring all your shipments. First, you can make some extra money by providing insurance. Second, it gives buyers peace of mind. Finally, if customers know their items are insured, they are less likely to complain about inflated shipping charges.

I recommend the services of DSI—Discount Shipping Insurance (www.dsiinsurance.com). DSI is a private discount insurer. Its rates are up to 60 percent less than those of the post office or private carriers, such as UPS or FedEx. Also, DSI gives you a little card that you can drop in the box to show the customer that his item was insured. Unlike the post office, you can claim losses much sooner and get paid in about five days instead of thirty to forty-five days. Another advantage of using both Endicia and DSI Insurance is that their systems are integrated. The Endicia Web site allows you to apply DSI insurance amounts; in addition, you can get a printout at the end of the month for your DSI billing.

BIZ BUILDER

If you will be shipping in large volumes—one hundred packages a month or more—consider calling DSI and asking for a customized quote. The company's toll-free number is 866–852–9956.

Here is an example of how you can make a little extra money each year by using a discount insurance company. Consider the following costs:

USPS Priority Mail cost	$3.90	What you charge for S&H	$4.90
Insurance cost ($100 item)	$0.40	What you charge for insurance	$1.25
Your actual cost	$4.30	Your profit	$1.85

This is not an unreasonable charge for shipping and handling. The key to getting this across to the buyer is to have a statement in your auction *and* in your end-of-auction e-mail that reads something like this:

Please note that our shipping and handling charge is designed to cover the cost of shipping the item, insurance on the value of the item and the shipping charge, and our cost for materials to properly package your item so it arrives safely.

If you ship two hundred packages a month and make an average of $1.85 on each one, that is $370 extra income per month, or $4,440 per year. Those monthly savings could cover a car payment for many people. If you are selling more expensive items, you can charge and make even more money on insurance. On a $300 item, I charge $3.75 for insurance. Since UPS insures the first $100 for free and DSI charges forty cents per hundred for the next two hundred, I make $2.95 ($3.75 – $0.80) on each transaction.

PRIVATE CARRIERS

If you are going to be a high-volume seller of items weighing more than five pounds, then you should open an account with a private carrier, such as UPS, FedEx, or DHL. My current favorite service is FedEx Ground. While UPS and DHL offer discounts on shipping to businesses, they do not discount shipments to residential addresses. FedEx Ground has a residential rate that is very competitive with UPS and DHL. However, I prefer DHL for overseas shipments, especially to Europe. DHL is the largest carrier in Europe and its rates and service are excellent. (We'll discuss shipping overseas in the next chapter.)

To receive available discounts, first go online to the carrier's Web site and open an account. Once you have an account, you will be given information on how to contact an account representative. Contact your rep by e-mail or phone, and give her an estimate of your shipping volume. The representative will usually get back to you within a few days with a discount quote. Make sure you let her know that you are also getting quotes from her competition.

SHIPPING POLICY

Whether you use eBay's Sell Your Item form or a private auction management service, there is a place for you to spell out your shipping policy. This is a very important step for several reasons. First of all, savvy eBayers always look for both the shipping cost and the method of shipment before bidding. If this information is not there, a lot of experienced bidders will not want to waste their time e-mailing you—they will just click away. Other bidders will e-mail and you will be wasting *your* time answering them.

Buyers sometimes become confused when looking at and bidding on multiple auctions. If there is a misunderstanding during the payment process, and you have specified a shipping policy in your auction, you can simply refer them back to the auction or copy and paste the specified shipping policy into an e-mail. Showing a buyer proof that he was informed of applicable costs usually circumvents any problem.

If you charge a handling fee in addition to shipping, this is the place to mention it. Remember: Don't just say, "We charge a handling fee on all sales." Instead, explain the reason for the extra cost: "I pack all our merchandise professionally in new packing materials. I add $1.25 to the actual shipping charge to cover the cost of shipping materials." At this point you should also explain your insurance policy—whether insurance is optional or required, and how much you charge per $100 of value.

SHIPPING STATION

To pack and ship items efficiently, set up a clean, organized shipping area in your home or office, with all your supplies nearby. This station should include boxes and packing supplies, a tape gun, a label printer, and a postage scale. Remember that your time is valuable. Having a dedicated and orderly shipping area can save you hours each week.

BIZ BUILDER

Experienced PowerSellers who manage large volumes of shipments often purchase cheap, secondhand computers for their shipping stations. To save time, you can connect such a computer to your postage scale and label printer. Also, because packaging items is so time-consuming, a lot of sellers hire neighborhood high school students to come over once a day and pack and ship their items. If the student has a car, she can even drop packages off at the post office for you.

HOW TO PACK GOODS

How you package your items is a major factor in your customers' satisfaction. Poorly packaged goods can lead to all sorts of headaches, from additional costs incurred to refund a customer's money or replace the original shipment, to negative feedback.

Here are some packaging tips: For DVDs or CDs—whether they're movies, music, or software—use CD mailers. These are cardboard packages of just the right size for sending such items. Tyvek mailers are ideal for shipping clothing and other soft goods. Wrap the clothing in blank newsprint or tissue paper, and then place the merchandise in these water-resistant, tear-proof mailers. Because Tyvek is so lightweight, shipping in Tyvek mailers is cheaper than shipping in boxes.

Postcards, photographs, stamps, and sports cards are also simple to mail. You can place the item between two flat, corrugated shipping blanks (sold at office supply stores) and then slide it into a bubble mailer, or you can purchase Stay Flat Mailers™. These mailers are difficult to bend and often come with self-adhesive strips on the flap.

For glass and other fragile items, I strongly recommend double boxing. This is your best protection against breakage. Here is the proper way to double box: First, wrap your item in bubble wrap and then place it in a box, leaving approximately two inches of space on all sides of your piece. Fill this void with packing peanuts, balled up blank newsprint, or craft paper. You should then place this smaller box inside a slightly larger one and again fill the extra space with Styrofoam peanuts or bubble wrap.

Packing and shipping with care makes a big difference in your success as an eBay seller. When your box arrives at the buyer's house or office, his first impression is based on the condition of the package. If you send his treasure in an old shoebox stuffed with yesterday's newspaper, that impression will be less than flattering. He may not leave you negative feedback, but he won't be inclined to leave you positive feedback, either.

SHIPPING MATERIALS

Shipping materials, such as boxes, tape, bubble wrap, Styrofoam peanuts, and so on, can be very expensive. It turns out that one of the best places to shop for these materials is right on eBay itself. A number of dealers sell these materials at very competitive prices. Although shipping supplies are typically not heavy (with the exception of large shipments of cardboard boxes), they are bulky. Oftentimes, the shipping cost will have a large impact on your total cost.

The trick here is to shop locally. Look for eBay sellers that are located close by. I am in Seattle. I once bought a large quantity of padded envelopes from a seller in Georgia and didn't bother to look at the shipping cost. By the time I received them, they ended up being more expensive than if I had just purchased them at my local office supply store at the regular retail price. I now purchase my shipping supplies exclusively from sellers located on the West Coast.

You should add a small amount to your shipping cost for packaging and handling, but this fee should not be excessive. Bidders get upset when they are charged $5.00 for shipping and they receive a package showing that the postage cost a mere $1.25. While it's acceptable to cover the cost of the box and the shipping material, the costs you pass on to the customer should be reasonable.

Your local gift shop is a treasure trove of free shipping and packing materials. These merchants receive daily shipments of fragile items requiring large amounts of bubble wrap, Styrofoam peanuts, and sturdy boxes.

Local laws may require these shops to recycle packing materials, rather than throw them away. This can be expensive. Believe me—store owners are usually happy to give these things away. Other stores that receive large quantities of shipping and packing materials include kitchen stores, gift shops, electronics stores (such as Radio Shack), and small neighborhood hardware stores.

If something requires special packaging, such as an odd-sized box or large amounts of packing material, explain these circumstances to the buyer when you provide the shipping cost—or, even better, specify this in the auction description.

POWER MOVES

❏ Set up a shipping station with tape, a tape gun, a scale, and any additional supplies you will need.

❏ If you decide to use Priority Mail, go online and order your supplies.

❏ Visit the Web sites for USPS, UPS, and FedEx Ground and compare the rates for the size and weight of the product you are shipping.

❏ If you decide to use a private courier service, visit the service's Web site or call Customer Service and open an account. If you will be shipping large quantities of packages each month, consider calling the company to get a customized quote.

CHAPTER 18

✦ BOOSTING YOUR PROFITS BY ✦ SELLING INTERNATIONALLY

The advantages of selling internationally depend on the type of product you are selling and how easy or difficult it is to ship. Not all products appeal to international buyers and some products are illegal or just too difficult to ship. For example you cannot export tobacco, alcohol, or certain electronic devices containing encryption algorithms. In general, you only want to ship products overseas that cost more than $50— otherwise, the shipping cost is too high, relative to the cost of the item.

Despite the challenges, opening your auctions to international buyers can greatly increase your profits. As we mentioned, eBay operates in twenty-seven countries across the globe, and sales outside the United States totaled over $25 billion in 2005. In addition, people from dozens of other countries surf the U.S. eBay site. The first year I started selling internationally, overseas orders accounted for more than 19 percent of my business; today that percentage is even higher.

In this chapter, we'll discuss how to maximize your profits by selling internationally, and how to reduce costs so that your margins more than compensate for the additional efforts and expense of selling overseas.

POWERFUL PROFITS

The main advantage of selling internationally is profit. International buyers, especially those from Europe and Japan, tend to pay more than American buyers do for the same products. And they don't seem to mind the high cost of shipping.

BIZ BUILDER

The best items to sell internationally are those with high dollar values, relative to their weight. These include collectibles like coins and stamps, jewelry, small electronics such as PDAs, MP3 players, automotive accessories, and sporting goods.

FIND YOUR MARKET

There are three major issues to consider when you sell internationally. The first is your product—does it appeal to international buyers? The only way to find out is to list your products in overseas markets. You do this by specifying *Ship-to locations* when listing your item for sale (see Figure 18.1). Simply check off each country to which you will agree to ship.

Figure 18.1 Ship-to Locations

If someone tries to bid from a country that you have not selected, her bid will be blocked by eBay. By listing internationally, you will be able to discern which parts of the world are viable markets for your product.

SHIPPING

The second consideration is shipping. Can you ship the product for a reasonable amount, relative to its cost? As a rule of thumb, if the shipping cost would exceed 20 percent of the estimated final value, I would probably not offer the item internationally.

BIZ BUILDER

Outside the United States, I only sell to Western European countries, Japan, Singapore, Australia, Israel, and Canada because credit card fraud is rampant in the other regions. These nations also have the largest overseas markets. If I do agree to sell to a country I have qualms about, I insist on being paid with an American Express money order in U.S. dollars.

Calculated Shipping

When we discussed shipping previously, I stated that I prefer to use fixed shipping rates. The rates to overseas countries are so varied, however, that this is often impractical. Therefore, you'll most likely find yourself offering calculated shipping when selling internationally. When you select this option, a shipping calculator will appear in your auction description. Overseas buyers can enter their country information, and the calculator will estimate shipping costs so they can see applicable rates before deciding to bid.

International Shipping and Customs

There are essentially two ways to ship internationally:

* **USPS AIRMAIL POST AND GLOBAL PRIORITY MAIL.** Shipping via the U.S. Post Office's Airmail Post or Global Priority Mail service has two distinct advantages—the costs are relatively low and you do not need a customs broker. Of the two, Global Priority is the faster service. While its rates are almost twice as high as those of Airmail Post, it is still less expensive than the express services offered by companies like FedEx. On the downside, there's no signature required, making it difficult to prove delivery. In addition, the service may be quite slow. Local post offices in foreign countries can hold up items for weeks, awaiting customs clearance, before notifying the recipients that their shipment has arrived. The lack of positive delivery confirmation is a real problem because you cannot take advantage of PayPal's Seller Protection policy without it. Furthermore, if the customer pays with a credit card (or pays via PayPal with a credit card) and claims he never received the product, he can initiate a chargeback. If you can't prove that the product was delivered, you have no recourse. For these reasons, I only use USPS for low-cost items. The other disadvantage of shipping overseas via USPS is that it's hard to collect on an insurance claim. It can take up to twice as long for the U.S. Postal Service to investigate and pay an insurance claim for an overseas shipment than it does for a domestic shipment.

* **INTERNATIONAL CARRIERS SUCH AS UPS, DHL, AND FEDEX.** The advantages of shipping with private international carriers are threefold: reliability, the ability to insure the shipment (and collect on claims), and positive delivery confirmation. The primary disadvantage is the cost—these carriers are more expensive than USPS and, in most countries, your shipment must go through a customs broker. This incurs brokerage charges that start at $25 and can run as high as 1.5 percent of the value of the shipment, or as high as $250. The $25 minimum brokerage fee makes it impractical to ship items overseas that cost less than $100.

A WORD OF ADVICE ON INTERNATIONAL SHIPPING

Whenever you ship overseas, you have to fill out a customs form that states the contents and the value of the item you are shipping. Buyers may ask you to mark the item as a gift or place a low value on the customs form, so that they incur a lower duty. *Do not do this!* First of all, you would be breaking the law if you were using the U.S. Postal Service. Second, if the item were lost or damaged, you could only claim the value stated on the form. Finally, eBay's policies state that you must obey the laws of *both* countries—the one you are selling from and the one you are shipping to. If you violate this policy, eBay will suspend you or, in repeated cases, cancel your account. When shipping internationally, I always place an invoice in the box, specifying the item description and the price the buyer paid. This prevents the customs official from having to guess at the item's value.

So, what *is* the best way to ship? Whenever I sell a low-value item overseas, I take my chances with the USPS. Yes, every once in a while a package goes astray and I lose money on the order. However, this does not happen often, and the extra cost is easily offset by the increased profits I earn from overseas buyers who do receive their merchandise.

When I sell an item worth over $100, I usually use UPS Calculated Shipping. In this scenario, I include a note in my auction that the buyer may have to pay a customs brokerage fee in addition to the shipping cost. I like to specify as many of the fees as possible in the item description. Be sure to be clear about the shipping method you'll be using, any risks associated with the item, the estimated delivery time, and if the buyer should expect any additional fees. eBay suggests that you advise potential buyers to research customs fees before placing a bid.

PAYMENT

The third and final point to consider when it comes to selling internationally is getting paid. Fortunately, PayPal is set up to collect funds from forty-five countries (see the PayPal site for a complete list), as well as in several currencies, including the yen, the euro, and the British pound. eBay automatically converts the cost of a product to the user's default currency. So, if a British bidder is viewing an item listed on the U.S. site, she will see the cost in U.S. dollars *and* British pounds. To see what your product will cost in other currencies, visit eBay's currency converter at http://pages.ebay.com/services/buyandsell/currencyconverter.html.

If an overseas buyer pays via PayPal, you don't have to worry about the conversion rate. The buyer will pay PayPal in his home currency, and PayPal will pay you in U.S. dollars (or the currency of your country). The currency converter is primarily helpful if the buyer wants to pay by money order, bank wire transfer, or certified check. Do not accept money orders or checks payable in a foreign currency. Some American and Canadian banks charge a $25–$50 fee, plus the currency exchange fee, to cash a check or money order in a foreign currency.

I would also not accept a credit card for any large overseas transaction, unless the buyer has an exceptionally high feedback rating (with excellent comments), and has been active on eBay for at least a year. Credit card fraud is much worse overseas than in the United States and Canada. The problem arises when someone pays with a credit card that clears, and then the credit card company discovers the card is invalid several weeks later—after you have shipped the product. In this case you are out the money, whereas with PayPal, you are still eligible for the *Seller Protection Program*, PayPal's antifraud insurance program. This program protects you from fraudulent credit card transactions processed through PayPal, up to $5,000 per year. (You can learn more about this program at www.paypal.com.)

POWER MOVES

I would not suggest that you start shipping overseas until you have mastered domestic selling and shipping. But, once you have successfully launched enough auctions that you know all the ins and outs of eBay selling, you should evaluate whether there is an international market for your product. You can do this in two ways:

- ❏ Search completed auctions on eBay. Look for successful auctions where the items sold at very high prices. Often these winning bidders are international buyers. Use this information to determine if there is an international market for your item. Also, evaluate the shipping policies specified by the sellers.

- ❏ Go onto overseas eBay sites, such as eBay.co.uk (the United Kingdom eBay site) or eBay.com.au (eBay's site in Australia). Unless you speak German, French, or Chinese, I would limit yourself to the English-speaking sites. Search completed items for the product you are selling and see if there is a market for it in these countries.

CHAPTER 19

✦ MONITORING AND REVISING ✦ YOUR AUCTIONS FOR SUCCESS

Professional eBay sellers like to stay on top of their auctions on a daily basis. They not only want to know how their auctions are doing, they may wish to revise an ongoing auction if it is not performing well. Fortunately, eBay makes monitoring and updating auctions easy for sellers. This chapter will take you through the various tools eBay provides to help you monitor, manage, and revise your ongoing auctions.

THE MY EBAY DASHBOARD

eBay provides a convenient tool for monitoring your auction activity, called *My eBay* (see Figure 19.1).

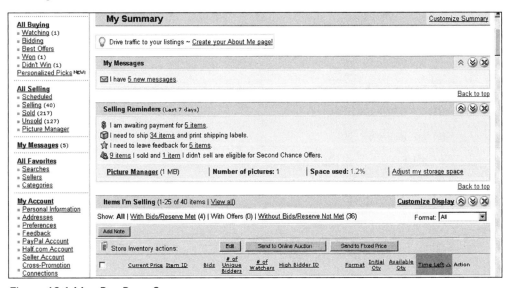

Figure 19.1 My eBay Page Summary

You can access My eBay from the top of any eBay page, by hitting the My eBay button. The first thing you will see is *My Summary*. This includes *My Messages*—clicking on this link will bring up any questions from buyers about your auctions.

Next you will see a list of symbols followed by notes:

* **UNANSWERED QUESTIONS (STAR):**
  How many questions from buyers you have left to answer

* **PAYMENT REMINDER (DOLLAR SIGN):**
  Number of items awaiting payment

* **SHIPMENT REMINDER (PACKAGE):**
  Number of items you have left to ship

* **FEEDBACK REMINDER (STAR):**
  Number of people for whom you need to leave feedback

* **SECOND CHANCE OFFER (TWO PEOPLE):**
  Number of closed auctions eligible for Second Chance Offers

After each of these symbols is a link. For example, if you click on the link after the dollar sign, you will arrive at a page listing all your auctions that are awaiting payment. Each listing includes a box you can click to send the seller an invoice.

If you scroll farther down your My eBay page, you will come across a list of all the items you are currently selling (see Figure 19.2). Each item is listed by its auction title. Below each title you will find the following information:

* **CURRENT PRICE**

* **NUMBER OF BIDS**

* **HIGH BIDDER ID**

* **NUMBER OF WATCHERS**

* **NUMBER OF QUESTIONS**

* **TIME LEFT IN THE AUCTION**

* **ACTIONS** (Here you'll find a series of boxes with applicable actions you can take)

This gives you a great snapshot of all your ongoing auctions. If you want further data, such as the number of hits your listing has received, you can simply click on that auction and look at your hit counter. If you see an auction without any bids halfway though the week and your hit counter shows few or no hits, you may have a problem with your auction title. You can revise your title in midauction, as long as you have no bids and there are more than twelve hours remaining until the auction ends. We will show you how to do this later in this chapter.

Figure 19.2 Items I'm Selling

On the left-hand side of every My eBay page are your main navigation links (refer back to Figure 19.1). These include:

* **ALL BUYING:** Clicking on this page will show you a complete list of all the items you are currently bidding on, the amount of your bids, the number of bids the item has received, and a link to contact the seller.

* **ALL SELLING:** This lists all your items currently for sale, whether at auction, listed with Buy It Now, or available in your eBay Store.

* **MY MESSAGES:** This is a link to all questions and messages from current and potential buyers.

* **ALL FAVORITES:** This is where you can store your favorite searches and links to your favorite sellers, as well as categories that you are watching.

* **MY ACCOUNT:** Here you can access your current account, past invoices, and preferences for both your eBay and PayPal accounts.

Also useful is the *Related Links* navigation box located below the *My Account* links. Here you can link to your PayPal account, eBay Stores, Buying and Selling

Resources, and more. From your My eBay page you may also link to the dispute console, where you can initiate and manage any disputes with sellers or report an unpaid item.

BIZ BUILDER

Every time I discover a competitor, I add him to My Favorite Sellers. When I am about to launch a new auction, I go to My Favorite Sellers and see what my competitors are selling the item for, if they have any clever new headlines, how many hits their auctions are getting, and so on. If someone has just launched an auction with a starting price of $19.99, I might start mine, offering a similar item, at $18.99 to attract more hits when our auctions run together.

When you monitor your auctions, you may notice some with numerous watchers and few (or even no) bids. Watchers are usually people who like to *snipe*—a term used for people who bid at the last second, or use special software programs to do this for them. Oftentimes, an auction will run all week with few or no bids, and then receive heavy bidding activity in the last few minutes. So don't despair if you look at your auctions days before they end and they do not seem to be getting bids—this is perfectly normal. Nevertheless, if you don't have any watchers, you might want to open the auction to see if it is getting any hits. If not, you might consider revising your auction—especially the title or the opening price. (See the next page for details on how to do this.)

SALES REPORTS

From your My eBay page, you can also link to *My Subscriptions.* Subscriptions are special tools and reports for which eBay charges additional fees. One such tool offered by eBay is a monthly sales report (see Figure 19.3). As of February 2006, eBay began offering these reports for free to eBay sellers.

eBay sales reports present a very detailed look at your sales. We spoke earlier about business metrics—how you measure your performance on eBay. You can determine most of your critical business metrics right from this report. The sales reports offered by eBay can help you understand and manage your business like a pro.

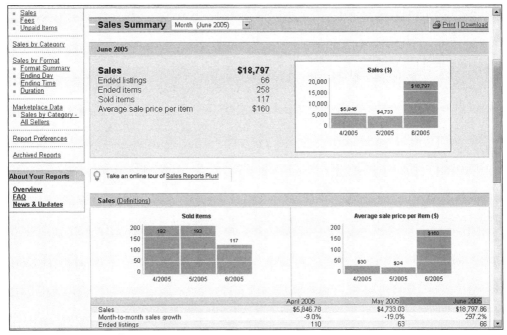

Figure 19.3 eBay Sales Report

REVISING AN ONGOING AUCTION

Once an auction has been launched, you can revise almost any part of it, provided the item has not yet received any bids. If it *has* received bids, you can add comments and images to the auction, but you cannot change anything listed in it.

The information that you can revise also depends on the time left before the auction ends. In most cases, you cannot change the listing format; that is, you cannot switch from an auction-style listing to an eBay Store listing. You also cannot change your listing from standard auction format to fixed price, or vice versa.

If your listing has not received any bids and has at least twelve hours left to run, you may:

✳ Revise any information in the title or description

✳ Remove the following optional features: Buy It Now, eBay picture services, reserve price, ten-day listing

✳ Add optional features to increase your item's visibility (for example, bold, highlight, or border)

✳ Add or change a gallery photo

If your item has received bids, you cannot change copy, images, or words in the description; however, you can add special features such as bold, gallery, or highlight, and you can add an additional image (although you cannot change or remove any of the existing images).

When you click on the link to revise your item, a new page will come up, as illustrated in Figure 19.4.

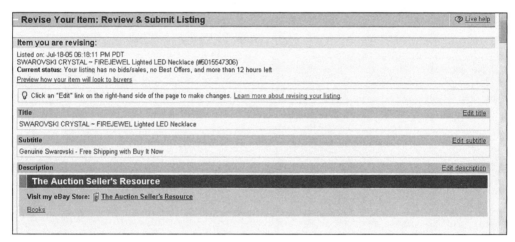

Figure 19.4 Review and Submit Listing

Simply click on the applicable links, such as *Edit Title* or *Edit Description*, to make whatever changes you deem necessary.

ENDING AN AUCTION EARLY

If you inadvertently launch an auction for something you don't have, or if you find a critical mistake in your description, and your item already has bids, you can still end your auction early.

If the auction has no bids, go to the eBay site map and select *End Your Listing* under the heading *Selling Activities*. If your auction has bids, select *Cancel Bids on Your Listing*. Remember that if you wish to end a listing early, you must first cancel any bids that have already been placed.

If you end a listing, correct it, and submit a new listing within twenty-four hours, make sure to e-mail eBay's billing department. Explain to the billing representatives that you made a mistake and ended your listing, and then ask for a refund of your listing fee. If you include the item number of the new listing, eBay will usually give you a refund (essentially applying the listing fee of the canceled auction to the new one).

POWER MOVES

❏ Familiarize yourself with the layout on your My eBay Page, and all the links and tools available to you there.

❏ Click on the Sales Reports link through the My Subscriptions link on your My eBay page to read and understand what kind of information this tool provides. Once you start selling on a regular basis, I recommend that you subscribe to this service.

CHAPTER 20

✦ GETTING PAID ✦

Getting paid is what it's all about on eBay. In the early days of eBay, there was no PayPal and very few eBay sellers were set up to take credit cards. I can still remember receiving checks, money orders, and envelopes stuffed with cash from customers. One buyer even sent me a box filled with rolls of dimes and quarters to pay for a rare naval history book I had sold him!

As we wrap up Week 2, we'll conclude by exploring the various payment methods available to you as an eBay seller and how to use them. In addition, we will show you how to deal with nonpaying bidders and expose some of the more common frauds and scams that unfortunately plague eBay from time to time—and reveal how you can avoid them.

PAYPAL

Today the vast majority of eBay buyers pay with PayPal. Now that PayPal is part of eBay (eBay purchased PayPal in early 2004), it's easy to integrate PayPal into your auctions.

How It Works

If you opt to place a PayPal button in your auctions, when your auction ends, the buyer will automatically receive an e-mail with a link to pay. When she clicks on the link, she will arrive at a page like the one shown in Figure 20.1.

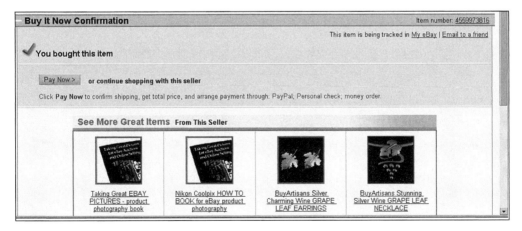

Figure 20.1 Pay Now Button

When buyers hit the Pay Now button, they are taken to the eBay checkout page, shown in Figure 20.2. On this page they can elect to pay with PayPal or other methods you've set up in your auction. In this case, buyers may pay via money order, cashier's check, or personal check. If the buyer selects Other Payment Methods, he will be shown your mailing address for the purpose of sending your payment. If he selects PayPal, he will proceed to the PayPal checkout page, shown in Figure 20.3.

Figure 20.2 eBay Checkout Page

Figure 20.3 PayPal Checkout Page

Once the buyer logs in and pays, you will receive an e-mail from PayPal, usually within minutes, notifying you that the auction ended and the buyer has paid with PayPal. It will also provide the buyer's shipping information. If you open your PayPal account, you will see that the money has been deposited.

If you look at the PayPal checkout screen, you will also see several credit card logos. A buyer does not have to have a PayPal account to use PayPal, because PayPal will also process your credit card transactions. If someone selects PayPal and does not have an account, he will be brought to a page where he can enter his credit card and shipping information. PayPal then processes the credit card transaction for you and you get paid right away, just as with any other PayPal transaction.

You're probably familiar with the popular AOL voice prompt, "You've got mail." Well, if you have Microsoft Outlook, you can set up the program to always give you a voice or sound alert whenever an e-mail from PayPal arrives. One of my friends has his computer set up to sound "Cha-Ching" every time an e-mail from PayPal arrives.

All kidding aside, it is a good idea to set up an alert like this. If you are near the computer, you can log on instantly and send the buyer an e-mail confirming that you received her payment and that her shipment is on the way. People are amazed when they buy something on eBay and receive a shipping notice minutes later. (This is a great way to boost your feedback rating.) In chapter 23 I will show you how to automate this process so buyers receive their confirmation e-mails instantly.

PayPal and Problem Transactions
Although there is some credit card fraud in the United States, it's much more prevalent overseas. If you receive a credit card payment via PayPal, and it turns out that the card the buyer used was invalid, PayPal will debit your account (unless the transaction met the requirements for PayPal's seller protection program). The same holds true if you have a merchant credit card account. With PayPal, you are also vulnerable to buyer disputes. A buyer can claim that she didn't receive your item, or that it arrived broken or was not as described. If she files a dispute with her credit card company or with PayPal, you will receive a chargeback until the dispute is resolved. Usually a thirty-day period is allowed for the dispute resolution; if the issue is not resolved by then, the chargeback becomes permanent. Unfortunately, the burden of proof is on you. You need to prove that you shipped the item, or that the item was as described in the auction, or—if it arrived broken—that you will take the item back or file an insurance claim.

PERSONAL CHECKS

When we discussed selecting payment methods in chapter 9, we addressed the issue of accepting personal checks. I accept personal checks up to $100 for immediate shipment—except from brand-new and overseas buyers. As long as someone has at least twenty positive feedback comments, I will usually ship an item right away after receiving a personal check. If someone has especially high feedback (100+ with a 99%+ positive feedback rating), I will even ship an item worth up to $250 right away. Above that, it is a judgment call. Most buyers will not issue bad checks for low-priced items, because banks generally charge bounced-check fees of around $25. Also, if I am cheated out of $25 (plus the fee my bank charges for receiving a bad check), it is not a disaster. If I am cheated out of a few hundred dollars, that's a different matter.

Lest you worry too much about this, let me reassure you that these kinds of problems are rare on eBay. Out of the millions of transactions that take place every day, only a tiny fraction result in disputes. During almost six years of selling, I can count the number of disputed transactions I have had on one hand.

NONPAYING BIDDERS

Nonpaying bidders are another story—and much more of a problem than disputed transactions or fraud. Depending on the category of merchandise you sell, nonpaying

.... BEST PRACTICES ....

THE SAVVY CAT AND THE FIRE PIT

Sometimes NPBs can come up with laugh-out-loud excuses. One day a bidder hit the Buy It Now button for one of my expensive ($250+) fire pits. Payment did not come through, so I sent her an invoice. Later that day, I received an e-mail back from the buyer, claiming that she had been looking at the auction when her phone rang. While she was on the phone, her cat had walked across the keyboard and somehow "bought" my fire pit. Now that is pretty funny when you consider that you must position your cursor directly over the Buy It Now button to activate it—and that once you activate the button, you are then taken to a *second* page with yet another button to confirm your purchase. I sent her a reply e-mail, congratulating her on having such a smart cat, and asking if the cat would mind participating in the dispute resolution process so I could get my fees refunded. She fessed up and admitted that she needed to back out of the auction because her husband had gotten mad at her when he found out that she had purchased the pricey fire pit.

bidders—or NPBs, as they are referred to by experienced eBayers—are fairly common. Sellers of low-cost merchandise, such as videos, CDs, DVDs, inexpensive jewelry, and the like, can often see NPB rates as high as 6–10 percent. For some reason, sellers of higher-priced merchandise experience lower NPB rates—usually closer to 1–2 percent. However, the eBay fees on higher-priced items are also much higher, so the dollar amounts at stake are often the same.

When a bidder doesn't pay, you can file a nonpaying bidder report with eBay through the dispute console. This will sometimes result in a payment; if not, eBay will credit your auction fees. The problem is that, in either case, the nonpaying bidder can and sometimes does leave you negative feedback. If the buyer refuses to participate in the process, eBay will neutralize any feedback he leaves. But, if he does participate and pay up, he can still leave negative feedback. There is nothing you can do about it, even if you did nothing wrong.

First let's review how the process works. Then I will show you a shortcut that can save you time and aggravation, and almost eliminate the negative feedback risk.

Seller Files an Unpaid Item Dispute

Sellers can report an unpaid item up to forty-five days after the transaction date (the date when the buyer commits to buying the item and the seller commits to selling it). Usually the seller must wait seven days after a listing closes to file an unpaid item dispute. However, in the following exceptional cases, the seller can file a dispute immediately:

* At the time of the filing, the buyer is no longer a registered user of eBay.

* The buyer is from a country to which the seller has indicated that she will not ship, as specified in the "shipping and payment details" section of the listing.

In these two cases, the buyer will receive an unpaid item strike and the seller will receive a final value fee credit without any additional steps.

eBay Contacts the Buyer

Once the seller files an unpaid item dispute, eBay sends the buyer an e-mail notification and displays a pop-up message if the buyer signs in to eBay within fourteen days of the filing. The e-mail and pop-up message will provide one of the following:

> A Friendly Reminder to Pay

The e-mail and pop-up message will remind the buyer that payment has not yet been received, and will provide simple instructions on how to respond or how to pay for the item. If the buyer does not respond to the e-mail or pop-up message within seven days, the seller may file for a final value fee credit. The seller also becomes eligible for a free relist credit. (*Note*: eBay does not refund the listing fee; you must relist the item using the Relist This Item button on your My eBay page to apply your listing fee from the disputed auction to a new one.)

When buyers receive the e-mail or pop-up message, they are presented with several options for communicating with the seller:

* *I want to pay now:* For listings where PayPal is available, the buyer can simply pay via PayPal to close the dispute. With other payment methods (such as checks or money orders), the seller is encouraged to wait until payment is received before choosing the appropriate option to close the dispute.

* *I already paid*: If payment has already been made, the buyer may provide details of the payment to the seller for review. The seller can then choose the appropriate option to close the dispute.

* *Communicate with the seller:* The buyer and seller can attempt to resolve the problem by communicating directly through the eBay Web site. The seller can close the dispute at any time by choosing the appropriate closure option.

> Mutual Agreement Indication

Another way to end a disputed auction is by mutual agreement. Both buyer and seller agree to end the auction. (It's sort of like having a marriage annulled.) The seller indicates through the dispute console that a mutual agreement has been reached with the buyer not to complete the transaction. When this occurs, eBay will ask the buyer through an e-mail to confirm this mutual agreement. One of three scenarios will then play out:

* The buyer confirms the seller's claim that the transaction was canceled by mutual agreement. The buyer does not receive an unpaid item strike and the seller receives a final value fee credit.

* The buyer disputes the seller's claim that the sale was canceled by mutual agreement. The buyer does not receive an unpaid item strike and the seller does not receive a final value fee credit. The dispute is closed immediately after the buyer responds, and the seller cannot refile an unpaid item dispute for that transaction.

* The buyer does not respond to the e-mail or pop-up message within seven days, and the seller is then able to close the dispute. The seller receives a final value fee credit and the buyer receives an unpaid item strike.

Closing the Dispute

The seller can close the dispute after the buyer has responded at least once, or if the buyer does not respond within seven days. There are several ways for the seller to close the dispute, each of which involves going through eBay's Dispute Console:

* *We've completed the transaction and we're both satisfied.* With this option, the seller does not receive a final value fee credit and the buyer does not receive an unpaid item strike.

* *We've agreed not to complete the transaction.* As discussed, with this option, the buyer does not receive an unpaid item strike, the seller receives a final value fee credit, and the item is eligible for a relist credit.

* *I no longer wish to communicate with or wait for the buyer.* With this option, the buyer receives an unpaid item strike, the seller receives a final value fee credit, and the item is eligible for a relist credit.

A dispute can only be open for sixty days after the transaction date. If the seller has not closed the dispute within sixty days, it will be closed automatically. When this automatic closure takes place, the seller does not receive a final value fee credit and the buyer does not receive an unpaid item strike.

Streamlining the Process

Normally, eBay requires you to wait seven days before filing an unpaid item dispute and then a total of thirty days before you can cancel the auction and get a refund of your selling fees. If you look closely at the *Report an Unpaid Item Dispute* form at the dispute console, there are several options to choose from as the reason for your claim. One of these options states, "We have both agreed not to complete the transaction."

Now here is the trick to making this work. Place the following text at the end of each auction description:

> *By bidding on this auction, you agree that if you have not paid for the item or contacted the seller to arrange payment within seven days from the end of this auction, then this auction is canceled by mutual agreement and neither party has any recourse against the other.*

What does this mean? Well, if the seller doesn't answer his e-mails, or claims he didn't bid on the auction or that it was some kind of mistake, you can file an unpaid item dispute and state that the auction was canceled by mutual agreement. So it will be as though the auction never happened.

As noted above, eBay will send an e-mail to the bidder, asking her to confirm the mutual agreement. In most cases the bidder will do this, since she probably does not want to pay for the item. If she does, eBay will immediately credit the final value fee (but not the listing or feature fees) to your account, and neither you nor the bidder can leave feedback. However, at this point you can relist the item for free, so you don't lose those listing and feature fees. (eBay does stipulate, however, that if the item doesn't sell the second time, you will not get the insertion fee refunded.)

If the buyer does not respond to the mutual agreement e-mail, eBay will refund your final value fee and you can relist the item for free. If, however, the buyer disputes the mutual agreement claim, you lose. eBay will end the dispute and will not refund your fees. This happens very rarely, however, so I have always found it worth the risk, unless it was a very large transaction involving a hefty fee.

Once eBay closes the dispute, neither party has the option of leaving feedback.

FRAUD WATCH

As previously noted, fraud is relatively rare on eBay, but it does exist and there are several scams you should watch out for. Most fraud is actually perpetrated by sellers, not buyers. However, there are certain schemes aimed at buyers that you, as a seller, should still be aware of. Below are some of the more common schemes affecting buyers and sellers. See Appendix G for additional safety tips.

Stolen or Phony Credit Cards

As discussed, sometimes people attempt to buy items with bogus credit cards. To protect yourself, consider only accepting credit cards from verified users and shipping to verified addresses. This will get you covered by PayPal's Protection Plan. (You can read about seller protection on eBay by clicking on the eBay Help tab and typing *seller protection* into the search box. You can also find this information at PayPal.) Whenever a buyer asks me to ship to a different address than the one specified on her credit card or eBay account, I check out her feedback and how long she's been on eBay. If the item in question is expensive and the buyer has a brand-new account, I may insist that she send me a money order. Also, I never accept credit cards from buyers in Eastern Europe (especially the Balkans), Russia, the Middle East (with the exception of Israel), any country in Africa except South Africa (and even there I am careful), and most of the developing countries in Asia and Central and South America. All these locations are hotbeds of Internet and credit card fraud.

The Foreign Agent Scam

This one was very popular in 2005. It still comes up in various forms but is not as prevalent today. A buyer clicks your Buy It Now button or wins an auction, typically for something over $500. Next, you get an e-mail from someone purporting to be the American agent of the buyer, who is actually located in Africa or the Middle East. The agent states that he is going to mail you a certified check for twice the amount of the purchase. The agent asks you to ship the item, cash the check, and send him (the agent) the excess funds—also by certified check. At first glance, that arrangement sounds pretty good. This international mystery man must really want your highly collectible jabberwocky (or whatever you were selling) and you are getting a certified check in payment for it. What could be wrong with that? The check arrives and you take it to your bank and deposit it. Next you withdraw the excess funds, make out a certified check, and send the check and the item to the agent (for some reason, all these guys seem to be located in the Washington, DC, area). All appears to be fine until, a couple of weeks later, your bank calls and a teller with a sweet voice says, "Mr. Jones, unfortunately the certified check you deposited was counterfeit. We are so sorry, but we have to debit your account."

If you ever sell an item and receive an e-mail similar to the one described here, e-mail eBay and report the user immediately. eBay knows about this fraud and will usually close down the user's account immediately and refund all your listing fees.

The Counterfeit Check Scam

This is a variation of the Foreign Agent Scam. Someone buys a very expensive item and mails you a counterfeit certified check. You ship the item and later find out that the check was fake. This one is easy to prevent. Before you ship the item, take the check to your bank and instead of depositing it, ask the bank to have it confirmed by the issuing bank. This will typically take about twenty-four hours. If the bank says the check is good, then ship your item. If the check later turns out to be fake, it is your bank that's on the hook for the funds, not you.

Counterfeit Postal Money Orders

This is similar to the counterfeit check scam, but you can't get your money back if you deposit it in a bank. (There is no way for your bank to confirm the validity of a postal money order.) The best way to identify a genuine postal money order is to look for the telltale watermark, which, when held up to the light, should reveal an image of Benjamin Franklin. Genuine postal money orders also have a security strip running alongside the watermark, just to the right. If held up to the light, a microfiber strip will show the letters *USPS* along its length.

In a typical swindle, the seller is sent a counterfeit postal money order in excess of the cost of the item being ordered. The seller is then asked to keep the cost of the purchase and ship back the balance in cash, along with the merchandise.

If you are at all suspicious about a money order, take it to the post office and try and cash it. If it is fake and the post office cashes it, it is their problem. In most cases, the postal workers will know how to spot a fake money order. If you receive a money order from another source, such as American Express or Western Union, you can also call and give the issuing company the number of the money order. Company representatives will verify when and where it was purchased—but not by whom.

Account Takeover (a.k.a. Spoofing or Phishing)

This is still one of the most prevalent and insidious frauds on eBay (and the rest of the Internet) today. You receive an official-looking e-mail from eBay (or PayPal), stating that there is some kind of problem with your account, that the credit card you have on file needs updating, or that your account has been compromised. The e-mail often threatens to suspend your account if you do not take immediate action. The e-mail contains a link you are requested to click to access your information so you can update it.

When you click on the link, you are taken to a page on "eBay" (or "PayPal") that asks you to enter your username and password, followed by your name, address, and credit card information—including the three-digit security code on the back. Well, this is kind of a pain, you think, *but what the heck?* The problem is that you are not on eBay or PayPal. You have been led to a spoof site hosted on a server in Guatemala or Slovenia that looks just like eBay, but it's not. The thieves now have your eBay and/or PayPal password and all of your credit card information, and are about to empty any money in your PayPal account and go on a shopping spree. The first time you realize anything is wrong is when you get your credit card statement, perhaps weeks later, and learn that *you* have purchased a top-of-the-line Rolex watch at the duty-free shop in Santo Domingo or Kuala Lumpur.

It's fairly easy to protect yourself from this type of scam. eBay and PayPal will never send you an e-mail directing you to click on an embedded link to enter either of their sites. Any legitimate e-mail from eBay or PayPal will instruct you to go to the main Web site and log on in the normal way. *Never click on any link in an e-mail directing you to a site where you are asked to enter security or credit card information.*

Phony Escrow Web Sites

Typically buyers are the victims of this fraud. I've included it here because, if you sell high-priced items, your bidders could be at risk.

Fake escrow Web sites may be one of the most successful Internet scams of all time. They prey on big-ticket auction winners and rely on the consumer's trust of escrow Web sites—once considered the safest way to make an exchange when an online auction involves an item of higher-than-average value. Victims of phony escrow sites can lose tens of thousands of dollars at a time; total losses incurred by big-ticket auction winners quickly add up to millions of dollars.

If you're a buyer, the best way to protect yourself is to use the escrow service listed on eBay itself. Sellers should encourage buyers to do the same. Never use an escrow service recommended by your buyer unless you know for certain that it is legitimate.

Stealing First Base

This scam only occurs if you are too slow in contacting your bidders after an auction ends. Here is what happens: The scammer watches auctions for expensive items ending in the next few minutes. When the auction ends with a successful bidder, he then e-mails the winner with a payment link. If the bidder doesn't happen to notice that the person sending the e-mail does not have the same username as the seller, she happily sends the money off via PayPal. A couple of hours later, when you contact the winning bidder, she indignantly informs you that she already paid for the item. There isn't too much you can do about this scam except report it to eBay. The problem is the buyer's—not yours. (However, if this happens to one of my buyers, I usually sympathize and let her out of the deal, if she agrees to end the auction by mutual agreement. This way she doesn't have to worry about owing me money or having an Unpaid Item strike against her, and I get to relist the item for free and have my final value fee returned).

With all scams, your best defense is to be on the lookout for anything that appears too good to be true. It probably is. While you don't want to be paranoid about every e-mail you receive, it does pay to be a little cautious—especially when you're doing business outside the United States and Canada.

POWER MOVES

❑ If you haven't yet signed up for PayPal, open an account and follow the steps to verify your account.

❑ Visit the Seller Protection page on eBay (via the site map or by clicking on Help at the top of any eBay page and typing *seller protection* into the search box). Familiarize yourself with the eBay and PayPal protection plans for both buyers and sellers.

❑ Type the phrase *online security* into the eBay Help search box. This will bring up a series of links relating to fraud protection on eBay.

BUILDING AND GROWING YOUR BUSINESS

You have your auctions up and running, and you've learned how to make them more efficient and to gain optimal sales potential. Now it's time to take your business to the next level. In this section, we'll show you how to reduce costs, manage your inventory, and automate routine tasks so you can run more auctions and increase profits. We'll also focus on special tools and upselling techniques, and e-mail marketing to your existing customer base.

In addition, we will show you how to make Fixed Price sales by setting up an eBay Store, and explore the nuances and limitless sales potential of consignment selling on eBay, a topic we introduced in chapter 3. As you'll recall, consignment selling means offering goods for sale on eBay for other people who don't know how—or don't have time—to sell on eBay themselves. I call this selling "OPM"—Other People's Merchandise. If you can master this strategy, you will have an endless supply of merchandise to sell with no investment or risk on your part.

Finally, we will examine a few techniques for using eBay as a vehicle to spread your market beyond eBay and into the rest of the Web.

CHAPTER 21

✦ COST CONTROL ✦

Controlling your costs is important in any business—selling on eBay is no different. There are two ways to increase your profits: Launch more successful auctions or cut your costs. So far we have dealt primarily with techniques to increase your sales. However, as your business grows, it is easy to lose sight of pesky little expenses that can eat into your earnings. eBay listing fees, for example, are small, but can add up quickly. The same goes for eBay photo hosting fees. Packing and shipping supplies are another major cost for eBay sellers. Let's examine some of your typical costs, and how you can get them under control and make more money on eBay.

FOR THE RECORD

The first step when you're trying to control your costs is to figure out what they are. While monitoring your costs, you can simultaneously track your sales and profits. If you are just starting out, create an Excel spreadsheet like the one in Table 21.1.

Table 21.1: Sales and Costs Worksheet

INCOME	JAN	FEB	MARCH	APRIL	MAY	JUNE
Sales	$1,400	$2,155	$2,855	$3,366	$4,125	$5,241
Cost of Goods Sold (COGS)	616	948	1,256	1,481	1,815	2,306
Gross Margin (Sales minus COGS)	784	1,207	1,599	1,885	2,310	2,935
EXPENSES						
eBay Fees	92	142	188	222	272	346
PayPal Fees	33	51	67	79	97	123
Cost of Shipping & Packing Materials	28	43	57	67	83	105
Shipping (UPS, USPS, etc)	62	95	126	148	182	231
Monthly ISP/DSL Fees, etc.	22	22	22	22	22	22
Office Supplies & Expenses	25	29	36	42	55	63
Miscellaneous	10	15	20	25	30	35
Total	272	397	516	606	740	925
PROFIT (Gross Margin minus Expenses)	$512	$810	$1,083	$1,279	$1,570	$2,010

The first line indicates total sales for the month. Only factor in payments you have actually received (not payments from sales concluded that month that have not yet arrived). So, for example, don't add payments to this month's sales from a deadbeat bidder who refuses to pay, or from an auction that closes on the last day of the month but for which you won't receive payment until the following month.

The next line, Cost of Goods Sold (COGS), represents the amount you paid for the merchandise you purchased that month, including any shipping costs. When you subtract your COGS from your total sales, you end up with your gross margin.

Next you want to list all expenses related to your eBay business. I have listed the most common expenses, but you may need to add a few more such as computer payments, car mileage to pick up and deliver goods, and advertising. Be sure to include these items in your total expenses for the month.

Once you total your expenses, subtract them from your gross margin to arrive at your profit for the month. As long as your eBay business is fairly small, this system will work quite well. If your business starts to grow, however, consider investing in a program like QuickBooks, an automated accounting system which costs about $200. While there are several other accounting software programs on the market, QuickBooks is the one used by most bookkeeping and accounting firms. Here's another advantage of using QuickBooks: If your business is successful, you will need to retain a Certified Public Account (CPA) or a tax service like H&R Block to help with your taxes. Most CPAs and tax services use QuickBooks; if you can deliver a QuickBooks file to them, they can prepare your taxes more efficiently—and usually for a lower fee. If you employ a part-time bookkeeper as I do, you'll discover that this program will easily pay for itself in money saved by avoiding having this person manage your books manually.

UNDERSTANDING YOUR EBAY FEES

Looking at Table 21.1, you can see that your eBay and PayPal fees represent a significant portion of your costs. There's not much you can do to reduce your PayPal fees; these fees are a fixed percentage of what you sell. If you were to stop accepting PayPal, your overall sales would drop—defeating the purpose of your cost cutting. However, there are some steps you can take to reduce your eBay fees. Understanding how eBay calculates its fees is essential to learning how to control them, so first you must have a good grasp of eBay's fee structure, and how the various costs relate to one another.

eBay has several categories of fees:

✳ Insertion fees, or the cost to post an item for sale

* Final value fees, or what eBay charges you for each item that sells
* Fees for additional listing options

Now let's explore the specific fees for each category. Note that the fees listed in this chapter were accurate when this edition went to press. However, eBay does change (translation: raise) its fees occasionally. You can find the current eBay fees at http://pages.ebay.com/help/sell/fees.html.

Insertion Fees

The first fee you'll encounter when listing an item for sale is the insertion fee. Insertion fees are a percentage of the starting price of your item. The percentage decreases as the price of your item increases. See Table 21.2 for a rundown of eBay's insertion fees.

Table 21.2: eBay Insertion Fees

BASIC INSERTION FEES	Item Starting Price	Insertion Fee
	$0.01 – $0.99	$0.20
	$1.00 – $9.99	$0.35
	$10.00 – $24.99	$0.60
	$25.00 – $49.99	$1.20
	$50.00 – $199.00	$2.40
	$200.00 – $499.99	$3.60
	$500.00 and up	$4.80
RESERVE PRICE AUCTION FEES	Reserve Price	Insertion Fee
(fully refunded if the item sells)	$0.01 – $49.99	$1.00
	$50.00 – $199.99	$2.00
	$200.00 and up	1% of reserve price (max.: $50.00)

BIZ BUILDER

The insertion fees for eBay Stores are, by comparison, much smaller. We will cover eBay Store fees in chapter 26.

Insertion fees for Dutch Auctions and Fixed Price listings are based on the opening value of your items. The opening value is the starting or fixed-item price, multiplied by the quantity you are selling. The maximum insertion fee for any multiple-item listing is $4.80.

Final Value Fees

Once your item sells, you will be charged a final value fee. As with the insertion cost, this fee is based on a sliding scale, as noted in Table 21.3.

Table 21.3: eBay Final Value Fees

CLOSING PRICE	FINAL VALUE FEE
$0.01 – $25.00	5.25% of the closing value.
$25.01 – $1,000.00	5.25% of the first $25.00, plus 3.00% of the balance
$1,000.01 or more	5.25% of the initial $25.00, plus 3.00% of the value from $25.01 to $1,000.00, plus 1.50% of the remaining closing value

Here's an example of how the final value fee works:

If an item sold for $1,450.00, you would pay 5.25% of the initial $25.00 ($1.31), plus 3.00% of the next $25.01–$1,000.00 ($29.25), plus 1.50% of the remaining balance ($6.75). Add up all three amounts ($1.31 + 29.25 + 6.75), and you have your total final value fee of $37.31.

BIZ BUILDER

Final value fees are much higher than insertion fees. Therefore, it is very important that you keep track of any nonpaying bidders and file a claim with the eBay dispute resolution console to get these fees refunded. Also, if a bidder doesn't pay, eBay will let you relist the item one time without an additional insertion fee. In other words you get one free relisting if you settled the dispute through eBay.

eBay only charges you a final value fee if your item sells. If an item fails to sell, you may relist it in the same category *once* without paying an additional insertion fee. You still pay a final value fee if the item sells.

The final value fee for a Dutch Auction is determined by taking the final value fee of the lowest successful bid and multiplying it by the number of items sold. To calculate the final value fee for a multiple-item, Fixed Price listing, eBay multiplies the final sale price of the item by the number of items sold.

The other final value fee you may encounter is the Buy It Now fee (see Table 21.4).

Table 21.4: Buy It Now Final Value Fees

BUY IT NOW PRICE	FINAL VALUE FEE
$0.01–$9.99	$0.05
$10.00–$24.99	$0.10
$25.00–$49.99	$0.20
$50.00 or more	$0.25

Optional Feature Fees

As we noted earlier, eBay offers several optional listing upgrades designed to make your listing stand out and to attract the attention of potential bidders. Table 21.5 shows the fees for these upgrades. (See page 164 for information about special feature "bundles.")

Table 21.5: Optional Listing Upgrade Fees

Gallery	$0.35	Border	$3.00
Listing Designer	$0.10	Highlight	$5.00
Item Subtitle	$0.50	Featured Plus!	$19.95
Bold	$1.00	Gallery Featured	$19.95
Scheduled Listing	$0.10	Homepage Featured	$39.95
10-Day Duration	$0.40	Dutch Auction Homepage Featured	$79.95
Gift Services	$0.25	List in Two Categories	Listing fees double

Additionally, you will incur expenses if you use more than one image in your listing or "supersize" any of your images (see Table 21.6).

Table 21.6: Image Hosting Fees

First Image	Free
Additional pictures	$0.15 each
Supersize	$0.75

REDUCING YOUR EBAY FEES

Now that you understand how eBay charges for its services, let's take a look at how you can reduce your fees.

Listing Fees

Right off the bat, you can see that eBay's listing fees increase at various price points. If your starting price is on the cusp of one of these breaks, always go with the lower value. For example, if you started a listing at $50.00, the insertion fee would be $2.40. However, start the same item at $49.99—just one penny less—and your listing fee drops by half to $1.20—you save $1.19.

In a Dutch Auction, the listing fee maxes out at $4.80. When you list a large number of items, you will usually hit this maximum. If you are listing only a few items for sale, you should once again place your starting bid at the lowest price point consistent with what you expect the item to sell for. Say you are selling popular, relatively low-end items that typically receive many bids. Consider starting your auctions at $0.99—the lowest possible listing fee. Keep in mind, however, that if you are selling a high-priced specialty item in a narrow niche, you cannot risk doing this. Therefore, you have two options: List at a higher starting price and pay the higher insertion fee, or launch a Reserve Price Auction and start the item at a much lower price. I prefer the second option. Remember that eBay refunds Reserve Price Auction fees if the item sells. Although the reserve fee is higher (1% for items over $200), as long as your reserve amount is reasonable and a high percentage of your auctions reach the reserve, the averages will work in your favor.

Special Feature Fees

We discussed how to use eBay's special features in chapter 16. Each of these features can potentially increase the number of bidders and the final value of your auction. However, you have to calculate the potential return on investment (ROI), based on the expected value of the item you are selling. If you sell something in the $20 range, paying $1 for the bold feature might get you a 10 percent increase ($2) in the final value, so this would be a good investment. However, the highlight feature, at $5, would not be a good value—even if it increased your final value by 20 percent ($4).

eBay offers statistics on how well certain of these features perform, but these figures are averages for *all* auctions. A feature that gets an average 10 percent ROI for all auctions might not perform as well for your particular item. The only way to know for sure is to run test auctions. Whenever I find a new product I want to sell on eBay, I run auctions both with and without special features to determine if the performance warrants the investment. This kind of ongoing product research is critical to success in most business ventures, and it's essential when you're building a business on eBay.

There are two other costs that bear mentioning: *picture hosting* and *scheduled listing* fees. eBay charges ten cents to schedule an auction to launch at a later time and fifteen cents per photo if you include more than one in your listing. If you use four photos in an auction, you will be paying forty-five cents, plus another ten cents (for a total of fifty-five cents) if you schedule the auction to begin at a later time. If you are launching one hundred auctions a month, this adds up to $55 a month. In chapter 23, we will discuss automated services that offer image hosting and scheduling solutions. These services cost as little as $16 a month—an excellent investment if you are launching lots of auctions.

As we discussed in chapter 15, you may be able to save money by hosting images on your own Web site, and just providing links to the images in your auctions. Many eBay sellers do this, but, in my opinion, it is too time-consuming to create and post the links every time you launch an auction.

The other major cost factor for eBay sellers is inventory—the products you buy to resell on eBay. We will discuss controlling your inventory costs in the next chapter.

POWER MOVES

❏ Set up a simple spreadsheet in Microsoft Excel and list your expenses. Be sure to include things such as your ISP and cable or DSL fees, as well as charges for telephone, postage, and office supplies. Take a step back and analyze your costs. Which line items are costing you the most each month? What can you do to reduce your monthly expenses?

❏ In chapter 10, you bookmarked the eBay fee schedule at http://pages.ebay.com/help/sell/fees.html. If you haven't yet, go to this page and print out the full schedule (or go to Appendix E to see the fee schedule as of this printing). Study the fee schedule until you are thoroughly familiar with how eBay charges fees. You don't have to memorize the fees, especially those for optional features, but you should have a good feel for what they are and when to use them.

❏ Now calculate the eBay fees for several items listed and sold at different prices. For example, calculate the fees for an item that listed at $9.99 and sold for $20.00. Now do the same thing for an item that started at $49.99 and sold for $75.00.

❏ Using this information, study the auctions you have launched thus far, and evaluate your pricing. Have you been paying higher fees than necessary? What sort of ROI have you been realizing for optional listing features you've used? List steps you can take to lower your eBay fees, and write them in the binder next to your computer.

CHAPTER 22

✦ INVENTORY MANAGEMENT ✦

Inventory consists of all the products you purchase to sell on eBay. Unless you engage in drop shipping (as detailed in chapter 7) or selling on consignment for others (see chapter 27), your inventory will represent your largest investment and potentially your biggest financial risk. You incur this risk by purchasing inventory that either does not sell, or cannot sell at a high enough price for you to make a profit. Business owners call this *nonperforming inventory*.

In chapter 4 we stressed how crucial it is to research a product before you purchase it, so you can determine if it will sell on eBay. Product research is your best defense against being stuck with nonperforming inventory—but even excellent research is not foolproof. You can still end up with products that sell well at first and then fall in price as others begin selling them. In this chapter we'll examine how to manage your inventory so that you reduce costs and increase your monthly profits.

DEALING WITH NONPERFORMING INVENTORY

Purchasing large amounts of inventory at one time has its risks and rewards. Although you can get better prices by purchasing in large quantities, you need to consider how long it will take you to move the inventory.

eBay bidders pay close attention to an item's supply. When bidders see many identical items listed, they are reluctant to place high bids. They know that if they miss an item in one auction, they can just bid on another one. If you put too many of the same or similar items on eBay within a short period, you will drive down prices by increasing the supply. When you do this, you end up competing with yourself.

Despite your best research, you might end up with a product that's just not selling at a price that's profitable. When this happens, the best thing you can do is sell it quickly for whatever you can get. When you are sitting on inventory that is not selling, you are tying up money that you could be spending on inventory that *will* sell.

Retail store owners understand the cost of nonperforming inventory and the value of inventory that makes them money. That is why every retail store has a sale table. If an item is not selling well, store owners mark the price down to move it out quickly and free up money and shelf space for inventory that will perform better. As an eBay seller, it is imperative that you do the same thing if you want to make a profit. When inventory isn't moving, you need to create a virtual sale table.

There are two strategies for getting rid of inventory quickly. One is simply to launch the items on eBay at a lower price. The problem with this approach is that listing a large number of similar items at one time could drive the price even lower than what you were hoping to get. A better way is to list the items in eBay's *Wholesale Lots* subcategory.

Almost every eBay category has a subcategory called Wholesale Lots. This is where people sell items in bulk. If, for example, you purchased a large lot of cell phone batteries from a supplier and were only able to sell a few of them before the price started dropping, you could take your remaining batteries and either break them up into small lots or sell them as one large lot. Small lots will usually realize a higher per-item price than large ones; there are many small eBay sellers who cannot afford to purchase a case of forty-eight batteries, but who would be willing to buy a dozen at a time.

TURN YOUR INVENTORY OVER OFTEN

Inventory turn refers to how often you replace your inventory in a given period. Keeping your inventory turning at a brisk pace is essential to making large amounts of money on eBay. Consider the following example:

You find a source for overstock designer blue jeans, and you can buy a pallet load of one hundred pairs for $7 a pair. When you check the prices on eBay, you see that similar jeans are selling for between $18 and $29 a pair. The normal response is to list the jeans at the higher price. So you start launching auctions for the jeans at $29 a pair and find that you can sell about ten pairs a week. You are making a gross margin of $22 a pair before eBay and PayPal fees. Because you are selling ten pairs a week, you are realizing $220 a week. At this rate, it will take you ten weeks to sell all the jeans.

Now, let's say you lower the price of the jeans to $25 a pair, and you begin selling twenty-five pairs a week, as opposed to ten. Your gross margin on each pair is now only $18, but you are realizing $450 a week because of increased volume. Plus, you will sell all the jeans in four weeks instead of ten. Your margin for the four-week period is $1,800. You can now turn around and invest that $1,800 in more inventory, which you can sell again in another four-week period at the same price. Compare the two scenarios: In the first one, you make $2,200 over a ten-week period at the higher price of $29. However, in the second scenario, you make $4,500 over the same ten-week period by selling the jeans at the lower price and reinvesting the profits. This is an example of using a lower pricing strategy to increase your inventory turn rate.

CONTROLLING YOUR INVENTORY

You can't control the flow of your inventory if you don't understand it. That's why it's important to keep good records. When you are just starting out, set up a simple Excel spreadsheet where you list your inventory (see Table 22.1). Create separate columns to list the item, the quantity you purchased, the quantity on hand, the date you acquired it, the cost per item, and the average selling price. (Every time you sell an item you should update the quantity on hand.) Keep a record of each sale in a ledger, so that you can determine the total final selling price for the entire lot.

Table 22.1: Sample Inventory Record

ITEM DESCRIPTION	INITIAL QUANTITY	QUANTITY ON HAND	DATE ACQUIRED	COST PER ITEM	AVERAGE (UNIT) SELLING PRICE
Men's Nautica Blue Jeans	44	17	12/1/2005	$19 pr.	$36.21
DKNY Silk Tops	12	8	1/7/2006	$24 ea.	$42.55
Nike Sneakers	36	33	2/14/2006	$47 ea.	$68.77
Nautica Blue Bathrobes, Unisex	12	4	2/22/2006	$14.20 ea.	$22
Fila Men's Running Suit	12	4	3/1/2006	$39 ea.	$76.88
Gloria Vanderbilt Women's Jeans	40	22	3/15/2006	$19.22 ea	$29.56

If you are going to run test auctions for the same item at different price points, set up a separate line item for each test. This will allow you to compare the performance of the different price points over time.

There are two other ways to track and control your inventory. If you decided to make an investment in QuickBooks, this program has a built-in inventory function whereby you can enter inventory cost and performance data. The QuickBooks inventory function is fairly basic, although it's fine for most small businesses. If you sell a large number of different products, consider the more sophisticated inventory management program, KwikInventory™, made for Windows by Worth Data (www.barcodehq.com). Worth Data's system retails for around $300. You may also want to invest in a bar code printer and reader. These systems go for about $600, but there are plenty of used systems available on eBay for under $300.

The other way to manage your inventory is with an online system. In the next chapter, we'll return to auction management systems, which we touched on in chapter 15. Most of these services, including the ones I recommend, allow you to track your inventory, connect images and descriptions to each item, and even launch eBay auctions directly from your online system.

When you are first starting out, you will most likely be selling very few products. Setting up an inventory control system might seem like overkill, but as your business grows, you will need to organize and track your products. Knowing how much inventory you have on hand, how much it costs, how long it is taking you to turn it over, and how much it is selling for are all integral to running a successful eBay business.

POWER MOVES

- ❑ Set up a spreadsheet to list and control your inventory. Be sure to track the dates you acquire your inventory, so you can assess how long it is taking you to move the inventory out.

- ❑ On this spreadsheet, track your average selling price (ASP) per item, so that you can identify your most and least profitable products. Use this information in determining which products (and how many units of each) to reorder.

- ❑ Determine and implement strategies for dealing with nonperforming inventory. Consider listing items in a Wholesale Lots category or lowering your price to clear out slow-moving items.

CHAPTER 23

✦ AUTOMATING YOUR AUCTIONS ✦

If you could hire a full-time employee for less than $50 a month, someone who would work with you in your eBay business—24 hours a day, 7 days a week—do you think that would be a good investment?

Uploading photos, writing descriptions, communicating with buyers, printing shipping labels, and posting feedback are just a few of the steps that you perform every time you launch or complete an auction. When you first start selling on eBay, you will be launching your auctions with the tools that eBay provides in the Sell Your Item form and managing your information from your My eBay page. As you grow your business, you should consider adding services and software that can automate some or all of these functions.

Automated services fall into three categories:

✳ **EBAY SOLUTIONS (ONLINE AND OFFLINE CHOICES)**

✳ **THIRD-PARTY OFFLINE SOFTWARE**

✳ **ONLINE AUCTION MANAGEMENT SERVICES**

Evaluating every product on the market to automate your auctions is beyond the scope of this book. Instead, let's look at the pros and cons of each type of service, and then evaluate one service that is fast becoming the choice of many full-time eBay sellers.

EBAY SOLUTIONS

eBay offers both auction management software and online systems. The three basic choices are Turbo Lister, Blackthorn, and Selling Manager. We now turn to these eBay solutions.

Turbo Lister

This is a free download that allows you to create listings offline and launch them onto eBay. Through Turbo Lister, you can list multiple items at once and save listings to reuse again and again. Convenient templates allow you to create listings easily with a WYSI-WYG (What-You-See-Is-What-You-Get) design editor. Turbo Lister can also schedule your listings to launch at a later time.

Blackthorne

Formerly known as *Seller's Assistant*, Blackthorne is a software program that comes in two versions, Basic and Pro. These are eBay's all-in-one desktop listing and sales management tools, designed to automate the process of launching auctions. Blackthorne's tools help medium-to-high-volume sellers launch auctions on eBay without requiring a constant Internet connection. Both versions offer several customizable features. The Pro version includes sophisticated inventory control tools and detailed financial reporting. eBay charges $9.99 a month for the Basic version and $24.99 a month for the Pro version. Unlike Turbo Lister, which is primarily a launching and scheduling tool, Blackthorn has record-keeping and financial reporting capabilities. Blackthorne also allows you to automate the process of sending e-mails to winning bidders.

Selling Manager

This is eBay's online (that is, Web-based as opposed to desktop-based) sales management tool. You access Selling Manager through your My eBay page, which makes this tool very convenient. Selling Manager also comes in a Pro version. Selling Manager is for low-to-medium-volume listers, while Selling Manager Pro is better suited for high-volume listers.

With Selling Manager you can relist multiple items at once; see a one-page snapshot of your business; track buying, selling, and account activities; create e-mails with custom templates; and print shipping labels and invoices. eBay charges $4.99 a month for this tool.

Selling Manager Pro gives you all these features, plus bulk relisting capabilities and sophisticated inventory management and financial reporting tools. eBay charges $15.99 a month for Selling Manager Pro.

The eBay Advantage?

With the various eBay solutions, all your auction management is integrated into your My eBay page. However, the major drawback of all three eBay systems is the lack of photo hosting. Remember that eBay gives you the first photo free and then charges fifteen cents for each additional photo. Most sellers use three or four photos in their auctions, so you can anticipate spending up to forty-five cents a listing on photography. If you list one hundred auctions a month, this adds up to $45—in addition to the monthly cost of whichever eBay listing management tool you choose. Another disadvantage is the inability to launch auctions in other (non-eBay) venues, such as Overstock.com Auctions or Yahoo! Stores. As you will see in chapter 28, once you have mastered eBay, you can easily increase your sales and profits by expanding beyond eBay.

THIRD-PARTY SOFTWARE

There are over a dozen companies selling software products that automate many of the common eBay functions. The three most popular are Spoonfeeder (www.spoonfeeder.com), Hammertap Manager (www.hammertap.com), and AuctionGenie (http://tinyurl.com/8b5qu).

All three systems include most of the features offered by eBay's Blackthorn. Hammertap includes free photo hosting as part of its monthly cost, which appears to make it a somewhat better value. All three are primarily Windows-based, although Auction Genie also has a Mac OSX version. The main advantage of these third-party systems over eBay's offerings is their ability to support multi-channel selling. So you can launch auctions on other sites as well, such as Yahoo! Auctions, Overstock.com Auctions, and Yahoo! Stores.

ONLINE AUCTION MANAGEMENT SERVICES

There are over a dozen companies offering Web-based automation solutions for eBay sellers. The leading companies and their Web addresses and costs are listed in Table 23.1.

Table 23.1: Leading Online Auction Management Services

Andale	www.andale.com
Marketworks	www.marketworks.com
Vendio	www.vendio.com
Mpire	www.mpire.com/asr
ChannelAdvisor	www.channeladvisor.com

All these companies provide basic automation services, although some do it better than others. My personal favorite for new sellers is Mpire. Mpire's basic service is called Mpire Launcher and it is a free utility. Mpire Launcher offers the following features:

* HTML templates to create your auctions.

* Free image hosting (up to 10 MB) and an editing utility. This allows you to avoid the fee eBay charges for adding extra images. In addition, you can upload your images directly from your camera to Mpire and edit them before storing.

* An auction-scheduling tool (saving you the ten-cent fee eBay charges for each scheduled listing).

- Tools to create an item in inventory, to be launched at a later time.

- Prewritten automated invoices, payment reminders, and shipping and feedback notices.

- My Mpire, a dashboard that shows the status of every item currently at auction, as well as all your closed auctions. Icons show if an item has been paid for, whether it has been shipped, and if feedback has been posted.

- An automated relisting tool.

- A contact manager that takes the guesswork out of tracking customer information and activity. With this tool, you can store customer information in one place, automatically track a customer's buying history, and easily e-mail or market directly to your customers. You'll never be left in the dark again.

Mpire Builder, the professional version, costs $29.95 a month and adds the following features to the above list:

- Integrated auction management that allows you to create and track your listings without ever needing to visit eBay. View all the items you're currently selling on a single page. You can switch from Auction-Style view to Fixed Price view to Store Listings view with a single click of the mouse.

- Cost tracking and sold-item data, detailed sales reports, and financial analysis tools to identify your best-selling and most profitable items.

- A consignment module that tracks consignor fees, commissions, and payments.

- Automatic feedback posting.

- An additional 250 megabytes of image hosting—enough to host over 1,000 images.

- Multiple eBay IDs (some eBay users have several accounts for their different product niches).

- A layout designer that allows you to create your own branded auction-listing templates.

- Automated second chance offers.

- Automated e-mail notifications.

When I contacted Mpire's customer service representatives for information for this chapter, they graciously offered a three-month free trial of Mpire Builder to readers of this book. If you would like to try this service go to www.mpire.com/asrbook. You will find specific instructions to sign up for your free trial.

Most of the auction management systems offer a free trial period. Personally, I favor the online systems: They save the most time and you don't have to worry about computer crashes and losing your data. Using such a system is like having a virtual employee—one who saves you time, helps you launch your auctions more efficiently, and keeps your costs under control.

POWER MOVES

❑ Visit eBay's Selling Resources pages and read the information about the eBay-based automation solutions Turbo Lister, Blackthorn, and Selling Manager.

❑ Visit Mpire.com and Vendio.com (or any of the other sites listed in this chapter) and take a tour of each one.

❑ Once you have selected an automation solution to try, either purchase a subscription or sign up for a free trial. Begin setting up your inventory and learning the system.

CHAPTER 24

✦ THIRD-PARTY ✦ PROMOTIONAL TOOLS

You have a great product that you can buy at a great price. You have mastered the art of headline writing, using keywords, taking great photos, and all the basic steps you need for success. In addition, you've reduced your eBay fees and improved how you manage your inventory. So what else can you do to increase your sales and profits?

eBay is a very competitive sales venue, so anything you can do to either stand out from the crowd or convince the customer to do business with you instead of clicking away to another auction will put money in your pocket at the end of the month.

Techniques for promoting your auctions fall into two categories: (1) those designed to drive buyers to your auctions, increasing your hits; and (2) those intended to generate buyer trust and confidence, increasing your bids. In this chapter, we'll explore some of the tools available from third-party vendors that can help lure buyers to your auctions and generate more and higher bids.

INCREASING AUCTION VIEWS

The single best way to boost the number of hits your auctions receive is by writing compelling, keyword-rich headlines. If your auctions are getting very few views, the first thing you need to do is review the material in chapter 14 and make sure you are writing the best headlines you can. The other factor that drives hits are the eBay promotional features covered in chapter 16, such as bold, highlight, subtitle, and so on.

Assuming that you've done the best job possible in these areas, what else can you do to increase hits?

The eBay Keywords Program

Several companies offer promotional tools that can send business to your auctions. One of them is the eBay Keywords Program, administered by a company called Ad Marketplace. You sign up for the program on the eBay site, under the Resources tab in Seller Central.

eBay Keywords is a pay-per-click advertising program. It works like this: You create a small promotional banner, which appears at the top of the Search Results page whenever someone searches for a keyword or a term that you have selected (see Figure

24.1). You bid against other sellers for the keywords. Bids start at ten cents. There are some very expensive keywords, such as *digital camera* or *diamond jewelry*, but most of them average between ten and twenty cents per click. You can control the number of clicks by setting a daily budget.

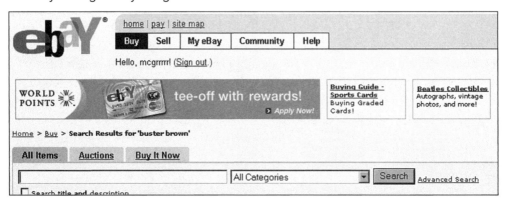

Figure 24.1 eBay Keywords Banners

The banner can be linked to a specific auction, although this is generally not a good idea, since you would have to discontinue the program every time an auction ends. You can also link to a list of all your auctions or, even better, to your eBay Store. Linking to your eBay Store is probably the best strategy, since your Store homepage displays both your eBay Store items for sale and all your ongoing auctions by category. The eBay Keywords program also allows you to link to one of your specific Store categories, such as Beatles Collectibles. So, if you sold NASCAR collectibles in addition to Beatles collectibles, when someone typed in *Beatles,* she would only see a list of your Beatles collectibles.

Web Site and E-mail Promotion

Another way to promote your auctions is with an eBay button that you can post on your Web site (if you have one) or attach to all your outgoing e-mails. If you go to the eBay site map under the heading Selling Activities, look for the link that says *Promote your listings with link buttons.* This will take you to a page where you can copy a snippet of HTML code that you can paste into a Web page or insert as your e-mail signature. The code will create a little button that says "Shop With Me" superimposed over an eBay logo. When shoppers click on this button, it takes them to a list of your auctions on eBay. There is no charge for this service; in fact, it can actually save you money.

Whenever someone arrives at your Store from an off-eBay location (such as from an e-mail link or your Web site), eBay credits 75 percent of the final value fee of anything the buyer purchases there.

Classified Ads

Here's another great way to promote your auctions that almost no one ever thinks of—classified advertising, both in newspapers and on the Web. This technique works best if you sell to a small, niche market. For example, let's say you collect and sell old fountain pens. You can take out small classified ads in newspapers that read something like this:

> *Old Fountain Pens for Sale on eBay. Just type 12345678 into the search box at www.ebay.com.*

The number could be the item number of a pen currently at auction or listed in your eBay Store. This is the easiest way to lead someone directly to you, because the complete hyperlink to your auctions is too long and complex to put in a newspaper ad. However, if you are posting classified ads on the Web, you can use a simple HTML command to create a link to your list of auctions. Your online ad would read like this:

> *Old Fountain Pens for Sale on eBay.*
> *<a href=your link to auctions goes here> Click Here</a> to see my auctions.*

When you use the <a href=> code, the reader of an online classified sees this:

> *Old Fountain Pens for Sale on eBay.*
>
> *click here to see my auctions.*

You can find plenty of Web sites that offer free classified ads by just typing *free classified ad* into the Google, Yahoo!, or MSN search boxes.

BUILDING TRUST AND CONFIDENCE

Once you drive prospective bidders to your auction, you want them to bid. There are plenty of studies that show that anything you can do to inspire trust and confidence in customers will increase bids on eBay auctions, boost purchases through your eBay Store, and increase purchases on a Web site. On eBay, your best strategy is to earn a high feedback rating and keep it at least 99 percent positive. But there are some interesting third-party tools to help you build buyer confidence as well.

SquareTrade

We discussed SquareTrade in chapter 11, when we reviewed feedback. SquareTrade (www.squaretrade.com) is an authorized eBay solutions provider that monitors your reputation and verifies your identity. Once you are accepted into the SquareTrade program, SquareTrade will automatically insert its seal in all your auctions. The seal appears just above your auction description as in Figure 24.2.

 eBay User ID
mcgrrrrr

Figure 24.2 The SquareTrade Seal

When someone clicks on the seal, she is taken to a page on SquareTrade's Web site that looks like the one in Figure 24.3.

Figure 24.3 SquareTrade Results Page for eBay User mcgrrrrr

The results show you that this seller (me) has been a SquareTrade member since 2002, that I continue to meet SquareTrade's standards, that I agree to use SquareTrade's Dispute and Mediation Service, and that my buyers are covered by SquareTrade's Buyer Protection Policy up to $250.

Experienced eBay bidders know what the SquareTrade seal stands for and, when they see it, they usually feel confident about placing a bid. The service costs $9.50 a month and can really help you attract more bids when your feedback is low. If you achieve a feedback rating in the high hundreds that is 99 percent (or more) positive, having the seal is less important, although it can still be valuable.

buySAFE

The bonding service buySAFE protects your buyers against fraud. If you sell low-value items (under $100), the service is probably not worth the cost (buySAFE charges a fee of 1 percent of the transaction value (final value) on each successful transaction). However, if you're selling big-ticket items, such as pricey antiques or collectibles, buySAFE certainly helps allay the fears of some prospective bidders who might otherwise hesitate to make a substantial bid on one of your pieces. Even if you have positive feedback in the thousands, someone considering buying an expensive antique has every reason to be cautious. When you sign up for and are accepted by buySAFE, the service automatically inserts a seal into your auctions informing bidders that they are protected against fraud, up to whatever limit buySAFE agrees to. If you are a fairly new seller, the fraud-protection limit will usually extend as high as $10,000. Once you gain more experience and your feedback rating climbs, buySAFE will often raise the limit to $25,000.

Figure 24.4 depicts the buySAFE Seal as it appears in an auction; Figure 24.5 (see next page) shows the results page bidders arrive at after clicking on the seal.

Figure 24.4 The buySAFE Seal

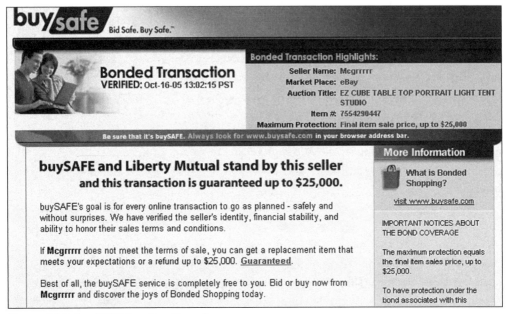

Figure 24.5 buySAFE Landing Page for mcgrrrrr

SellersVoice

Silent auctions may be going the way of silent movies. Voice technology has been around for several years, but a relatively new company called SellersVoice has made adding audio clips to your auctions a breeze. SellersVoice has set up a special page for readers of this book at www.sellersvoice.com/skip to demonstrate how I use the technology in my auctions. Like other links cited in this book, this can be found at the book's Web site, www.skipmcgrath.com/3_weeks. Using SellersVoice is easy. Once you sign up for an account (you can get a three-week trial for $1 at the link specified above), you call a toll-free number and record a message. I have found that a thirty-to-forty-five-second message is ideal. After recording your message, you return to the SellersVoice Web site and copy a snippet of HTML code to your computer's clipboard. Now when you list an auction, simply paste the code right into your item description. This will place an audio toolbar into your auction text. See the example in Figure 24.6.

I have performed several blind tests in which I launched identical auctions with and without a voice recording. The results varied, depending on the products I was selling, but in all cases I achieved more bids and higher final values when I used the voice feature. In one test, selling Starbucks collectible mugs, I averaged 19 percent more bids and achieved a 14 percent higher final value.

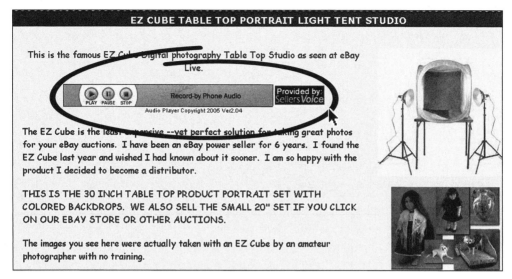

Figure 24.6 SellersVoice Toolbar in an Auction

The service seems a bit expensive at $29.95 a month. However, if you are currently realizing monthly profits of $2,000.00 or more, and you can increase that by even 10 percent, you'll see an extra $200.00 in sales per month. Subtract the $29.95 fee, and you have an additional monthly profit of $170.05. If you really build your business and take your sales up to the $10,000-a-month level, using audio could put $970 or more into your profit column each month.

Don't worry if you don't have a professional-sounding voice or don't know what to say. The idea is to "humanize" your auction to increase bidder trust and confidence. The SellersVoice Web site has excellent tutorials and best practices to help you get started.

POWER MOVES

❏ As soon as you qualify, sign up for the SquareTrade program at www.square-trade.com.

❏ Visit the other resources mentioned in this chapter, including:

> The eBay Keywords Program

> buySAFE (www.buysafe.com)

> SellersVoice (www.sellersvoice.com/skip)

Become familiar with their offerings and determine if any of these resources could benefit your business.

❏ Begin running online and newspaper classified ads for your auctions. Track the increase in sales to determine your ROI.

CHAPTER 25

✦ UPSELLING AND E-MAIL ✦ MARKETING TO YOUR CUSTOMERS

eBay has very strict rules regarding e-mail—especially when it comes to e-mail marketing to eBay members. In the early days of eBay, you could get any member's e-mail address right off the site. Now eBay has a system whereby you can only e-mail members through eBay. Furthermore, you can only see the recipient's e-mail address if he replies to you and checks a box allowing his e-mail address to be revealed. This may sound a bit draconian, but it is actually for the best. From eBay's point of view, the company makes money when people buy and sell through eBay. From a buyer's point of view, eBay is now much safer, because, under the previous system, there used to be a lot more fraud and bid stealing.

.... BEST PRACTICES ....

RIGHT ITEM, WRONG SELLER

One popular scam worked like this: I see an auction end for a very expensive product, for which you are the winner. Because I can see your e-mail address, I immediately send you an e-mail claiming that I am the seller and providing a link you can click to pay me now. I am banking on the real seller failing to send out an authentic payment notice upon the auction's close, and that you are gullible enough to click on my link and pay me via credit card. Upon receipt of the payment, I promptly close the eBay account and disappear—until tomorrow, when I open a new account. eBay's current system reduces this once-popular form of fraud. It also attempts to keep spammers from getting your e-mail address and scamming you in other ways, or from trying to sell you who-knows-what.

Once a customer buys something from you on eBay, that customer is now "yours," in the sense that you have established a direct relationship with him. You can now freely communicate with him and make offers to him outside the eBay platform. This is perfectly within eBay's guidelines. (Actually, it's the law and there is nothing eBay can do about it.)

Does this mean you should now start deluging your customers with all sorts of offers? Not unless you want them to write back and ask to be taken off your mailing list. However, there are plenty of other ways to reach out to these customers. In this chapter, we'll explore profitable ways to go about building and marketing to your customer base. We'll also examine how to *upsell* (also known as *cross-sell*), by getting winning bidders to increase the quantity of their orders—or add related products to their original orders.

END OF AUCTION E-MAILS

The most common form of upselling is done in your end of auction e-mail. If you use an auction management system like Mpire, you can create e-mails that go out to winning bidders and link to your eBay Store or your Web site, if you have one. In the e-mail message, you can offer customers an incentive to buy more of the same product or another related item. Typical incentives include free shipping if customers buy a second item, or a discount on the second item purchased.

Here is a sample e-mail, designed to upsell, which you can send to a winning bidder:

> Dear (Winning Bidder's username),
>
> Thank you for purchasing the Weber combined gas/charcoal barbecue grill, eBay item #123456789 from our auctions. Your winning bid was $126.50 + $12.50 shipping and handling. The total is $139.00. I have provided a link below that you can click on to pay via PayPal.
>
> Almost everyone who buys one of these grills purchases a cover to keep the grill clean and dry when it sits outside during inclement weather. We offer a fitted cover for $24.00 plus $4.90 for shipping. However, if we ship it with your order, we will waive the additional shipping charge. If you want to take advantage of this offer, please click on the second link below that says **Barbecue + cover.**
>
> <u>Payment link barbecue</u>
>
> <u>Payment link barbecue + cover</u>
>
> Please <u>click here</u> to visit our eBay Store, where we sell a wide range of barbecue tools and accessories to go with your grill.
>
> Thank you once again for your business. We will ship your order immediately upon receiving payment and send you an e-mail with the tracking information.
>
> Best regards,
>
> Skip McGrath, Bidmoreoften

Note that the underlined words in the e-mail are clickable links to the payment gateway and to your eBay Store.

The advantage of upselling from your Web site is that you raise your average selling price without incurring any additional eBay fees. If you upsell from your eBay Store, you must still pay a final value fee.

E-MAILING CUSTOMERS ABOUT NEW PRODUCTS

Let's say you sold a quality product to someone at a decent price, posted glowing feedback about her, and provided her with a positive customer service experience all around. You now have the opportunity to market to that customer again.

There is nothing wrong with sending customers *occasional* e-mails when you have something special you think they would be interested in. For example, my wife and I sell Starbucks collectibles—Starbucks City mugs, Bearista Bears, and Starbucks coffee cards. Now I don't want to send my customers an e-mail every time I'm auctioning a new Starbucks collectible, since I list several items every week. However, every once in a while I come across an unusual item—perhaps a mug with a spelling mistake on it, or a rare or hard-to-find Bearista Bear. In these cases, I send out an e-mail to my list of several hundred people who have purchased Starbucks merchandise from me in the past and alert them to the auction.

Invariably, I get one or two people who reply and ask not to be mailed to again. Because my e-mails do not go for the hard sell, these requests are usually polite. For example, a customer might write something like this: "Hi, I bought a mug from you as a gift for someone and am not really a collector. So could you please take me off your mailing list? Thank you . . ."

Now let's look at a few other ways you can market to your customers.

BUILD AN OPT-IN MAILING LIST

A more effective approach than mass e-mailing is to ask your customers if they would like to be notified of future promotions, sales, and unusual or hard-to-find items. Every time you make a sale, after you post feedback and ship the item, send your customers an e-mail like this:

> *Dear eBayusername,*
>
> *Thank you for purchasing the Aviator Bearista Bear through my auction. I hope your bear arrived in good condition and you are delighted with it. If you have any problems, please let me know immediately and I will do my best to make it right.*

I have posted positive feedback for you and hope you will do the same for me.

Living in Seattle, the home of Starbucks, I often pick up hard-to-find Starbucks collectibles. Please reply to this e-mail if you would like to receive my monthly sales notice or an occasional e-mail if I come across a very special item.

Using this method, you will get fewer names to add to your list, but they will be highly qualified names. In addition, if you have an eBay Store or a Web site, you can add a line to the e-mail with the store's and/or Web site's URL, and invite the customer to peruse your other offerings and purchase from you directly.

Obviously, this method of marketing only works if you have built a specialty niche. If you are selling used blue jeans one week and DVD players the next, there isn't much use in pursuing this type of marketing.

USING YOUR WEB SITE

Another form of upselling involves capturing your customers' e-mail addresses, with an eye toward sending them future promotional offers available through your Web site. I do this using a service from PayPal that allows me to create a promotional code. For example, I can e-mail all my customers with a special code entitling them to 10 percent off any purchase from my Web site. When a customer visits the Web site and buys something, he is directed to the PayPal–enabled shopping cart. Once he enters his credit card or PayPal account information, a box comes up where he can enter the promotional code. PayPal then deducts the percentage I specified from the customer's order. You can also set the promotional code to disable the shipping calculation, thereby offering free shipping.

Several auction management services have special upselling tools. For example, Vendio provides a scrolling marquee that moves across the bottom of your auctions, as in Figure 25.1.

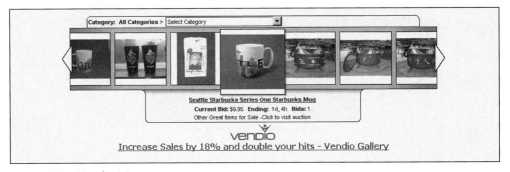

Figure 25.1 Vendio Marquee

Vendio and other services incorporate a Web store (separate from your eBay Store) as one of their offerings. When an auction ends, an automated e-mail is sent to the winner, directing her to click on a link to pay. When the buyer clicks on the link, she is taken to a payment gateway located in your Web store, where she can see all the items you have listed there. Here again, you have a chance to entice the buyer with a discount or free shipping to get her to purchase an additional product.

NEWSLETTER AND WEB SITE MARKETING

Another variation on the same theme is to start a subject-oriented newsletter. Many specialty sellers—especially those selling collectibles—create monthly or bimonthly newsletters and invite buyers to sign up for a free subscription. Here's how this works: First, you create a Web site to sell products in the same category as those you're listing on eBay. Then you publish your newsletter right on the site. The navigation bar on your homepage includes an internal link to your newsletter, and you might put a "teaser" box about the newsletter on the homepage to entice visitors to check it out. You then send out the newsletter's table of contents in an e-mail, with a link taking readers right to the applicable page on your site. This strategy is designed to drive prospective buyers to your Web site. Once they look around, you're counting on them purchasing something.

Don't worry if you can't write well enough to produce a newsletter. You can always produce a digest of news and articles about your topic. For instance, let's say you sell mineral specimens to rock collectors. Conduct a Google search on several terms related to rock collecting and use the News tab of the Google search feature. Whenever you find a relevant article, include the headline and the first sentence or two in your newsletter, with a link to the full article. It would look something like this:

> *GEM SHOW'S POOL OF TREASURES INCLUDES 96-YEAR-OLD'S AGATE WHITTIER, CA — Clarence Pool has been an avid rock hunter for more than half a century. He became a dedicated Rockhound in his 20s, at the urging of another collector . . . Read More*

The words <u>Read More</u> would be a hyperlink to the article itself. You can include a series of these on your newsletter page. Consider writing your own comments below each article.

You can also find free articles on hundreds of subjects at Web sites where authors post articles. In most cases, you are free to post the article on your Web site as long as you attribute the material to the proper source and include a link to the author's Web site. (Consult each site's Terms of Use policy.) Here are several Web sites from which you can copy or download articles:

www.findarticles.com
www.articlecity.com
www.goarticles.com
www.ezinearticles.com
www.articleworld.net
www.aracontent.com

Your goal is to build a content-rich Web site that makes your customers come back again and again.

CAPTURING E-MAIL ADDRESSES FROM NONBIDDERS AND NONBUYERS

Did you know you can also capture e-mail addresses of people who just *look* at your auction, even if they don't bid or buy? The trick is to give something away for free. Yes, I said "free." What you are going to give away is a free report. For example, suppose you are in the wedding business. You have a Web site that offers wedding gowns and supplies for sale, and you also sell some of your merchandise on eBay. At the bottom of every auction for a wedding-related item, you include a statement along the following lines: "As a FREE GIFT for looking at my auction, please click on my <u>About Me</u> page, where you can download my free e-Book, *A Checklist for Planning the Perfect Wedding*."

The underlined words would be a clickable link to your eBay About Me page. While eBay does not allow you to link to other Web sites from your auctions, it does allow you to do this from your About Me page. So, once you set up your About Me page, include a link to the area of your Web site where customers can download the free report. Many people who look at your auctions without bidding on them will bite on your free offer. Once they arrive at your Web site, you provide the free report and hope that they bookmark the site or buy something. Or, even better, you can set up a subscription form for your newsletter and require a visitor to enter her first name, last name, and e-mail address before she can access the free report. Now you really have a prospect you can market to (until the wedding is over, that is).

THE EBAY E-MAIL MARKETING SYSTEM

In 2005, eBay figured out that many sellers were using the strategies outlined above and decided to try to compete for your business—and keep you and your customers on eBay—by offering a free e-mail marketing service.

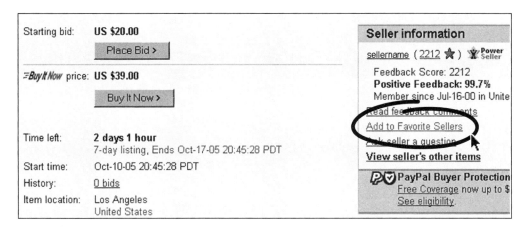

Figure 25.2 Add to Favorite Sellers Option

If you look at Figure 25.2, there is a box on the right with a link that says "Add to Favorite Sellers." When a member viewing your auction clicks on that link, he is taken to a page that looks like the one in Figure 25.3. At this point, he can sign up to receive e-mails from you. If you sell in several categories, there is a box where the buyer can select which category of products he is interested in.

Add to My Favorite Sellers and Stores

Please select any preferences and click the **Add to Favorites** button below.

Seller
sellername1

My Note:

250 characters left.

Email Communication Preferences

Favorite Sellers Top Picks email (sent by eBay)
Receive an email summary of new items available from your Favorite Sellers. You can set the frequency of this email through the Favorite Sellers page in My eBay.
☑ Add sellername1 to my Favorite Sellers Top Picks.

Add To Favorites   Cancel

Figure 25.3 Add to Favorite Sellers Screen

Once a buyer adds you to his "Favorite Seller" list, you can e-mail him through your My eBay page or the Manage My Store control panel. If you open an eBay Store (see chapter 26), eBay allows you to build and market to your mailing lists in the following ways:

* Buyers can sign up to receive your e-mail "newsletters" when they add you to their Favorite Sellers list.

* Using a simple tool, you can create e-mails with links to your eBay Store and your auctions and then send them to your subscribers. You can control which subscribers receive your e-mails, based on their interests, purchase history, and so forth.

* You can create up to five mailing lists that target different interests or types of promotions. For example, you could have a DVDs mailing list (alerting buyers to new DVDs you have in stock) and a Sale Notifications mailing list (alerting buyers to special discounts you are offering). Buyers choose which of your mailing lists to sign up for when they add you to their Favorite Sellers lists.

* You can measure the success of a targeted e-mail by viewing statistics, such as the number of bids and Buy It Now purchases it generated, and use this information to reach out more effectively to customers.

Depending on your eBay Store subscription level (Basic, Featured, or Anchor; see chapter 26), eBay will allow you to send a certain number of free monthly e-mails to your subscribers. If you exceed your monthly allocation, you will be charged a per-recipient fee for additional e-mails. Monthly allocations and additional e-mail charges are outlined in the Table 25.1.

Table 25.1: eBay Store E-mail Allocation Breakdowns by Store Type

SUBSCRIPTION LEVEL	MONTHLY FREE E-MAIL ALLOCATION	ADDITIONAL COST PER RECIPIENT (OVER ALLOCATION)
Basic Store	100 e-mails	$0.01 per e-mail
Featured Store	1,000 e-mails	$0.01 per e-mail
Anchor Store	4,000 e-mails	$0.01 per e-mail

For more on eBay Store fees, see chapter 26.

E-mail marketing, both on and off eBay, allows you to generate more business. And more sales mean more profits. If you can use your eBay auctions as a means of advertising for your eBay Store, where listing and selling fees are lower—or, even better, for your Web site, where there are no listing or selling fees at all—then your profits will increase exponentially.

POWER MOVES

❏ Evaluate the products you currently sell. See if you can come up with combinations that would lend themselves to upselling; in addition, write up a list of products you could buy or create for the purpose of cross-selling. Once you have identified these items and determined their pricing, start featuring them in your e-mails to customers at the end of your auctions.

❏ Learn about eBay's e-mail marketing program. (To find out more information about the program, click on the Help tab at the top of any eBay page and type *e-mail marketing* into the search box.)

❏ Visit www.topica.com and read about Topica's programs for newsletter publishers. Consider how to create newsletters that would appeal to bidders and buyers of your specific product(s).

❏ Set up a system to capture and record e-mail addresses from your successful bidders.

CHAPTER 26

✦ OPENING AN EBAY STORE ✦

An eBay Store is basically a "mini" Web site on eBay, where you can sell products to eBay members at fixed prices. You can list your merchandise in an eBay Store for thirty days or you can select *Good 'Til Canceled.* If you select the latter option, your listing will automatically renew every thirty days until you cancel it.

WHY SET UP AN EBAY STORE?

The key reason is to garner bigger profits. According to eBay's research, Store sellers realize, on average, a 25 percent increase in sales the first three months after opening their Store. As a Store seller, you'll also save on listing fees—just two cents a listing for each thirty-day period. Optional features are also much less expensive if you have an eBay Store; for example, it costs only one cent for the gallery feature in a Store, as opposed to thirty-five cents to insert the gallery feature in a regular auction listing.

An eBay Store can also save you time relisting items that haven't sold. Instead of relisting unsold items, stock your Store with Store Inventory listings that last for longer durations—thirty days or even Good 'Til Canceled!

BIZ BUILDER

eBay provides a dedicated search box within your eBay Store, enabling buyers to search through your items and find exactly what they want. There's no other way on eBay for buyers to do such targeted searching— and finding.

You control the look and feel of your Store. A professional-looking Store gives you credibility as an online retailer—and makes shopping easier for your buyers. eBay offers a Business Resource Center where you can access tools to establish your Store brand by downloading templates for business cards and more. This helps you build your brand on eBay and develop repeat business.

Since an eBay Store is essentially a Web site, it has its own URL that you can use to drive buyers directly there, from both on and off eBay. You can even optimize your Web address so that it shows up in search engine results. (You can find complete instructions for doing this through the *Manage your store* link, once your eBay Store is set up.)

An eBay Store also allows you to cross-promote your products to prospective auction bidders. With an easy-to-use tool, you can control which items are cross-promoted; links to selected items appear at the bottom of your auctions. See Figure 26.1 for several examples.

Figure 26.1 eBay Store Cross-Promotions

TYPES OF STORES AND FEES

eBay charges less to sell through its fixed-price Store format than through auctions. There are three kinds of fees for eBay Stores:

* **MONTHLY SUBSCRIPTION FEES**

* **LISTING AND FINAL VALUE FEES**

* **SPECIAL PROMOTIONAL FEES**

Let's look at each type, and what you get for your money.

Subscription Fees

eBay charges all sellers monthly subscription fees for their eBay Stores. There are three subscription levels for eBay Stores:

> Basic: $15.95/month

> Featured: $49.95/month

> Anchor: $499.95/month

With a *Basic Store* subscription, you can showcase all your Auction, Fixed Price, and Store Inventory listings in a custom storefront that you design. In addition, you can list an item in your Store for just two cents for thirty days, and use the cross-promotion tool to cross-sell your inventory on all your Item, Bid Confirm, and Purchase Confirmation pages. The Basic subscription level also gives you free monthly Seller Reports on the performance of all your eBay sales.

With a *Featured Store* subscription, you get all the Basic Store benefits plus additional exposure, including:

* Priority inclusion in the "Shop eBay Stores" section on search and browse pages.

* Featured placement on the eBay Stores homepage (http://stores.ebay.com).

* Prime positioning in the Stores Directory pages.

* A free subscription to Selling Manager Pro, eBay's online sales management tool.

* Marketplace data and sophisticated traffic statistics, allowing you to see where your traffic is coming from.

At $49.95 per month, a Featured Store may seem expensive, but eBay softens the financial impact somewhat by giving you, for free, $30 a month of eBay Keywords advertising (see chapter 24). Most large sellers use eBay keywords to promote their Stores anyway, so this effectively lowers the cost of the Featured Store to $19.95. Given all the features included in the Featured Store subscription, you can make a case (eBay does) that upgrading to a Featured Store is practically free.

If you have a Featured Store, eBay allows you to choose up to twenty categories of merchandise to sell. This is helpful if you are selling different types of products and you want to direct customers to the right place in your Store. For example, if you were selling men's, women's, and children's apparel, you could have a separate category for each one. This would spare a woman visiting your Store from having to page through dozens of men's and children's items. Similarly, if you were selling after-market car accessories, you could have separate categories for all the popular car companies—such as Nissan, GM, Toyota, Chrysler, Honda, Ford, Mazda, and so on.

The *Anchor Store* is quite expensive at first glance. However, if you are selling products with high keyword potential (that is, items that are frequently searched for), this option actually could be a good value. With an Anchor Store subscription, you get all the Basic and Featured Store benefits, plus:

* One million banner impressions per month for your Store throughout eBay.com—including on the eBay homepage.

* Placement of your logo on the eBay Stores homepage.

* Premium placement in the "Shop eBay Stores" section on the search and browse pages.

When you open a Store for the first time, eBay gives you the first thirty days of your Store subscription for free. After the first thirty days, you're billed the normal monthly subscription fee. You can pay this fee through your primary eBay account by credit card, PayPal, or check.

Listing and Final Value Fees

When you list an item (either for auction or at a fixed price), the listing will automatically appear both in your eBay Store (all subscription levels) and on eBay's search and browse pages, at no extra charge. When a potential bidder clicks on View Seller's Other Items, he will see both your Store listings and your auction listings.

By contrast, *Store Inventory listings* are Fixed Price listings that only appear in your eBay Store and on Store search pages. They will not be included in the search results prompted by a search of all eBay listings.

The standard insertion fee for Store items is only two cents a listing per month. This fee covers any quantity of items with a single listing, whether you list one, one hundred, or one thousand of the same item. The fees vary based on the *duration* of your listing—not on the *quantity*.

While eBay Store listing fees are much lower than those for eBay auctions, the final value fees are higher. Table 26.1 is a schedule of final value fees for Store listings as of this printing (for the most recent fees, go to http://pages.ebay.com/help/sell/storefees.html).

Table 26.1: eBay Store Final Value Fees

CLOSING VALUE	FINAL VALUE
$0.01–$25.00	8% of the closing value.
$25.01–$1,000.00	8% of the initial $25 ($2.00), plus 5% of the remaining closing value balance.
Over $1,000.01	8% of the initial $25 ($2.00), plus 5% of the next $25.01–$1,000.00 ($48.75), plus 3% of the remaining closing value balance.

Table 26.2: Optional Feature Fees with an eBay Store

FEATURE	30 DAYS	GOOD 'TIL CANCELED (price per 30 days)
GALLERY	$0.01	$0.01
ITEM SUBTITLE	$0.02	$0.02
LISTING DESIGNER	$0.10	$0.10
BOLD	$1.00	$1.00
HIGHLIGHT	$5.00	$5.00
FEATURED PLUS	$19.95	$19.95

Finally, as with insertion fees, optional feature fees for Store Inventory listings are much lower than those associated with auction-style listings (see Table 26.2).

SETTING UP SHOP

No matter which subscription level you opt for, setting up and branding your eBay Store is fairly simple and only takes a few minutes. Best of all, you have complete control over the look and feel of your Store. eBay allows you to:

* Customize your Store's homepage.
* Select a color scheme for your header and left navigation bar.
* Insert your own custom graphics into your header.
* Choose the default option of how you want your items displayed.
* Create up to twenty custom categories within your Store.
* Provide additional information to your buyers, including descriptions about your Store, yourself, and your Store's policies.

Creating custom graphics for your Store is important for branding purposes. If you don't have any experience in the field of online graphics, there are plenty of people on eBay who can do this for you. Simply type *eBay Store graphics* into the eBay search engine, and you will find dozens of auction listings for people who offer this service. Most sellers charge between $50 and $150 for this service, but some may charge higher fees for more sophisticated graphics.

Promoting Your eBay Store

The biggest PowerSellers on eBay generate the bulk of their sales from their eBay Stores. The trick is to launch auctions that generate plenty of interest and traffic—and then convince everyone who looks at your auctions to visit your eBay Store.

There are two ways that eBay lets bidders know you have a Store: by placing a small Store icon after your username, and by including a link in all your auctions to *View seller's other items.* Unfortunately, very few buyers actually click on these links. Your challenge is to change that—to encourage buyers to click through to your Store.

As noted above, Featured and Anchor Stores allow you to set up separate categories in your Store, like departments in a department store. The goal is to drive people viewing one of your auctions to a specific category in your Store. Here's how it might work: Let's say you sell bird feeders and other bird-related products. You launch a few auctions for high-end bird feeders and promote them with some of eBay's special features, such as Category Featured, Homepage Featured, Bold, and Highlight, in hopes of generating a lot of traffic. Now in your auction, right under your product description, you include a paragraph that describes all the other bird-related items you sell. The paragraph would contain both an invitation and a clickable link to a specific category in your eBay Store, like the one below:

> *If you love songbirds, please visit my eBay Store,*
> *<a href=http://www.your_store_link_goes_here> BirdsForAll</a>, where you*
> *will find a large selection of bird feeders, bird baths, bird houses, and books*
> *on birds and birding.*

The HTML code is the clickable link right to the appropriate category in your eBay Store. The name *BirdsForAll* will appear in light blue with an underscore, indicating to prospective buyers that they can just click on the link to visit your Store. Bidders will read it as follows: "If you love songbirds, please visit my eBay Store, BirdsForAll, where you will find a large selection . . ."

Another technique for turning auction browsers into Store customers is to offer something for free. For instance, you could add the following sentence to the paragraph above with the clickable link: "As a free gift for looking at my Store, you can download the e-Book, *How to Attract Songbirds to Your Yard.*" In this case, you would simply create a short PDF file that anyone could download from your About Me page.

(If you don't know how to attract songbirds to your yard, you can buy a book on the subject from the U.S. Government Printing Office and reproduce it. The GPO has books on thousands of subjects that you can freely reproduce because the copyright is in the public domain.)

Another way to attract visitors to your eBay Store is to offer free shipping. I often do this by adding a statement to my auctions like this:

FREE SHIPPING FOR MY EBAY STORE CUSTOMERS

You do not have to wait for the auction to end to buy this Garmin GPS unit. They are available in my eBay Store for immediate shipment. If you buy this item now from my eBay Store, I will ship it for FREE anywhere in the US. If you are in Canada or overseas, I will give you a $5.00 credit toward the shipping cost. I also have several other Garmin models in my Store in different price ranges. Click Here to buy now or to see all the items in my Store.

While you'll have to pick up the cost of shipping, you'll be generating sales you would not have made otherwise. Many Store sellers deliberately set the prices in their Stores a bit higher to cover the cost of this giveaway. Once you get the bidders to check out your Store, be sure to make it as easy as possible for them to buy. As we mentioned above, you need to direct the buyer to the correct category, because this saves him time and, hopefully, prompts him to buy other items of interest.

BIZ BUILDER

I make it a point to prominently feature the search box that allows buyers to search my Store. Once a potential bidder is in your Store, anything you can do to get her to the product she is looking for as quickly as possible will produce the best results. If you were selling apparel, for instance, you could invite buyers to search by size. If you sold different brands of cameras, you could place a message next to your search box inviting customers to search by brand, such as Nikon or Sony or Kodak.

You can also promote your eBay Store from outside eBay. eBay automatically submits your Store's URL to several search engines, such as Google and Yahoo!. Be sure to use keywords in your Store description and in each item title to increase your chances of getting hits from search engines. To encourage you to bring in outside business, eBay offers a 75 percent discount on the final value fee of any item sold to someone who reached your eBay Store from outside of eBay. This can translate into huge savings. For example, if you sold an item for $75.00, the final value fee would be $4.50. If the sale came from outside of eBay, the fee would only be $1.12. See chapters 24 and 25 for more ways to drive traffic to your Store from outside of eBay.

POWER MOVES

❏ Visit the eBay Stores link from the eBay homepage. Click on several of the Store listings and become familiar with how Stores are listed and how other sellers promote their Stores.

❏ From your My eBay page, click on the *Manage My Store* link and sign up for a Basic Store subscription.

❏ Place some merchandise in your Store, and start linking from your auctions to your Store. Consider ways to entice bidders to your Store, such as offering free shipping or a giveaway.

CHAPTER 27

✦ EBAY CONSIGNMENT SELLING ✦

I like to call selling goods on consignment for others the "perfect eBay business." Oftentimes, the biggest problem eBay sellers face is finding products that they can resell at a profit. Luckily, there's an alternative. If you're finding it difficult to locate products of your own, you may be able to make money selling items for others.

For every successful eBay seller, there are others who can't figure out how to sell effectively or profitably on eBay. Also, believe it or not, there are still people who are not convinced that eBay really works, are afraid to try it, and/or are computer illiterate. There are also plenty of people who just don't have the time to learn the skills needed to sell successfully on eBay. That's where you come in.

In 2002, eBay launched the Trading Assistant program. A trading assistant is an eBay seller who sells products for eBay members who either don't know how to or don't want to sell their goods themselves. If you go to the eBay site map and look under the Selling Resources heading, you will see a link to Trading Assistants. By 2005 there were 80,000 trading assistants helping others sell on eBay. In fact, consignment selling is currently the fastest-growing segment of eBay's business. While becoming an eBay trading assistant will take you more than three weeks, you can start selling on consignment at any time—and it's useful to understand how the Trading Assistant program works, so that, if you choose, you can incorporate this program into your long-term success plan.

THE TRADING ASSISTANT PROGRAM

When you join the Trading Assistant program, you tell the world that you are willing to sell for others. Trading assistants charge fees or commissions for their services. Selling as a trading assistant allows you to leverage your selling expertise without having to find products yourself—clients provide the products and you are compensated for your efforts on mutually agreed-upon terms. Many sellers already do this as a way of making money on eBay; profit margins can be significant, especially for higher-priced items.

Do You Qualify?

To join the Trading Assistant Directory (see Figure 27.1 on page 248), you must have sold at least ten items in the last three months, have a feedback rating of 100 or higher, and at least 97 percent of your feedback must be positive. You also must be in good standing with eBay. Joining the directory is free.

Figure 27.1 *The eBay Trading Assistant Directory*

eBay does not endorse the assistants listed in the directory. As eBay states in its description of the program: "Including yourself in our Trading Assistant Program directory is a lot like running a classified ad for your services. Trading Assistants are not employees or independent contractors of eBay. Nor do we endorse or approve them. Each Trading Assistant runs his or her own independent business free from any involvement by eBay."

How It Works

Through the Trading Assistant program, eBay gives any eBay seller who qualifies an opportunity to start a consignment business. When an eBay member is looking for a trading assistant, she goes to the directory, where she can type in her location and search for an assistant in her area. Once the seller performs a search, she receives a list of trading assistants and their contact information. If your name comes up in the list, the seller (in this case the *consignor*, or the person who supplies your products) can either e-mail or call you to work out a deal directly.

BIZ BUILDER

If you specialize in certain products, you can say so in your Trading Assistant Directory listing. For example, if you state that you specialize in antiques and collectibles, someone looking to sell a used printing press most likely would not call you. However, a person with a collection of old HO trains (or an *antique* printing press) probably would.

---

eBay also provides trading assistants with promotional material. There is a *Toolkit* link on the Trading Assistant page, leading to a section called *Marketing Tools*. From here you can download posters and flyers in Microsoft Word format that you can personalize, print out, and use in your marketing efforts.

Signing up to be an eBay trading assistant should be your first step in starting a consignment business.

THE TRADING ASSISTANT BUSINESS

There are thousands of eBay sellers running consignment businesses. These range from regular sellers who sell on consignment as a side business to full-time, large commercial businesses operating out of retail storefronts. A recent story in AuctionBytes (www.auctionbytes.com), a weekly newsletter for the online auction industry, reported that there are now over 4,000 eBay drop-off stores open in the United States. (A drop-off store is a retail storefront set up to provide consignors with a convenient place to drop off merchandise for consignment sellers to list on eBay.)

A woman in my hometown used to own a consignment shop right in the heart of the retail district. She sold good-quality antiques and collectibles on consignment and had a very nice business for several years. Three years ago she tried selling some of the goods in her shop on eBay. After some trial and error, she began doing very well. Earlier this year, she closed the shop; she now sells exclusively on eBay.

Like many consignment sellers, she finds people with goods to sell by placing ads in the local paper and on free community bulletin boards, approaching previous customers who know her, and by word of mouth.

Consignment selling on eBay is not a new idea. While eBay professionals have been doing it for several years, it is now becoming a large business that is attracting many professional sellers. Recently, I was in San José, visiting relatives. While driving North on the 101 Freeway, I saw a billboard that said:

Drop Off Your Item and We'll

Sell It on eBay

Call 1-866-DROP-IT-OFF

When I got home, I called the number to ask about the service. The company, called AuctionDrop™, is a professional consignment service. The founders raised $500,000 in startup venture capital to build the business, and they have raised another $2.5 million to expand the business to Los Angeles and New York. AuctionDrop plans to go public in 2006. You can visit its Web site at www.auctiondrop.com. In 2005, AuctionDrop partnered with UPS to establish UPS stores as drop-off locations for merchandise that they will sell on eBay.

This business will certainly invite competition. You can start doing eBay consignment selling with very little capital, and you'll find few barriers to entry. AuctionDrop's strategy is obviously to grow fast and dominate the market with prime locations, a big-time advertising push, and a well-known brand name.

Does this mean you shouldn't enter the market? Not at all. Starbucks dominates the coffee market in the United States, but, according to the Motley Fool, Starbucks still accounts for only 16 percent of all the premium coffee outlets in the country and less than 2 percent worldwide. Plenty of other people are making good money selling coffee for $1.75 a cup. AuctionDrop will have lots of competitors, too.

How big can an eBay consignment business grow? That really depends on several factors: how big you want your business to grow, what resources you have, and how much you can invest. AuctionDrop is a private company, and the officers do not release their sales figures. But, by watching their auctions on eBay, I estimate they are closing about $50,000 worth of auctions a week. Their basic commission schedule is 40 percent, so that works out to a gross margin of $20,000 a week. Now, you aren't going to take in this much without a sizable investment, several full-time employees, a hefty advertising budget, and so on. But I firmly believe that anyone who is well skilled at selling on eBay can develop a small business that can realize a gross margin of $1,000 to $3,000 a week. This would require you to launch an average of twenty to fifty auctions a week. Many PowerSellers today routinely launch over a hundred auctions a week, so twenty to fifty auctions a week is certainly doable. In chapter 23, we discussed automating some of the common tasks that allow you to do this.

MARKETING YOUR EBAY CONSIGNMENT BUSINESS

Once you have honed your eBay selling skills, it's not hard to market your services. If you want to find consignors, you have to go looking for them. The eBay Trading Assistant Directory may bring you some business, but probably not enough to live on.

Finding consignors takes little time and money. Here's how I market my eBay consignment services:

✳ Classified ads: I run small newspaper classified ads that read something like this: "I will sell your treasures on eBay. Call Skip 360-555-1111" or "Raise cash by selling your unwanted merchandise on eBay. Professional eBay seller does all the work for you. Call Skip at 212-555-2222." Many newspapers offer deals on multiple placements of classified ads. Speak to your newspaper's classified ad rep about working out a volume discount.

✳ Networking: I like to use what I call the "three-foot (0.9m) rule." Everyone who comes within three feet (0.9m) of me learns what I do for a living. I always carry business cards or even a small flyer that explains what I do. Whenever I meet people, I tell them that I am a professional eBay seller and that if they have something they would like to sell, I would be glad to help them.

* Free bulletin boards: This works the same way as classified ads. Just create short ads on three-by-five cards and place them on community bulletin boards in supermarkets and laundromats. I always carry push pins or thumbtacks so I'm ready whenever I come across one of these corkboards.

* Direct mail to attorneys: Create a short letter that explains the services you offer and mail it to all the estate and bankruptcy attorneys in your county. When an attorney has to settle an estate or sell off the proceeds of a bankrupt individual or company, he often works with a local auctioneer. If you explain to an attorney that you can raise far more money for the estate or the creditors by exposing the merchandise in question to over 50 million prospective eBay buyers—rather than relying on the couple of hundred people who show up for a local auction—he will most likely be all ears.

There are many other ways to market your eBay consignment service, but these four techniques should net you enough business to keep you busy—and profitable—for quite a while.

POWER MOVES

❏ If you would like to try consignment selling, visit the eBay Trading Assistant page (on the site map, click on *Trading Assistant Program,* under Selling Resources) and read the requirements to see if you qualify.

❏ Create some small classified ads and three-by-five cards advertising your services as a consignment seller, and start placing the ads in local papers and the cards on community bulletin boards in supermarkets, laundromats, and the like.

❏ Once you have some experience as a consignment seller, if you decide to pursue this business more aggressively, visit my Web site, www.skipmcgrath.com, where you'll find my book on this subject, *How to Start and Run and eBay Consignment Business.*

CHAPTER 28

✦ BEYOND EBAY ✦

eBay is a great place to start an online business. It has a low barrier to entry and you can learn while you're making money. But there is life beyond eBay. My wife and I started selling on eBay in 1999. Today we still sell on eBay every day—but now we also sell on Overstock.com and maintain three different Web site offering a variety of products.

While eBay is certainly the largest online auction site, there are a number of other successful sites such as Bid4Assets, Overstock.com, and E-Pier. In addition to auction sites, you can sell from your own Web site or create a Web store (see below) at CityMax.com.

OTHER AUCTION SITES

Once you master eBay, you might want to explore selling your goods in other venues. If you sell very expensive items, one of the best auction sites is www.Bid4assets.com™, which deals almost exclusively in high-priced goods. If you specialize in sports-related collectibles and memorabilia, check out Web-based auction sites that focus on those items, including www.bidz.com.

Overstock is a popular online shopping site that launched an auction format in early 2005. Since then it has grown substantially, and is now the second-largest auction site behind eBay in terms of gross merchandise sales. The Overstock auction site is separate from the Overstock.com site. You can find it at www.auctions.overstock.com.

In addition to auctions, there are all sorts of targeted selling sites. AbeBooks.com™ is a high-traffic site for selling books. Craig's List (www.craigslist.com) is a well-known classified ad site, which allows you to sell goods regionally.

YOUR OWN WEB SITE

In the past, setting up your own Web site was a daunting challenge. If you didn't know how to write HTML code and upload pages, you would have to hire a Web designer to do it for you. This could cost anywhere from five hundred to several thousand dollars— and once the site was designed and launched, you needed help to maintain it. Over the past two years, an array of new Web services have come on the market, allowing anyone with minimal computer skills to design and maintain an e-commerce Web site. If you have the skills to launch an eBay auction, then you can build a Web site.

These companies use a system of pre-designed templates and shopping carts. All you have to do is point and click to select colors and designs and to upload photos, and then just type text into an HTML editor that looks like a Microsoft Word document to create the headlines and text for your Web site.

Here is a list of some of the more well-regarded Web site–creation companies:

* www.citymax.com
* www.bigstep.com
* www.register.com
* www.homestead.com

Using the first site on the list, CityMax, I was able to design and upload an e-commerce Web site in less than two hours. (You can check out the Web site I designed with CityMax at www.ezauctiontools.com.) CityMax has over two hundred color and design combinations, as well as offering e-mail accounts, newsletter and auto-responder functions, FAQ pages, photo albums, message boards, and a shopping cart that allows you to use PayPal so you don't need to apply for a merchant credit card account.

CityMax also offers several tools to help promote your Web site, such as free Web site submission to major search engines like Yahoo! and Google; the ability to add titles, keywords, and meta tags to your Web pages to make it easier for search engines to find you; free submission to Google's online shopping engine Froogle; and discounts for Yahoo's Overture keyword advertising program.

As of this writing, CityMax charges $19.95 a month or $203.40 ($16.95/month) if you pay annually in advance.

There are many advantages to having a Web site. As we've discussed, you can capture customers on eBay and drive them to your Web site, where you can sell products to them without paying additional eBay fees. As you build a customer base, you can market to them from your Web site as well. A Web site can also help build your credibility and brand your business.

I use eBay to drive traffic to my Web sites, and I use my Web sites to drive traffic to my eBay auctions and stores. Once you get the hang of managing Web sites and auctions, you will see how easy it is to make your business venues complement and support each other.

ONWARD AND UPWARD

I hope by now you are well into your third week of activity and closing auctions successfully. The most important advice I can give you at this point is this: Don't give up!

Things will go wrong—they always do. As with any new venture, you will certainly make mistakes and they can frustrate and demoralize you. Whenever you make a mistake, go back to the basics and analyze what you did and what you can do differently the next time. Take risks and experiment—but remember to stay within eBay's guidelines when you do. When you take risks, such as selling a new product, remember to take lots of small risks instead of one large one. Don't commit to buying a large amount of inventory until you have thoroughly tested the market.

Finally, remember that eBay is a community. eBay members love to help each other. If you are having problems, go on the eBay message boards and ask for help. You'll be amazed at how many people will reach out to assist you with terrific advice.

Besides being profitable, selling on eBay is supposed to be fun. If you always try to view your business in this context, you will enjoy yourself, your mistakes will be less frustrating, and you will probably make more money in the end.

Good luck on eBay!

✦ APPENDICES ✦

✦ AUCTION CHECKLIST ✦

Here is a short checklist you should consult before launching your auctions:

- ❏ Have I checked my listing for any spelling or grammatical errors?
- ❏ Is my type readable? Is it too large or too small?
- ❏ Did I use short paragraphs with breaks between them?
- ❏ Are my photos clear and not too big to cause slow loading?
- ❏ Have I checked all my fees and options?
- ❏ Did I use the correct auction duration (number of days)?
- ❏ Does my auction end at a good time and on a good day (such as Sunday at 11 p.m. EST)?
- ❏ Did I include clear shipping information, costs, and terms?
- ❏ Is my item description accurate, clear, and complete?
- ❏ Did I include information as to the product's size, weight, and so forth?
- ❏ Did I mention any flaws or discrepancies?
- ❏ Did I clearly spell out the payment terms?
- ❏ Does my headline communicate what I am selling?
- ❏ Does my headline contain the appropriate keywords for item searches?
- ❏ Did I invite bidders to e-mail me with questions?
- ❏ Did I include active links to my eBay Store and About Me page?
- ❏ Is my About Me page up to date?
- ❏ Did I include a Buy It Now price?

✦ POPULAR SOURCES OF ✦ WHOLESALE MERCHANDISE

Here is an annotated list of popular sources for merchandise at wholesale prices. eBay PowerSellers often buy from these wholesalers. Some of these companies require you to have a state resale license (or sales tax ID number). You can also find this list and click through to the sites directly at www.skipmcgrath.com/3_weeks (don't forget the underscore!).

LIQUIDITY SERVICES INC. (www.Liquidation.com) is one of the largest closeout and surplus dealers on the Web. Its customers include major department stores, such as Macy's, Target, and BJ's Wholesale, as well as small businesses looking to move out surplus merchandise from their stores.

Using an auction format similar to eBay's with comparable fees, Liquidation.com holds hundreds of bulk auctions at any given time. In addition to providing access to an assortment of lot sizes—pallet loads, box lots, and trailer loads—the site also sells a variety of surplus merchandise, including overstocks, closeouts, shelf pulls, and refurbished products. Best of all, this company has excellent customer service.

The merchandise available at Liquidation.com is available for a wide range of prices: A typical pallet can cost anywhere from $200 to $2,000. Recently, I saw a pallet of video game sets carrying several Game Boys, Xboxes, and PlayStations that were selling for an average of $40 each. Another pallet had a thousand pairs of new, name-brand blue jeans—Polo, Lee, Hugo Boss, and the like—selling for less than $1.70 each.

Merchandise at Liquidation.com changes every day and you can sign up for e-mail alerts to make sure you don't miss any specials that would be of interest to you. The company also owns and operates **GOVERNMENT LIQUIDATION.COM** (www.govliquidation.com), which is the official Web-based auction site for the Department of Defense. Through this site, the DoD clears out their military surplus goods, unneeded office equipment, computers, appliances, tools, and just about anything else you can imagine. In 2005, the U.S. Air Force sold more than 10,000 surplus Palm M515 units. I bought a lot of twenty-five for just $70 each—about one-quarter of the retail cost.

WARNING #1: Before bidding on an item at Liquidation.com, be sure to check the shipping cost. Because dealers who list with this site are located all over the country, the cost of shipping a pallet load of goods can get very expensive; so try to buy from suppliers who are nearby. For example, if you live on the East Coast, you should expect that a pallet sent from California would be subject to high shipping prices. Before placing a bid, either get a shipping estimate or be sure to bid from sellers who are fewer than one thousand miles from your location.

WARNING #2: Be wary of *returns*. If you are unsure about the quality of merchandise you're considering bidding on, e-mail the seller to ask if the goods you're interested in contain *product returns* or *warranty returns*. *Product returns* are merchandise that customers returned to the store for some reason. The reasons for return could be anything: maybe the item was the wrong color or size, or maybe the customer found it defective. *Warranty returns* are items that were brought back to the manufacturer for warranty repair. Some manufacturers will simply ship a new item to the customer and sell the returned item as is, rather than pay the cost of repair. In general, I would not buy warranty returns unless you either have the ability to repair the product yourself or plan to sell it for its parts.

VIA TRADING (www.viatrading.com) is another large closeout dealer that buys and sells surplus, overstocks, and returns from major department store chains. In my own dealings with Via, I've found that company representatives are very honest in describing their merchandise; that is, you won't be surprised about the quality of the goods you order. However, there is one caveat: Via Trading only deals by the pallet load. And though many of its pallets sell for as little as $250, whenever you're considering pallet loads of merchandise, always be sure to check the shipping charges first.

LIQUIDXS.COM is the place to find brand-name merchandise by some of the biggest retailers on the market. LiquidXs acts as a wholesale gateway for major manufacturers, such as Mattel and Liz by Liz Claiborne, as well as kitchen and housewares manufacturers like KitchenAid, Calphalon, and Cuisinart. When you place a bid, you're actually dealing directly with the manufacturer—LiquidXs just facilitates the bidding and payment between buyer and seller. This site does not sell returns or warranty items; all merchandise is new (generally referred to in the trade as *shelf pulls* or *surplus*). It takes a little time to register and become eligible to bid, but it's well worth the wait. I've purchased goods from LiquidXs that I was able to sell on eBay at a markup of more than 200 percent.

BUYLINK (www.buylink.com) is a collective of several hundred small distributors and manufacturers' reps. You have to register, enter your sales tax ID number, and wait about two business days for a confirmation e-mail before you can get a rundown of prices. But once you're online, you can place orders for a variety of gift products, home and garden accessories, and new collectibles.

AMERICAN TOP LEATHER (www.americantopleather.com) is a manufacturer of leather goods specializing in apparel and accessories. This is definitely *not* your source for those cheap, $17 leather jackets you'll see selling on eBay. American Top Leather produces merchandise in several qualities, ranging from average to excellent. The company has a great line of motorcycle jackets and outstanding saddlebags that sell extremely well on eBay at a very nice markup.

LUXURY BRANDS, LLC (www.luxurybrandsllc.com) is the best-known supplier of designer goods among eBay PowerSellers. Luxury Brands sells all the famous designer labels—and, best of all, you can purchase them in small quantities. I recently bought a lot of six Prada Tessoto handbags for about $450 total, and they retailed for between $150 and $175 each.

Luxury Brands offers a PowerSeller Starter Lot for newcomers, which is a great introduction to the company. The Starter Lot is available in three sizes—$499, $749, and $999. I bought the $799 lot myself and sold all the items for a nice profit, with the sole exception of a belt that ultimately cost me $10. My lot realized a total profit of $1,494.00. In the end, I almost doubled my money—even after eBay and PayPal fees. Other sellers I've spoken with have made anywhere from 60 to 110 percent with the PowerSeller Starter Lots.

Not all Luxury Brands products sell well on eBay, though. Once again, before committing to a large purchase, research the items on eBay to make sure they are selling well. Hint: Always search "completed auctions" so you can find out what something actually sold for instead of merely what the current high bid is.

MADISON AVENUE CLOSEOUTS (www.madisonavenuecloseouts.com) is a great source of quality clothing for men, women, and children. The company also carries men's big & tall and women's plus sizes, which are great sellers on eBay.

The pricing here is excellent, and you'll frequently find great specials. In addition, in my experience, the product descriptions are very honest in terms of the quality and makeup of the goods. However, you do have to request that information via e-mail, as it's not readily available on the Web site.

CHILDREN'S WHOLESALE APPAREL (www.childrenswholesale.com) has a better supply of children's clothing than Madison Avenue Closeouts.

T-SHIRT WHOLESALE (www.t-shirtwholesaler.com) sells a lot more than just T-shirts. This is a great source for name-brand men's and women's tops of all kinds.

THE SILVER SOURCE (www.silversource.com) is one of the largest and most reliable sources for jewelry on the Web. The Silver Source has been supplying flea market dealers and jewelry stores for more than twenty years and the company expanded to eBay sellers in 1998. The Silver Source literally has thousands of styles of almost every type of jewelry—rings, pendants, necklaces, toe rings, and more. Sterling silver rings start at less than $2 each, and the minimum order is $100.

TEEDA (www.teeda.com), another jewelry company, specializes in cubic zirconium, marcasite, and sterling silver jewelry at excellent wholesale prices.

LIK SANG INDUSTRIES (www.lik-sang.com) is a Hong Kong exporter of accessories for Game Boy, Xbox, Dreamcast, DVD players, PC programs, and lots of great electronic goodies and accessories. The Web site serves as the basic retail site; however, when you click on a specific product, there's another link for wholesale bulk pricing. You can get decent discounts on quantities as small as a dozen, but the pricing gets much better when you order fifty units or more. Please note: You'll need to e-mail the company to request better pricing, but company representatives usually get back to you quickly.

MBK WHOLESALE (www.mbkwholesale.com) is a large general wholesaler that carries a wide range of gifts, collectibles, and As-Seen-On-TV (ASOTV) items. MBK is a regular source for many large PowerSellers.

DRAGON DISTRIBUTING (www.dragondistributing.com) is a leading, noncompeting wholesale distributor specializing in the distribution of automotive and consumer electronics to independent dealers. Dragon carries all the hot brands of car audio amps, speakers, cables, and accessories. You'll need a sales tax ID number and a commercial checking account to do business with Dragon.

Dragon is headquartered in Asia, but they have warehouses in the United States. Before you buy, make sure to determine where the goods will be shipped from and get a shipping estimate. If they are coming from overseas, you will need a customs broker to clear the shipment and pay any duties involved. A&A Contract Customs Brokers (www.aacb.com) is very experienced at working with eBay sellers and can handle all your importing needs.

TELEBRANDS WHOLESALE (www.telebrandswholesale.com) is the leading supplier of ASOTV goods for eBay sellers. There are several companies in this industry, but, in my opinion, TeleBrands is the best. They sell most products in one-case lots and the prices are typically 50–60 percent below the advertised-on-TV price.

   The other big ASOTV supplier is Salco, which runs a drop-shipping operation for eBay sellers at http://ezdropshipper.com.

BOONE'S ANTIQUES (www.boonesantiques.com) is a wholesaler of antiques—yes, you *can* buy antiques wholesale. This company supplies antiques dealers and decorators all over the country. Boone's main store is in Wilson, North Carolina. (Actually, *store* is something of an understatement; this sprawling outlet covers about two acres).

✦ THIRD-PARTY RESOURCES ✦ FOR EBAY SELLERS

eBay has spawned an entire industry of companies that supply products and services exclusively for eBay sellers. Some of the most popular companies are listed below; you can also find links for them on my Web site for this book: www.skipmcgrath.com/3_weeks.

AUCTION MANAGEMENT SERVICES

Auction management services allow you to automate the auction process, which gives you time to list more items for sale and, consequently, make greater profits. Valuable features provided by most auction management services include the following:

Predesigned templates	Image hosting and placement
HTML editors	Image editing
Bulk listing tools	Tools to print shipping labels
Automated payment notification	Automated checkout
Auction scheduling	Recurring launching
Sales reporting	Access to other auction venues
Inventory reporting and control	Hosted online stores

The main advantage of online auction management systems is that they work 24/7, even when you're not online. Also, if your computer crashes, your data is still safely stored on the Web. However, the main disadvantage of an online service is the cost: Auction management services charge by the month, by the transaction, or both. You should carefully compare costs before selecting a service. Some of the best-known auction management services on the Web are listed below:

Andale	www.andale.com
AuctionHawk	www.auctionhawk.com
Auctiva	www.auctiva.com

Channel Advisor	www.channeladvisor.com
MarketWorks	www.marketworks.com
Mpire	www.Mpire.com/asr
Vendio	www.vendio.com

Readers of *Three Weeks to eBay Profits* can take advantage of special free offers from these online management services by accessing them through the Web site for this book, www.skipmcgrath.com/3_weeks.

AUCTION MANAGEMENT SOFTWARE

The auction management systems described above are all Web-based, but you also have the option of purchasing auction software for use on your computer. These software programs offer many of the features of an online service, with only a few exceptions. Software will only allow you to handle automated checkout, automated payment notification, and image hosting when you're connected to the Internet. This means you must manage and revise your auctions offline and then connect to the Web when you're ready to make updates, upload images, send payment notices, and so on. The main advantage of software is the cost—once you've purchased the program, you own it (as opposed to online services, which charge by frequency of use). However, as with any software, you're relying on your home computer: If you don't sufficiently back up your sales records and your computer fails, you risk losing your data. Here are the most popular software products and their corresponding Web sites:

AuctionGenie	http://www.luxcentral.com/auctiongenie/
AuctionSubmit	www.auctionsubmit.com
e-Lister	www.blackmagik.com/elister.html
Marketblast	www.marketblast.com
Shooting Star (Foo Dog Software)	www.foodogsoftware.com

PRODUCT RESEARCH SERVICES

Hammertap Deep Analysis (www.hammertap.com)

Hammertap's Deep Analysis2 is an invaluable research tool for eBay sellers. By sorting through the multitudes of auctions, the program identifies top-selling items up for bid in your particular niche of the eBay market. Deep Analysis allows you to drill down and narrow your search to find the most successful brand or product feature within a category of merchandise—information that will help you effectively evaluate your products' sales potential.

This software can also uncover auction trends that will yield higher sell-through rates in your own auctions. For instance, use the data available on Deep Analysis2 to discover which day of the week is best to end your auction listing, assess whether or not you should use a reserve, choose starting prices that attract more bids, and much more.

In addition, Deep Analysis has an "Auction" tab on its search results page that enables you to investigate successful auctions via a variety of factors, including their popularity, starting price, total sales, number of bids, seller's reputation, reserve sell-through rate, or category. It's a great way to learn exactly what determines an auction's success.

Terapeak Research Service (www.terapeak.com)

Terapeak is one of the newest research services for eBay sellers. It offers all the features of Hammertap plus a new keyword analysis tool.

Terapeak provides the following information about a product:

- TOTAL LISTINGS
- TOTAL BIDS RECEIVED
- TOTAL SALES
- AVERAGE SALES PRICE
- SUCCESS RATE
- DEMAND FOR THE ITEM
- PRICES REALIZED ON EBAY
- BEST TIME OF DAY TO SELL
- TOP-RANKED SELLERS AND TOTAL BIDS THEY HAVE RECEIVED
- TOTAL SALES MARKET SHARE
- SELL-THROUGH RATE

Terapeak also allows you to download the data to Excel for further offline analysis.

Andale (www.andale.com)

Andale (pronounced ON-da-lay), which is Spanish for "get going," is best known as an auction management company. However, Andale has also developed a number of online services and tools that are sold separately. You do not have to use Andale's auction management service to take advantage of the following features:

✳ **WHAT'S HOT** This research tool allows you to search by product, so you can see the traffic and sales a specific item generates; you can also browse by category to identify popular markets and the top-selling products in a particular category.

✳ **PRICE FINDER** Price Finder collects information from closed auctions to provide three valuable services for eBay sellers. You can research the average selling price of an item to help determine your starting price; compare your selling prices to the competition's prices; and follow price trends to see if your products are holding steady or falling in price. Price Finder also tells you the high, low, and average selling prices of items you plan to sell, as well as which eBay promotional features (bold, highlight, etc.) the top sellers use.

✳ **ANDALE SUPPLIERS NETWORK** The Andale Suppliers Network connects eBay sellers in need of merchandise with suppliers who stock that kind of merchandise. Buyers and sellers create profiles that describe their businesses and the types of products they are looking to buy or trying to sell. Andale surveys the Network profiles for auto-matches based on common product categories. When a buyer-supplier match is found, Andale sends an email notification so the two parties can make contact.

✳ **SALES ANALYZER** This is a useful tool that provides a snapshot of your eBay U.S. sales history for the last ninety days, including your total number of listings, the number of items sold, and your sell-through rate. It also displays your fees, margins, and the selling prices of competitive items. With Sales Analyzer, you can compare your sales from month-to-month and track your fees and expenses.

Auction Niches

(The main site is www.auctionniches.com. However, at the following Web address you'll find a special offer for readers of this book: http://tinyurl.com/9fymy. You can also access this offer through links on the Web site for this book, www.skipmcgrath.com/3_weeks.)

Auction Niches is a monthly service that researches hot keywords used in more than one hundred narrow product niches. This is a great way to discover new niches and pinpoint the best keywords for any niches you select.

AUCTION NEWS AND INFORMATION

AuctionBytes (www.auctionbytes.com)

AuctionBytes, run by David and Ina Steiner, is the authoritative news source for eBay and the online auction community. The Steiners publish a daily newsletter and a weekly wrap-up featuring longer stories, advice, and articles by online auction experts. The site also contains several free resources and links to hundreds of Internet services.

AUCTION PROMOTION TOOLS

SellersVoice (www.sellersvoice.com/skip)

SellersVoice is an online service that allows you to easily add audio to your eBay auctions. According to research conducted by SellersVoice, adding audio can increase the number of bids received by as much as 30 percent and final values by as much as 19 percent. For testimonials, links to my auctions featuring audio, and a free trial from SellersVoice, visit http://tinyurl.com/49wff, or go to the Web site for this book, www.skipmcgrath.com/3_weeks, where you will find links to all of the specials and offers mentioned here.

buySAFE (www.buysafe.com)

buySAFE is a bonding company that provides your buyers with protection against fraudulent transactions on eBay and the Internet. This is very useful if you sell high-priced merchandise, because it gives your customers confidence in you as a seller. Buyers can shop for merchandise that is insured by buySAFE via the company's online store.

Google Adwords (https://adwords.google.com)

Google Adwords is a pay-per-click service that you can use to drive business to your eBay store. The ads appear as small boxes on the right side of every Google search results page that relates to your search term. For example, let's say you're selling digital camera supplies and someone Googles the term *tripod*; if you have purchased the keyword *tripod* through Adwords, a sponsored advertisement for your store will appear next to the natural search results. When the consumer clicks on your ad, she will be taken directly to your store.

In addition to the one-time activation fee, Adwords users have two payment options. If you select *cost-per-click pricing*, Adwords will charge you when someone clicks on your Google ad; if you opt for *cost-per-impression* advertising, you'll be charged when your ad is viewed on the Google search page. Advertisers' fees are determined by their bids on specific keywords that, when searched by Google users, will call up their paid advertisement. The higher the keyword bid, the more prominent placement on the Google page.

Yahoo! Search Marketing (www.content.overture.com)

This is another pay-per-click advertising service that puts a link to your eBay store just ahead of the natural Yahoo! search results. The ad is formatted so that it looks more like an actual Yahoo! listing, although it's preceded by the heading *Sponsored Results* directly above it.

Free Keyword Research Tool (http://inventory.overture.com/d/searchinventory/suggestion)

Need help determining which keywords to bid on? When you enter a keyword into this free research service, it calls up dozens of other frequently used keywords in similar searches.

✦ A BASIC HTML PRIMER ✦

As we've discussed, eBay provides sellers with an easy-to-use HTML editor, so that you can create listings without ever entering in a single line of code. However, more advanced sellers can use HTML coding to get a leg up on the competition and further stylize their listings—as well as their feedback comments and community postings. In addition, if you're going to expand your eBay business by creating a Web site, you'll find knowing a little HTML to be a big help in formatting your site so it reflects your business' message and style.

Here you'll find a basic HTML tutorial, as well as resources for learning more about HTML, should you find it to be a useful tool for your eBay auctions.

WHAT IS HTML CODING?

HTML is an abbreviation for *hypertext markup language*. HTML coding consists of writing software instructions to change the font, color, paragraph style, and so forth of the text on a Web page. It is surprisingly simple to do; in fact, you can learn it in about one hour of practice. Go to www.draac.com for an easy-to-understand tutorial on HTML, image hosting and loading, and over two thousand free images and backgrounds you can upload to your auction pages. Draac.com also offers a free online course in Web design right on its Web site. Another useful Web site is www.davesite.com, which offers an interactive tutorial for beginners.

In addition to the above Web sites, there are many good books on the subject of HTML coding. My manual, *The Basic Seller's Guide to eBay* contains a good introduction to HTML, focusing on what you need to know to improve the appearance and performance of your eBay listings.

GETTING STARTED

HTML is easy to learn and a lot of fun—and much simpler than what you probably envision when you think of programming. Basically all you do is insert formatting instructions in front of your words as you type them, and these instructions change the appearance of your text on the Web. Web pages, such as eBay, look for the HTML signal, which is a set of brackets ("<" and ">"). Whenever the Web page encounters that symbol, it follows the instructions inside of it. Anything you type between < and > will not show up as text on the Web page; rather, it will affect the look of the type.

If you prefer, you can create your HTML coding in a word processing program, such as Microsoft Word, and then copy and paste it into your eBay ad. (Note that you cannot use HTML in your auction title. HTML is only permitted in the item description.) You can also paste banners, images, and photos into your ads.

CREATING AN ACTIVE LINK IN YOUR AUCTION DESCRIPTION

If you would like a word or phrase such as *click here* or *See my other auctions* to be an active hyperlink to any Web site or Web page, use the following command with the Web page address in quotation marks:

<a href="http://www.mywebpage.com"> click here </a>

This would make the words *click here* an active link to the Web page you specified. Here is an example: To get someone to click on your About Me page, you would type the following into your auction item description:

Please visit my

<a href="http://www.ebay.com.aboutme/username.com"> About Me Page. </a>

The words *About Me Page* would appear in blue in the auction description as a hyperlink. The best way to prevent mistakes is to go to your About Me page (or any page you want to link to) and copy and paste the URL from the address bar into the space between the quotation marks.

TYPEFACE CUSTOMIZATION

There are many, many typefaces that can be used in creating an auction ad. Most, if not all, of the fonts in your Microsoft-compatible word processor can be created in an auction. Table D.1, the Font/Typeface Cheat Sheet (see page 276), lists the most popular typefaces and shows how they will appear when displayed. They should work in the vast majority of browsers, but will occasionally default to Times New Roman if not compatible. To create a different look in your ads, use the following coding:

<font face="onyx">This is a test</font>
The above will result in: This is a test

<font face="impact">This is a test</font>
The above will result in: **This is a test**

<font face="copperplate">This is a test</font>
The above will result in: THIS IS A TEST

As you can see, the text affected is positioned between the two HTML commands (tags). In this case, the first one is the *font face* command. At the end of this text, you must insert the closing tag *</font>*. Note the slash indicating the end of this formatting.

BOLD, ITALICS, AND UNDERLINE

You can make many formatting changes to your auction text with HTML commands, including making the text **bold**, *italicizing* it, underlining it, changing its color, and adjusting its size.

Again, all HTML commands are enclosed in < > symbols. To end the specific formatting, you must include the </xxxx> tag (note the slash) at the end of the text. (The xs represent the command name).

For italics the command is <i>. To end italics, use </i>. So, for example:

This is a test
results in *This is a test*

To make text bold, the tag is . To end the bold, use . For example:

This is a test
results in **This is a test**

To underline text, the command is <u>. To end the underline, use </u>. For example:

<u>This is a test</u>

results in This is a test

You can also use multiple commands: To make text bold, italicized, *and* underlined, use all three commands listed above. So, for example:

<u>This is a test</u>

results in ***This is a test***

You can also combine these commands with font face commands. For example:

<font face="garamond"><u>This is a test</u></font>

results in **This is a test**

Table D.1: Font/Typeface Cheat Sheet

Arial Black	*Forte*
Arial	Garamond
Arial Narrow	Helvetica
Bauhaus	**Impact**
Bell MT	*Mistral*
Brush Script MT	Onyx
Comic Sans MS	Papyrus
COPPERPLATE	Perpetua
Cooper Black	Rockwell
Courier	**STENCIL**
Curlz MT	Times New Roman
ENGRAVERS MT	Verdana

TEXT COLOR CHANGES

There are many colors and font sizes you can use to format your text. For more obscure colors, consult a book on HTML coding. Here we'll cover the most common ones. To change a color you use the *font color* command. The opening HTML tag is <font color=xxx>; the closing tag is </font>. Here's an example:

<font color=red>This is a test</font>

When displayed in a browser, the enclosed text, "This is a test," will be red.

Black is the default HTML color. The other, most common colors are:

Blue	Red	Green	Orange	Gray	Yellow	Aqua	Teal
Fuschia	Lime	Maroon	Navy	Olive	Purple	Silver	White

We unfortunately can't illustrate these colors on this black and white page. But you can imagine the possibilities for improving the aesthetics of your auction listings.

TEXT SIZE CHANGES

To change the font's size, you need to use the *font size* command. The default font size is twelve point. Using HTML coding, you can add to or subtract from that size in increments. You make the type larger by using the "+" command and smaller by using the "−" command. Simply enter the number of points by which you wish to enlarge or reduce the default type size. The format is as follows:

<font size=+2>This is a test</font>

The above results in:

This is a test

This creates a font that is two points larger than the twelve-point default.

Here's another example:

<font size=-3>This is a test</font>

The above results in:

This is a test

This is a great command for creating the fine print at the end of your auctions, where you may discuss items such as your back order policy, applicable taxes, and any restrictions. The key is to remember to input the relative size increase or decrease you want. Play with this command for a while and it'll start to make sense.

Of course, you can combine any and all the commands we've discussed so far. Here is an example:

<font face="Garamond" size=+2 color=orange><u>This is a test</u></font>

The above commands result in *This is a test* (and the text would appear orange on the Web page).

Note that we included only one *</font>* end tag, since we combined all the font subcommands.

Another, more interesting example:

<font face="verdana" color=blue><u>This is an even <font size=+4>bigger test</font> than before</u></font>

The above coding results in:

This is an even *bigger test* than before (The text would appear blue in one's browser).

In this example, we changed the text within the sentence, too. As long as you include the opening and closing tags, you can be as creative as you like.
Of course, any and all of the text formatting commands can be used together in any combination. For example:

<hr><p><font face="comic sans ms" color=gray> This is a neat test
more text for this neat example</font><p><font face="impact" size=+4><u>and even more text</u></font><hr>
<font face="brush script mt"> and one last line of text </font>

results in:

This is a neat test
more text for this neat example
and even more text

---

and one last line of text

Study the above HTML commands and the results they create, and you'll see how it all works. Notice how the closing tags turn off the formatting that was created previously. Also note the difference between the break command *
* and the new paragraph command *<p>*. By the way, "This is a neat test" above would appear in gray coloring when displayed in a browser. See Table D.2 for a cheat sheet of basic HTML tags.

Table D.2: Basic HTML Tags

ACTIVE LINKS: `<a href="http://www.mywebpage.com"> click here </a>`

BOLD: `<b>text</b>`

CENTER: `<center> text </center>`

FONT SIZE—
DECREASE: `<font size=-1> decreases default type size by one point </font>`

FONT SIZE—
INCREASE: `<font size=+1> increases default type size by one point </font>`

HEADINGS: `<h1>Biggest Heading</h1>` through `<h6>Smallest Heading</h6>`

HORIZONTAL RULE: `<hr>` (no end tag)

ITALICS: `<i>text</i>`

LINE BREAK: `<br>`

LIST, ORDERED
(NUMBERED):   `<ol>`

         `<li> item 1 </li>`

         `<li> item 2 </li>`

         `</ol>`

LIST, UNORDERED
(BULLETS):   `<ul>`

         `<li> first item </li>`

         `<li> second item </li>`

         `</ul>`

MAIL LINK: `<a href="mailto:username@host.com">email me</a>`

PARAGRAPH: `<p> paragraph text </p>`

UNDERLINE: `<u>text</u>`

✦ THE EBAY FEE SCHEDULE ✦

The eBay fee schedule changes periodically. As we've discussed, to find the most up-to-date schedule, visit http://pages.ebay.com/help/sell/fees.html, or http://pages.ebay.com/help/sell/storefees.html to see eBay Store fees. Below you'll find the fee schedule as of February 22, 2006. We've also included PayPal fees you may encounter for easy reference.

Understanding eBay's fees is the first step to understanding how to manage them, and thus reduce your cost of doing business on eBay. See chapter 21 for tips on managing your eBay seller's fees.

BASIC EBAY SELLER FEES

Here are the fees that you, as a new seller, are most likely to encounter:

Insertion Fees

STARTING PRICE	FEE	STARTING PRICE	FEE
$0.01 – $0.99	$0.20	$50.00 – $199.00	$2.40
$1.00 – $9.99	$0.35	$200.00 – $499.99	$3.60
$10.00 – $24.99	$0.60	$500.00 and up	$4.80
$25.00 – $49.99	$1.20		

Reserve Price Auction Fees*

RESERVE PRICE	INSERTION FEE
$0.01 – $49.99	$1.00
$50.00 – $199.99	$2.00
$200.00 and up	1% of reserve price (max.: $50)

*Note: These are fully refunded if the item sells.

Final Value Fees

CLOSING PRICE	FINAL VALUE FEE
$0.01 – $25.00	5.25% of the closing value.
$25.01 – $1,000.00	5.25% of the first $25.00, plus 3.00% of the balance
Over $1,000.01	5.25% of the initial $25.00, plus 3.00% of the value from $25.01 to $1,000.00, plus 1.50% of the remaining closing value

Buy It Now Fees

BUY IT NOW PRICE	FEE
$0.01–$9.99	$0.05
$10.00–$24.99	$0.10
$25.00–$49.99	$0.20
$50.00 or more	$0.25

Optional Listing Upgrades*

Gallery	$0.35	Border	$3.00
Listing Designer	$0.10	Highlight	$5.00
Item Subtitle	$0.50	Featured Plus!	$19.95
Bold	$1.00	Gallery Featured	$19.95
Scheduled Listing	$0.10	Homepage Featured	$39.95
10-Day Duration	$0.40	Dutch Auction Homepage Featured	$79.95
Gift Services	$0.25	List in Two Categories	Listing fees double

* For $0.65, you can purchase a *Value Pack*, which includes the gallery, listing designer, and subtitle features. The *Pro Pack* offers the bold, border, highlight, Featured Plus! and Gallery Featured upgrades for $29.95.

Image Hosting Fees

First Image	Free
Additional pictures	$0.15 each
Supersize	$0.75
Picture Pak	$1.00 for up to 6 pictures or $1.50 for 7–12 pictures

Fees for Seller Tools*

TurboLister	Free
Selling Manager	$4.99
Selling Manager Pro	$15.99
Blackthorne	$9.99
Blackthorne Pro	$24.99

*Fee-based tools include a free 30-day trial

EBAY STORE FEES

Should you expand your business by launching an eBay Store, you will encounter different types of fees. Here are the most common fees for eBay Store sellers:

Store Subscription Fees

BASIC	$15.95/month
FEATURED	$49.95/month
ANCHOR	$499.95/month

eBay Store Insertion Fees

DURATION	INSERTION FEE
30 days	$0.02
Good 'Til Cancelled	$0.02 every 30 days

eBay Store Final Value Fees

CLOSING VALUE	FINAL VALUE FEE
$0.01–$25.00	8% of the closing value
$25.01–$1,000.00	8% of the initial $25 ($2.00), plus 5% of the remaining closing value balance
Over $1,000.01	8% of the initial $25 ($2.00), plus 5% of the next $25.01–$1,000.00 ($48.75), plus 3% of the remaining closing value balance

Optional Feature Fees for Store Inventory Listings

FEATURE	30 DAYS	GOOD 'TIL CANCELLED (PRICE PER 30 DAYS)
Gallery	$0.01	$0.01
Item Subtitle	$0.02	$0.02
Listing Designer	$0.10	$0.10
Bold	$1.00	$1.00
Border	$3.00	$3.00
Highlight	$5.00	$5.00
Featured Plus	$19.95	$19.95

PAYPAL FEES

If you accept PayPal as a payment method, you'll pay the following fees:

Fees for Personal and Premier/Business Accounts

ITEM	PERSONAL ACCOUNT	PREMIER/BUSINESS ACCOUNT
Open an Account	Free	Free
Send Money	Free	Free
Withdraw Funds	Free for bank accounts in the US	Free for bank accounts in the US
Add Funds	Free	Free
Receive Funds	Free	1.9% to 2.9% + $0.30 USD

✦ EBAY EXPRESS ✦

In spring 2006, eBay will roll out eBay Express, a new program for sellers with feedback ratings of 100 or higher. As a relatively new seller, it may be a while before you can take advantage of this program. However, it's worth understanding a bit about eBay Express, as you may want to incorporate this new venue into your business plan as your eBay business develops. As this is a new program, keep checking eBay's help pages and http://express.ebay.com for further developments. (All information included here is current as of this book's printing; however, details may change after publication.)

WHAT IS EBAY EXPRESS?

eBay Express is a completely new selling venue on eBay. It even has its own URL (http://express.ebay.com). Operating more like a traditional e-commerce site, eBay Express will allow a buyer to purchase several items from one or multiple sellers, place the items in a shopping cart, and make one payment using either PayPal or a credit card. The expectations are that eBay Express will be a boon for eBay Store operators and those sellers who use Fixed Price listings, as eBay is promoting this site as a venue for customers to buy on eBay at fixed prices.

Although millions of people use eBay, there are still millions that don't—many of them for two reasons: They don't like or understand the auction format and they are afraid of fraud. eBay Express addresses both of these issues.

The fixed price format makes it simple and quick to buy something. In addition, eBay has set higher requirements for feedback. To have your items listed on eBay Express, you need a feedback rating of at least 100 and a positive score of 98 percent or better. As most fraud is committed by sellers with low feedback numbers, this requirement should reduce the incidence of fraud on eBay Express.

This is another good reason to have an eBay Store. If you place several Fixed Price listings for a seven- or ten-day period, you will incur a lot of burdensome listing fees. With an eBay Store, you'll pay fewer fees and gain exposure on eBay Express for a month.

It's easy to get listed on eBay Express. Here are the requirements from eBay:

1. You must maintain a feedback score of 100 or more, with your feedback being 98 percent positive or better. (Note that this is consistent with PowerSeller requirements.) Your feedback profile must be public, rather than private.

2. You must support your listings with a PayPal Premier or Business account, and set your PayPal account to ship to unconfirmed addresses or make sale-by-sale decisions.
3. You must be a US registered seller.
4. Your listings should be in Fixed Price or Store Inventory format. You must indicate in the item condition field if the item is new, used, or refurbished. You must also include shipping costs, as well as a picture or gallery.
5. You are required to use eBay's checkout or the new checkout integration API.

Feedback from eBay.com will carry over to eBay Express and vice versa. (Any feedback you earn on eBay Express will carry over to eBay.) This is the one worrisome feature: eBay Express is designed to attract buyers new to eBay. Many of these newbies will not understand the feedback concept and, unlike more experienced eBayers, they may potentially leave negative feedback for very minor reasons. As mentioned throughout this book, always be careful to explain your return policy, shipping and tax information, and any item flaws *clearly* throughout your listing. This is always your best defense against negative feedback.

✦ SAFETY TIPS FOR ✦ BUYERS AND SELLERS

Compared to the rest of the Internet, eBay is actually one of the safest venues for online buying and selling. Fraud is quite rare and affects a tiny fraction of the millions of dollars of business done on eBay every day. Nevertheless, with 85 million potential buyers, eBay does attract its share of online criminals—dishonest people bent on stealing your money any way they can. Below are some strategies you can use to ensure a safe buying and selling experience.

BUYING ON EBAY

The most common type of fraud on eBay occurs when someone sells an expensive item that he doesn't possess and/or has no intention of delivering. For example, let's say you have been looking at one of those new Hitachi plasma TVs that sell for over $4,000. You see one from a seller for under $3,000 and you bid on it. You send the money and the TV never arrives. A week later you e-mail the seller and get no reply. When you check the seller's account on eBay, it has been terminated. Your money is gone and so is the seller.

While this scenario may sound frightening, this type of fraud is easily prevented if you follow these simple steps:

1. CHECK THE SELLER'S FEEDBACK

In chapter 11, we discussed the concept of feedback. eBay's feedback reports on other members can tell you a lot about the sellers with whom you are considering doing business. Look at an eBay member's username; a number in parentheses immediately follows it. That number is that member's unique feedback score.

If you look at Figure G.1 (see page 288), you can see this user's feedback score is 4505 and his feedback is 100 percent positive.

Below that is the number of users who left positive comments and the number who left negative ones. The next line reveals the *total* number of positive feedback left. Note that this aggregate number is higher than the positive feedback number above it. This is because eBay only counts positive feedback *once* from any given member. So the difference between these two numbers represents the number of transactions that were from repeat buyers. The fact that over five hundred people came back to buy from this seller inspires confidence in his past performance.

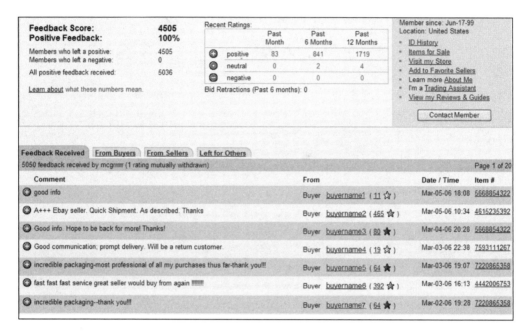

Figure G.1: A Sample eBay Feedback Report

If you are buying a T-shirt or a coffee mug for $20, the chance of out-and-out fraud is pretty slim. Most fraud-minded sellers tend to focus on items with high values, such as diamond rings or plasma TVs. So I wouldn't hesitate to buy a low-cost item from a seller who may have a low feedback score as long as it is primarily positive. If you look again at Figure G.1, you can see that eBay displays the actual comments that buyers left. If someone has recently received negative feedback, I sometimes scroll down the page to read the actual comment.

2. Don't Buy Expensive Items from New Sellers

If you look at the top, right-hand section of Figure G.1, you can see how long a member has been registered on eBay and the member's ID History. Most fraudulent transactions are by sellers who have been registered for fewer than thirty days. I would be very hesitant to bid on or buy an expensive item from a brand-new seller. If you are considering bidding on an item, you can also click on the link that says *ID History*. This page will show you if the seller has changed her username since she registered.

3. Never Send Cash, a Money Order, or a Certified Check for an Expensive Item

Most legitimate sellers accept PayPal and/or credit cards as payment methods. There are a few sellers who demand money orders or certified checks, but they are in the minority. Only if a seller had a high positive feedback rating—and had been selling on eBay for at least a year—would I consider this type of payment. However, I would first look to see if the same item was available from another seller who *did* accept PayPal.

4. Always Ask Sellers for a Tracking Number or Delivery Confirmation

UPS and other shipping services track all packages to their destinations. Similarly, the US Postal Service offers delivery confirmation. Positive tracking prevents a seller from claiming he sent a package when he actually did not.

5. Make Sure You Pay the Correct Seller

In another popular scam, an eBay member monitors auctions for expensive items during the final few seconds of bidding. When a bidder wins an auction, this unscrupulous interloper sends her an immediate e-mail requesting payment. The responsible bidder pays right away—only to later receive a payment notice from the legitimate seller. To avoid this scenario, before sending a PayPal payment for an expensive item, I always check the username of the person I am paying to make sure it's the same as that of the person who sold me the item.

Another variation on this scam is an e-mail that arrives from a purported eBay seller demanding immediate payment for an item you bought—or else the "seller" will report you to eBay and leave you negative feedback. You panic and send him the money, only to realize later that you never bought anything from that seller.

6. Read the Auction Description Carefully

One recent scam involved some sneaky members selling the empty box that the popular Microsoft Xbox game system comes in. The auction description would describe the Xbox system in great detail with lots of photos. Unfortunately, buried in the text was the statement "you are bidding on the box only." Buyers reading this line assumed that, by "box," the seller was referring the Xbox—when, in fact, the seller was only offering the empty box in which the product was originally packaged.

7. Make Sure You Are Buying Authentic Products

Unfortunately, there are a lot of knockoffs and outright counterfeit items for sale on eBay. eBay aggressively polices this through their Verified Rights Owner (VeRO)

Program, but they can't catch everyone. If you are bidding on a brand-name item, such as a Rolex watch or a Prada handbag, this is another situation where you might want to check the seller's feedback and ID history very carefully.

8. Look for buySAFE-Bonded Sellers

As we discussed in Chapter 24, buySAFE is a bonding service underwritten by the Liberty Mutual Insurance Company that insures buyers against fraud. Whenever you see the buySAFE seal in an auction, you know two things: the seller has been thoroughly vetted by buySAFE, and, if that seller defrauds you, buySAFE will reimburse you for your loss up to the amount of the seller's bond. If you click on the buySAFE seal in the seller's auction, you can see the amount of the bond, which can be anywhere from $5,000 to $25,000. (If you are selling expensive merchandise, you may want to consider using buySAFE so potential bidders feel more comfortable buying from you).

9. Report Suspicious Auctions to eBay

If you come across an auction that looks suspicious—such as a seller from Taiwan who has only been on eBay for a few weeks, and who is selling an expensive piece of jewelry and demanding cash as payment—take action. In this situation, you should not only refrain from bidding on the item, you should click on the link at the bottom of every auction that says *Report this listing to eBay*. Upon receiving the report, eBay's Trust & Safety department will examine the listing and cancel it if they think it may contain a high risk of fraud.

10. Safeguard Your Registration Information and Password

Phishing is jargon for sending out spoof e-mails designed to lure recipients into entering their eBay passwords and credit card information into spoof Web pages that look just like the PayPal or eBay sites. To avoid falling victim to these online predators, remember a couple of simple pointers: Neither eBay nor PayPal will ever send you an e-mail asking you to click on a link to update your account information. Legitimate e-mails will always be addressed to you by name and will direct you to the eBay or PayPal homepage to log in as you normally do.

11. Beware of the Evil Twin

A more recent method of stealing your personal information is the "Evil Twin." This scam takes advantage of wireless connections in airports and coffee shops. The Evil Twin is essentially a wireless version of a phishing scam—you think you're connecting to a genuine hot spot, but are actually connecting to some guy with a laptop and a wireless network card sitting perhaps a few feet away. Because he is closer to you than the base station, you might actually log onto his network instead.

Once you are logged on, the thief can capture a record of your keystrokes. Therefore, you want to be careful of entering personal information such as passwords and credit card information when you are on one of these networks.

12. Pay with PayPal or Other Secure Methods

For items covered by PayPal's *Buyer Protection Program*, your purchases are protected against fraud—including sellers that do not deliver your merchandise as promised, or delivered items that differ significantly from the auction description—up to $1,000.00. (See www.paypal.com for more information.) Also, investigate any protection policies your credit cards may offer.

SELLING ON EBAY

Like buyers, sellers can also fall victim to scams such as phishing and the Evil Twin. However, other scams specifically target eBay sellers. Here are some important tips for anyone considering selling on eBay:

1. Be on the Lookout for Counterfeit Certified Checks and Money Orders

This is a larger problem when receiving payments from overseas. American criminals rarely use this method because it is a federal crime and carries very serious penalties. Whenever I receive a money order, I cash it instead of depositing it into my bank account. That way the responsibility for determining the money order's authenticity falls with the post office or whoever cashed it. I never ship the buyer's goods until I have the cash in my hand.

Certified checks are slightly more problematic. If I receive a certified check (also know as a *bank check*), I take it to my bank and ask a representative to contact the issuing bank to determine if the check is good *before* I deposit it. This usually takes about twenty-four hours. If the bank says the check is good and it turns out to be counterfeit, then it becomes the bank's problem—not yours.

2. Always Ship Using a Service That Provides Tracking

Just as some sellers will *claim* they shipped your unreceived item, there are some buyers who will claim they never received their item and demand a refund or a replacement. That's why I usually ship with a service such as UPS or FedEx that provides positive tracking for all packages. If the item I am shipping is expensive, I check the box on the shipping form to require a signature upon delivery. Whenever I ship via USPS, I always opt for *delivery confirmation*, which is the USPS tracking service. If you insure the package with the US Postal Service, then it is signed for at each step of the way. You don't get a signature from the customer, but the postal carrier who delivers it signs a form certifying the delivery.

3. Carefully Select the Locations to Which You Will Sell

I have been selling internationally for several years now, but there are some countries I simply will not sell to because fraud is so rampant. Chief among those are Russia, Thailand, and Nigeria. When you launch an auction on eBay, there is a form that comes up where you can select the countries or parts of the world where you will do business. Until you gain some experience, I would limit your sales to the United States and Canada. Later you may want to add European nations and Australia.

4. Use a P.O. Box or Postal Service as Your Registered Address on eBay

Once you conduct a transaction with someone, she can find your address within the eBay system. As I mentioned, I once had someone who purchased an item from me show up at my front door. It's generally not a good idea to have your address available anywhere on the Internet if you can help it.

5. Take Detailed Photographs of and Insure Expensive Items

There are some unscrupulous buyers who receive something and then decide they didn't really want it. So they may break it or put a scratch on it and then demand a refund. If the item is insured and the buyer breaks it, you can simply file an insurance claim and the insurance company will take over from there. The company will almost always investigate the claim, especially if the item was expensive. If the buyer put a scratch on the item or otherwise damaged it, you will have a photograph to prove it was fine when you shipped it.

✦ GLOSSARY AND GUIDE ✦
TO COMMON ABBREVIATIONS

active user: An eBay member who has bought or sold merchandise at least once in the last twelve months.

ADDY: An abbreviated term for *e-mail address*.

Adwords: Google's term for *pay-per-click advertising*.

AG: An abbreviation for the term *about good*, used to describe the condition of an item.

a.k.a.: An abbreviation for *also known as*. (Also sometimes written as *a/k/a*.)

A/O: An abbreviation for *all original*, an auction term used to describe the condition of an item. *A/O* is often used in the auction title to save space.

ASAP: An abbreviation for *as soon as possible*.

as is: A term identifying auction items that are sold without warranties as to the condition of the property. Items sold without warranties may be damaged or have missing parts. See also *caveat emptor*.

ASOTV: An abbreviation for *as seen on TV*.

ATM: An abbreviation for *at the moment* (not to be confused with *automated teller machine*).

auction: The standard selling format on eBay. A seller offers one or more items at a set starting price; buyers then visit the listing page and bid on the item during an established period of time. When the auction ends, the high bidder (or bidders) buys the item from the seller for the amount of the winning bid.

average selling price (ASP): The average price at which an item sells, or the average price of all items sold by a particular eBay seller in a given period. When calculating ASP, only count items that have actually been paid for; do not count sales to winning bidders who have not yet paid.

BC: An abbreviation for *back cover.*

bid increment: The amount by which you must increase your bid over the current high bid in order to bid on an item at auction. The bid increment is established by the current bid price.

bid rigging: The unlawful practice whereby two or more bidders conspire to influence an item's value either by not bidding at its auction or by placing fake bids. See also *collusion* and *shilling.*

BIN rate: The percentage of items sold with BIN (Buy It Now) or any fixed-price format.

blocked bidders: A seller's list of specific eBay members who are prohibited from participating in that seller's auctions.

BTW: An abbreviation for *by the way.*

Buy It Now (BIN): The BIN option allows a seller to set a purchase price that, when selected by a bidder, ends an auction immediately and sells the item on the spot.

B&W: An abbreviation for *black and white*, generally used in reference to photos.

calculated shipping: A seller's option that posts a shipping calculator in an auction description. When a buyer enters her zip code, the calculator estimates applicable shipping costs.

caveat emptor: A Latin term for "Let the buyer beware"; also a legal maxim stating that the buyer incurs all the risk in a transaction.

COA: An abbreviation for *Certificate of Authenticity;* a legal guarantee that an item is genuine (usually certified by an expert).

collusion: A practice in which two or more eBay bidders conspire to influence an item's value either by placing fake bids (to inflate the price of the item) or by refusing to bid at all (to deflate the price of an item). See also *bid rigging* and *shilling*.

consignment selling: An arrangement in which one person sells merchandise on eBay on behalf of the item's owner, and in turn receives a commission for his efforts should the item sell. See *Trading Assistant*.

CONUS: An acronym for the continental United States (not including Alaska and Hawaii).

conversion rate (CR): The percentage of auctions closed successfully (i.e., with items sold) out of the total auctions listed by a seller.

DBA: An abbreviation for *doing business as*. This is the legal term for using a business name instead of your real name. For example, you incorporate as John Jones, Inc., but the name you do business as is *The Sell More Company*.

deadbeat bidder (DBB): A winning bidder who fails to complete a transaction.

dingbat bidder: A bidder who doesn't yet understand how eBay works; known to send e-mails with such basic questions as "What does *new with tag* mean?"

Dispute Console: The eBay service that allows members to report and track all transaction problems. For instance, sellers can report auction winners who have neglected to pay for their items, and buyers can report sellers who have failed to ship items that have been paid for.

DNR: An abbreviation for *one dollar no reserve*; a listing that starts at $1 with no reserve.

DOA: An abbreviation for *dead on arrival*; a term used when the item you just purchased doesn't function properly upon receipt.

drop shipping: A business model in which a seller hires a wholesale vendor to ship products directly to the seller's customers. With drop shipping, the seller lists the item on eBay at a price that is higher than the drop shipper's wholesale price. Once a sale is made, the seller collects the payment and shipping fee from the buyer, and then sends a payment to the drop shipper, who in turn ships the item directly to the seller's customer.

DSL: An abbreviation for *digital subscriber line;* a high-speed Internet connection through a dedicated phone line.

Dutch auction: An auction format for selling multiple quantities of identical items in one auction. Bidders indicate the number of items they want to buy when placing their bids. Naturally, the highest bidders win; but the final *price* is determined by the *lowest* bid among all the winning bidders. For example, if ten belts are selling at a Dutch auction and the top ten winning bids range from $3 all the way up to $12, the ten winning bidders each pay the lowest successful bid price—in this case, $3 per belt.

eBay store: An individualized "mini" Web site on eBay where sellers can market their products to eBay members at fixed prices. Sellers list their merchandise in an eBay store for varying lengths of time—30 days or Good 'Til Cancelled, with an option to renew the listing when the specified time is up.

emoticon: A specific group of characters used to form facial expressions in e-mails. For example, :-) is a smiley face.

escrow: A buyer's deposit or fund entrusted to a third-party that will hold the payment for an item, or items, until the seller makes delivery of merchandise to the buyer.

FAQ: An abbreviation for *frequently asked questions;* a list of common questions and their answers made readily accessible for new and inquiring users.

feedback (FB): Short comments posted by parties in an eBay transaction regarding their satisfaction with the transaction. A feedback comment becomes a *permanent* part of a member's reputation and is open for public viewing by the eBay community.

file transfer protocol (FTP): A method of exchanging files over the Internet.

final value (FV): An item's final selling price, not including shipping costs.

final value fee (FVF): The eBay seller's fee upon making a successful sale.

Fixed Price listing: An item for sale at a Buy It Now price. There is no bidding with a Fixed Price listing; buyers can purchase items immediately at the set price.

flame: A series of angry e-mails or posts to a message board, often written in all capital letters.

free on board (FOB) (also known as *freight on board***):** A term indicating that goods will be placed onto shipping transport without a loading fee. The *FOB location* is the point at which the buyer takes ownership of goods while they are in transit; consequently, this is when the buyer becomes responsible for shipping charges. For example, if I quote a price for a pallet of goods as "FOB Trenton, NJ," the buyer's total price includes the cost of freight from Trenton to the delivery location.

gently used: A term indicating that an item was previously owned, but shows little wear.

gross merchandise sales (GMS): The total dollar value of your sales over a specified period of time.

HP: An abbreviation for *homepage.*

HTML: An abbreviation for *hypertext markup language.* This is the code that computer programmers use to create what you see when you view a Web page.

HTML Editor: An eBay application that appears in the *Sell Your Item* form; it allows you to enter text in plain English and insert objects and images much like you would into a word processing document. The HTML editor then converts the text into HTML code. This feature allows you to create attractive listings and to create or modify your *About Me Page* without taking the trouble to learn HTML.

hyperlink: A clickable photo or line of text on a Web page that takes you to another page on the Internet (also known simply as a *link*).

IE: An abbreviation for Internet Explorer.

IMHO: An abbreviation for the phrase *in my humble opinion.*

IMO: An abbreviation for the phrase *in my opinion.*

Internet service provider (ISP): A business or organization that offers users access to the Internet and related services. Well-known ISPs include Earthlink, AOL, MSN, Yahoo!, and some telephone companies. Sometimes called Internet access providers.

jpeg: An acronym for *Joint Photographic Experts Group* (often abbreviated as *jpg*); the preferred file format for pictures on eBay; pronounced JAY-peg.

link: See *hyperlink*.

LOL: Laughing out loud (sometimes seen as ROFL, for *rolling on the floor laughing*); this abbreviation is used frequently in e-mails to and from buyers and in posts on the eBay message boards.

lot or lots: Similar items sold in bulk quantities. Lots are normally sold at discount or wholesale prices.

LTD: An abbreviation for *limited edition*.

MIB: An abbreviation for *mint in box*; see *Mint*.

MIMB: An abbreviation for *mint in mint box*; see *Mint*.

MIMP: An abbreviation for *mint in mint package*; see *Mint*.

Mint: An item that has never been opened or used and is in perfect condition.

MIP: An abbreviation for *mint in package*; see *Mint*.

MNB: An abbreviation for *mint no box*; see *Mint*.

MOC: An abbreviation for *mint on card*; see *Mint*.

My eBay: An eBay page that displays your ongoing auctions, their status, and your auction history.

NARU: An abbreviation for *not a registered user* (i.e., a suspended eBay user).

NBW: An abbreviation for *never been worn.*

NC: An abbreviation for *no cover* (i.e., a book missing its dust jacket or, in the case of a paperback, its cover).

newbie: A term for someone who is new to eBay.

NM: An abbreviation for *near mint;* a very subjective term. See *Mint.*

NPB: An abbreviation for *nonpaying bidder.* See also *deadbeat bidder.*

NR: An abbreviation for *no reserve;* used frequently in auction titles to indicate that there is no reserve price for the item being auctioned.

NRFB: An abbreviation for *never removed from box.*

NWT: An abbreviation for *new with tag.*

OEM: An abbreviation for *original equipment manufacturer.*

OOP: An abbreviation for *out of print.*

PayPal: The payment service owned by eBay; more than 75 percent of eBay users are registered with PayPal, and it is the only payment service that is integrated with the eBay checkout system.

PayPal verified buyer: A buyer whose address and account information have been confirmed through PayPal. This status qualifies a user for the PayPal fraud protection plan.

phishing: A fraudulent practice whereby an unscrupulous person (or group of people) attempts to gather personal (usually financial) information about an unsuspecting eBay user. In a typical scenario, you receive a counterfeit e-mail that appears to come from eBay, PayPal, or your bank, and contains a link leading you to a fake Web site, which is designed to look like a well-known, branded site but has a slightly different URL. This tactic is used to trick online shoppers into disclosing their credit card numbers, bank account information, social security numbers, passwords, and other personal information, which can lead to identity theft. If you receive a suspicious e-mail, you can simply forward it to spoof@ebay.com and they will track down the sender and work with the ISP to block the Web site. All genuine e-mails from eBay will appear in the *My Messages* folder on your *My eBay* page.

PM: An abbreviation for *Priority Mail.*

PPC: An abbreviation for *pay per click.*

Primail: An abbreviated term for *Priority Mail.*

private auction: An auction in which neither the buyers' nor the seller's identities are disclosed.

proxy bidding: eBay's bidding system. A bidder enters the maximum amount he is willing to spend on an item. The auction begins at a low starting price and, as it continues, eBay automatically increases the high bid in set increments, until the bidder emerges as the winner or his maximum price is exceeded.

relisting: The process of listing an unsold item again.

reserve not met: An auction term that means no bid is high enough to match the seller's minimum acceptable price; see *Reserve Price Auction.*

reserve price: The minimum price a seller is willing to accept for an auction item.

Reserve Price Auction (RPA): An auction in which the seller sets a minimum acceptable price. Sellers sometimes disclose the reserve price to prospective bidders.

retaliatory feedback: Negative comments posted by an eBay member in response to another member's negative feedback. This term is also used when a nonpaying bidder posts feedback in response to a seller's complaints to eBay.

RMA: An abbreviation for *Return Merchandise Authorization;* a seller's authorization of a product return. Many sellers require buyers to e-mail them first and get an RMA before returning an item for a refund.

RSVP: An abbreviation for the French term *répondez s'il vous plaît* (please reply).

second chance offer (SCO): An option that allows sellers to offer identical items to losing bidders after an auction ends—either because the winning bidder was unable to complete the transaction or because the seller has more than one of a particular item for sale.

Seller Central: An area of the eBay site map featuring valuable resources for sellers—from advice on effective selling strategies, ways to promote your merchandise, and shipping options, to eBay news and updates, and tips on category trends and marketplace research.

shilling: A practice in which a seller conspires with another eBay member to place phony bids to artificially inflate the price of an item. See also *bid rigging* and *collusion*.

SIG: An abbreviation for *signature*.

siphoning: The practice whereby a third party contacts bidders and offers them the same item they are currently bidding on in an ongoing auction—thus drawing bidders away from the legitimate seller's auction. If eBay receives a report of siphoning, they will investigate and cancel the violator's account should they see evidence of this activity.

site map: A Web page that presents a visual and organizational guide to all features on a Web site. The eBay site map offers links to all resources and tools available on eBay.

SKU: An abbreviation for *stock keeping unit;* a numerical identifier used to distinguish individual items in an inventory. Most auction management systems, including eBay's Turbo Lister, have a field for SKU.

snail mail: A slang term for regular mail delivered via the U.S. Postal Service.

sniping: The practice of bidding in an auction at the last possible moment so that others don't have the opportunity to place a higher bid. Several companies actually make automated software that will snipe for you if you are not on the computer during the final minutes of an auction.

spam: Unwanted e-mail designed to sell something; on eBay, spammers send unsolicited e-mail to bidders in auctions with which they have no involvement. eBay will suspend your account for doing this.

spoof Web site: See *phishing*.

TM: An abbreviation for *trademark*.

trading assistant (TA): An experienced eBay seller who meets eBay requirements and will sell another person's items on eBay for a fee or commission. See also *consignment selling*.

unwanted bid: A bid that does not meet the seller's terms stated in the auction. For example, a seller states in her auction that the item will only be shipped to U.S. locations; however, the bidder is located overseas. In this situation, the eBay seller may cancel the bid without any adverse repercussions.

UPS: An abbreviation for *United Parcel Service*.

Upselling: The tactic of offering a winning bidder an additional quantity of his item or a related product (such as a set of earphones to someone who buys an MP3 player) upon purchase. If you use an auction management system, this can be done automatically during the checkout process. Otherwise, you can make the offer via e-mail when you send the winning bidder payment instructions.

URL: An abbreviation for *Uniform Resource Locator;* the address that identifies a Web site on the Internet. The URL comprises the protocol (e.g., http://), followed by the domain name (e.g., www.skipmcgrath.com) and the specific file reference (e.g., /ebaynews/).

USPS: An abbreviation for *United States Postal Service*.

VeRO: An acronym for eBay's *Verified Rights Owner* program, which enforces copyright and trademark laws within the eBay marketplace. If you sell counterfeit goods on eBay, the rights owner can file a VeRO complaint and have your auctions shut down.

VG: An abbreviation for *very good*

VHTF: An abbreviation for *very hard to find*.

wholesale: The practice of purchasing a quantity of goods at a discount, for the purpose of reselling at a (hopefully) higher retail price.

winning bidder notification (WBN): Notification sent to the winning bidder at the end of an auction. The e-mail may be sent by eBay, PayPal, a seller, or a seller's auction management system. The WBN typically tells the buyer the final value of the item he has won and the shipping cost, and either includes instructions or provides a link to a payment page.

WYSIWYG: An abbreviation for *What You See Is What You Get;* a program that displays what your final HTML page will look like while you're creating it. eBay and other auction management services provide WYSIWYG HTML editors to help sellers create their auction listings.

Yahoo! Shops (or Yahoo! Stores): A shopping portal operated by Yahoo! (not to be confused with Yahoo! Auctions).

✦ INDEX ✦